S0-ALE-986

World Almanac

Children's
Atlas
of the
United
States

Maps created by
MapQuest.com. Inc.

MAPQUEST

WORLD ALMANAC®

Updated and reprinted in 2006.
Copyright © 2003

MAPQUEST.

ISBN 0-8343-0203-9 (hardcover)
ISBN 0-8343-0202-0 (softcover)

This product contains proprietary property of MapQuest.com, Inc. Unauthorized use, including copying, of this product is expressly prohibited.

While every care has been taken to trace and acknowledge copyright, the publishers tender their apologies for any accidental infringement where copyright has proved untraceable.

Cover images: © CORBIS

Photographs on pages 10–11 (from Nature, Landscapes, Hawaii, Caribbean disks), 14–15 (from Arctic disk) Copyright © 2002 Corel Corp. and their suppliers.

Photographs on pages 10–11 (from Vols. 16, 44), pages 14–15 (from Vols. 16, 44) Copyright © 2002 PhotoDisc, Inc.

Photograph on page 10 (Tundra) Copyright © Tom Dew, National Park Service; Alaska Division of Tourism.

World Almanac editorial direction:
   Mark J. Sachner
World Almanac art direction/cover design:
   Tammy West

All rights reserved. No part of this book may be reproduced, stored in a retrieval system, or transmitted in any form or by any means, electronic, mechanical, or otherwise, whether now or hereafter devised, including photocopying, recording, or by any information and retrieval system, without express written prior permission from the Publisher.

Printed in the United States of America

2 3 4 5 6 7 8 9 08 07 06

Political. 4–5

Physical. 6–7

Landform Regions 8

Elevations. 9

Climate Regions 10–11

Weather
   Average January Maximum Temperature 12
   Average July Maximum Temperature 12
   Average Annual Precipitation 13
   Average Annual Snowfall. 13

Natural Vegetation. 14–15

Land Use 16–17

Population Density 18–19

First Americans
   Migration of Early People 20
   Ancient Civilizations 20
   North American Culture Areas
      During the Pre-Columbian Period. 21

Exploration and Colonization
   Early European Exploration 22
   Around the World with Magellan 22
   Exploration of North America 22
   European Claims in North America:
      About 1615, 1713, 1754, 1763 23

Colonial America
   Economy of the Thirteen Colonies 24
   Colonial Trade Networks 24
   American Revolution, 1775–1781. 25
   North America, 1783 25

Westward Expansion
   Louisiana Purchase, 1803. 26
   United States, 1820 26
   Texas Revolution, 1835–1836 27
   California Gold Rush. 27
   Trails to the West 27

Civil War
   Slave and Free States, 1861. 28
   Slavery and
      the Underground Railroad, 1860 28
   Civil War, 1861–1865 29

Territorial Growth and Immigration
   Territorial Growth. 30
   U.S. Immigration for Select Periods 31

U.S. and the World
   World Trade Organizations. 32
   Major U.S. Trade Partners 32–33

Regions of the United States 34–35

Alabama 36–37
Alaska 38–39
Arizona 40–41
Arkansas 42–43
California 44–45
Colorado 46–47
Connecticut 48–49
Delaware 50–51
Florida 52–53
Georgia 54–55
Hawaii 56–57
Idaho 58–59
Illinois 60–61
Indiana 62–63
Iowa 64–65
Kansas 66–67
Kentucky 68–69
Louisiana 70–71
Maine 72–73
Maryland 74–75
Massachusetts 76–77
Michigan 78–79
Minnesota 80–81
Mississippi 82–83
Missouri 84–85
Montana 86–87
Nebraska 88–89
Nevada 90–91
New Hampshire 92–93
New Jersey 94–95

New Mexico 96–97
New York 98–99
North Carolina 100–101
North Dakota 102–103
Ohio 104–105
Oklahoma 106–107
Oregon 108–109
Pennsylvania 110–111
Rhode Island 112–113
South Carolina 114–115
South Dakota 116–117
Tennessee 118–119
Texas 120–121
Utah 122–123
Vermont 124–125
Virginia 126–127
Washington 128–129
West Virginia 130–131
Wisconsin 132–133
Wyoming 134–135
District of Columbia 136
Puerto Rico 136
American Samoa 137
Virgin Islands 137
Northern Mariana Islands . . . 137
  Saipan and Tinian 137
  Rota 137
Guam 137
Index 138–144

Using the index and grid to find information quickly

All of the political maps in the *World Almanac Children's Atlas of the United States* use a grid system to help you locate specific cities or points of interest. There are numbers across the top and bottom of each map and letters along both sides. These numbers and letter are used in the index to give you directions to find what you are looking for. For example, to find out where Cleveland, Ohio, is located, you would look up Cleveland in the index. The index entry for Cleveland shows the page number of the map in bold and the grid location next to it: Cleveland...**104** B4. To find Cleveland, go to page 104, draw an imaginary line across from B and down from 4, and you'll find Cleveland.

About This Atlas

World Almanac Children's Atlas of the United States is the perfect introduction to our country and the states that make it unique.

Begin with the United States political and physical maps that detail state and international boundaries, capitals, mountain ranges, bodies of water, and other geographical features of the country.

Follow that with the thematic maps that give you insight into the country's diverse characteristics and history. Landforms, weather, climate, and vegetation maps highlight the country's natural resources. A series of historical maps shows you how the land that is now the United States evolved from the times of the first Americans. You'll see how exploration, colonization and territorial growth formed the country. Historical maps help you visualize the great changes that have shaped American history.

With this picture in mind, you can explore the states in each of the country's six regions: New England, Middle Atlantic, Southeast, Midwest, Southwest, and West.

Arranged alphabetically, each two-page state entry contains a political, physical and economic map. You'll see cities, counties, parks, mountains, rivers, and major industries. An "almanac" fact box and a brief description of the state's history, people, way of life, and tourist attractions help you discover what's fun and unique about each state. For instance, did you know that the highest and lowest points in the contiguous U.S. are both in California?

Colorful and up-to-date, this atlas is a wonderful way to discover the many diverse states that make up the U.S.A. It will help make basic geography and social studies concepts interesting and easy to understand.

WASHINGTON (WA)
Seattle
Olympia ★ Tacoma
Spokane •

River

OREGON (OR)
Vancouver •
Portland •
★ Salem
Eugene •
Columbia

Great Falls •
Missouri River

MONTANA (MT)
Helena ★
Billings •

NORTH DAKOTA (ND)

Bismarck ★

IDAHO (ID)
Boise ★
Pocatello •

WYOMING (WY)
Casper •

SOUTH DAKOTA (SD)
Pierre ★

Reno •
Sacramento ★
Carson City ★
Oakland •
San Francisco • • Stockton
San Jose •

NEVADA (NV)

Great Salt Lake
Ogden •
Salt Lake City • • Provo

UTAH (UT)

Cheyenne ★

NEBRASKA (NE)

Fort Collins •
Boulder ★
Denver ★ • Aurora

Colorado River

COLORADO (CO)
Colorado Springs •
Pueblo •

KANSAS

Fresno •

CALIFORNIA (CA)

Las Vegas •
Henderson •

Flagstaff •

PACIFIC OCEAN

Los Angeles •
Long Beach • • Anaheim

San Diego •

ARIZONA (AZ)
Phoenix ★ Scottsdale •
Tempe • Mesa
Tucson •

Santa Fe ★
Albuquerque •

NEW MEXICO (NM)

Amarillo •

Lubbock •

El Paso •

Rio Grande

TEXAS (TX)

ALASKA inset
RUSSIA
ARCTIC OCEAN
70N

ALASKA (AK)
Nome •
Fairbanks •
Arctic Circle
60N
Bering Sea
Anchorage •
Gulf of Alaska
Juneau ★
CANADA
N W E S
PACIFIC OCEAN
170W 160W 150W 140W
0 200 400 Miles
0 200 400 Kilometers

HAWAII inset
HAWAII (HI)
Honolulu ★
PACIFIC OCEAN
20N
Hilo •
N W E S
160W 155W
0 100 200 Miles
0 100 200 Kilometers

110W

MEXICO

San Antonio

Lar

100W

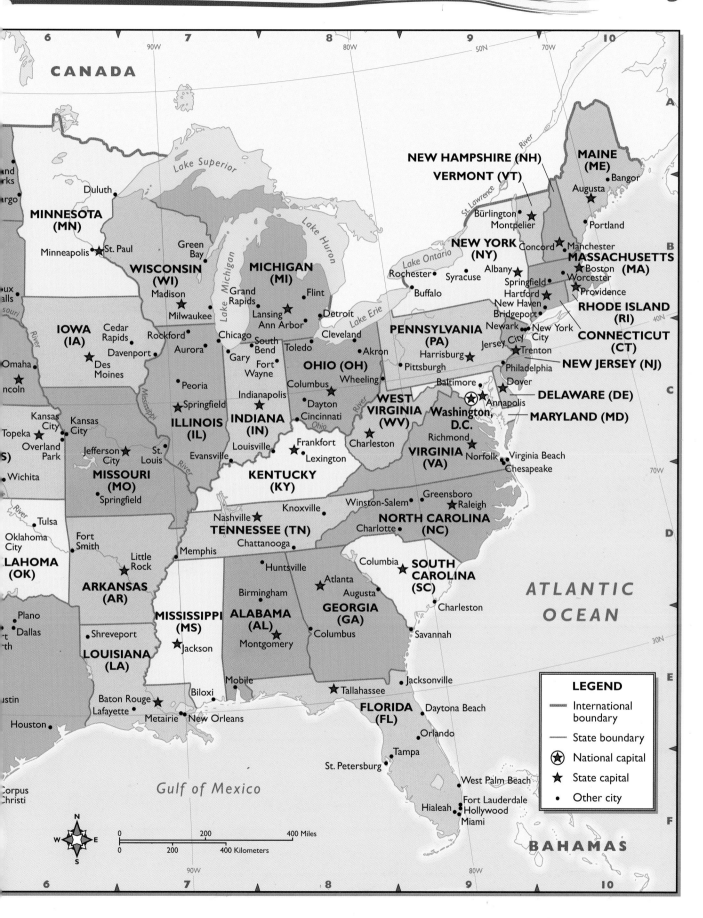

CANADA

Duluth

MINNESOTA (MN)
Minneapolis • ★ St. Paul

Green Bay

WISCONSIN (WI)
Madison ★
Milwaukee •

Lake Superior

Lake Michigan

Lake Huron

MICHIGAN (MI)
Grand Rapids •
Lansing ★
Ann Arbor •
Flint •
Detroit •

Lake Ontario

Lake Erie

NEW HAMPSHIRE (NH)
VERMONT (VT)
Burlington •
Montpelier ★

Augusta ★

MAINE (ME)
Bangor •

Portland •

NEW YORK (NY)
Rochester • Syracuse •
Buffalo •
Albany ★
Springfield •
Hartford ★
New Haven •
Bridgeport •

Concord ★ • Manchester

MASSACHUSETTS (MA)
★ Boston
Worcester •
Providence ★

RHODE ISLAND (RI)

CONNECTICUT (CT)

Fargo
...rks
...and

...ux
...lls

Omaha •
...ncoln •

IOWA (IA)
Cedar Rapids •
Davenport •
Des Moines ★

Rockford •
Aurora •
Chicago •

South Bend •
Gary •
Fort Wayne •

Peoria •

Cleveland •
Toledo •
Akron •

PENNSYLVANIA (PA)
Harrisburg ★
Pittsburgh •

Wheeling •

Newark •
Jersey City •
New York City •
Trenton ★

NEW JERSEY (NJ)
Philadelphia •
Dover ★

DELAWARE (DE)

Kansas City
Topeka ★
Overland Park •

Kansas City •

Jefferson City ★
St. Louis •

MISSOURI (MO)
Springfield •

ILLINOIS (IL)
Springfield ★

INDIANA (IN)
Indianapolis ★

Columbus •
Dayton •
Cincinnati •

OHIO (OH)

WEST VIRGINIA (WV)
Charleston ★

⊛ ★ Annapolis

Baltimore •

Washington, D.C.

MARYLAND (MD)

Richmond ★
Norfolk •
Virginia Beach •
Chesapeake •

VIRGINIA (VA)

...S)

• Wichita

Evansville •
Louisville •
Frankfort ★
Lexington •

KENTUCKY (KY)

Knoxville •

Winston-Salem •
Greensboro •
Raleigh ★

River
Ohio

River

OKLAHOMA (OK)
• Tulsa
Oklahoma City
Fort Smith •

Little Rock ★

ARKANSAS (AR)

Nashville ★
Chattanooga •

TENNESSEE (TN)

Memphis •

Charlotte •

NORTH CAROLINA (NC)

Columbia •

SOUTH CAROLINA (SC)

Charleston •

ATLANTIC OCEAN

Plano •
Dallas •
...rt
...th

Shreveport •

Jackson ★

MISSISSIPPI (MS)

Huntsville •
Birmingham •

ALABAMA (AL)
Montgomery ★

Atlanta ★
Augusta •

GEORGIA (GA)
Columbus •

Savannah •

...ustin

Houston •

LOUISIANA (LA)
Baton Rouge ★
Lafayette •
Metairie •
New Orleans •

Biloxi •

Mobile •

Tallahassee ★

Jacksonville •

Daytona Beach •

FLORIDA (FL)
Orlando •

Tampa •
St. Petersburg •

West Palm Beach •
Fort Lauderdale •
Hollywood •
Hialeah •
Miami •

...orpus
...hristi

Gulf of Mexico

LEGEND
┅┅┅ International boundary
──── State boundary
⊛ National capital
★ State capital
• Other city

BAHAMAS

N W E S

| 0 | 200 | 400 Miles |
| 0 | 200 | 400 Kilometers |

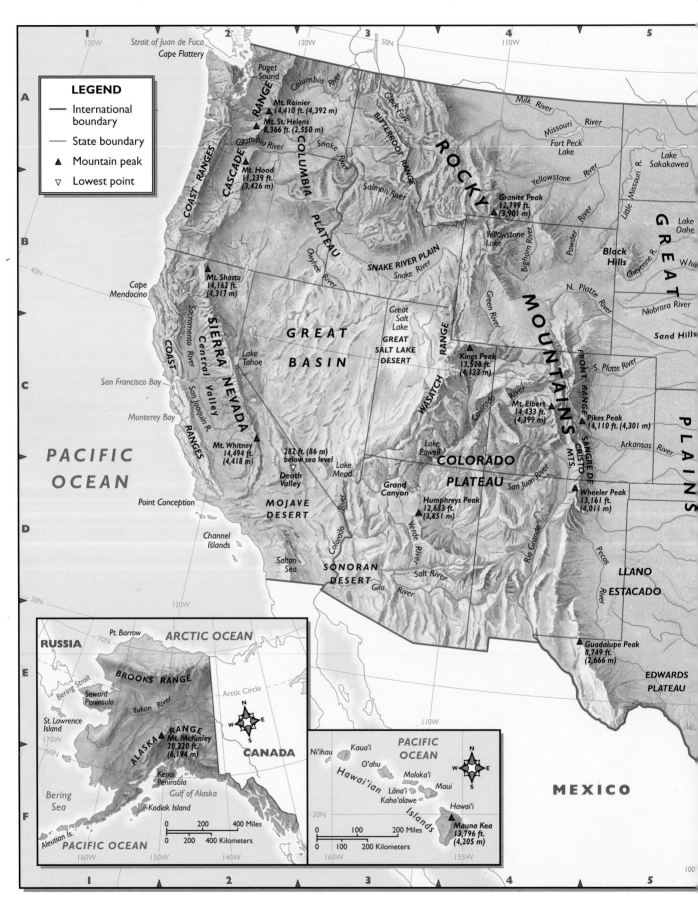

LEGEND
— International boundary
— State boundary
▲ Mountain peak
▽ Lowest point

Strait of Juan de Fuca
Cape Flattery
Puget Sound
Columbia River
Clark Fork
Milk River
Missouri River
Fort Peck Lake
Lake Sakakawea
Mt. Rainier 14,410 ft. (4,392 m)
Mt. St. Helens 8,366 ft. (2,550 m)
BITTERROOT RANGE
Columbia River
Snake River
Salmon River
Yellowstone River
Little Missouri R.
Lake Oahe
ROCKY
CASCADE RANGE
COLUMBIA PLATEAU
Mt. Hood 11,239 ft. (3,426 m)
Owyhee River
SNAKE RIVER PLAIN
Snake River
Yellowstone Lake
Granite Peak 12,799 ft. (3,901 m)
Bighorn River
Powder River
Black Hills
White
GREAT
COAST RANGES
40N
Cape Mendocino
Mt. Shasta 14,162 ft. (4,317 m)
Great Salt Lake
GREAT SALT LAKE DESERT
Green River
N. Platte River
Niobrara River
Sand Hills
MOUNTAINS
Sacramento River
SIERRA NEVADA
Central Valley
Lake Tahoe
GREAT BASIN
WASATCH RANGE
Kings Peak 13,528 ft. (4,123 m)
Colorado River
FRONT RANGE
S. Platte River
San Francisco Bay
COAST
San Joaquin R.
Mt. Elbert 14,433 ft. (4,399 m)
Pikes Peak 14,110 ft. (4,301 m)
Arkansas River
PLAINS
Monterey Bay
RANGES
Mt. Whitney 14,494 ft. (4,418 m)
282 ft. (86 m) below sea level
▽ Death Valley
Lake Powell
COLORADO PLATEAU
SANGRE DE CRISTO MTS.
PACIFIC OCEAN
Lake Mead
Grand Canyon
Humphreys Peak 12,633 ft. (3,851 m)
San Juan River
Wheeler Peak 13,161 ft. (4,011 m)
Point Conception
Channel Islands
Colorado River
Verde River
Rio Grande
Pecos River
Salton Sea
MOJAVE DESERT
30N
120W
SONORAN DESERT
Salt River
Gila River
LLANO ESTACADO
Guadalupe Peak 8,749 ft. (2,666 m)
EDWARDS PLATEAU

RUSSIA
Pt. Barrow
70N
ARCTIC OCEAN
BROOKS RANGE
Bering Strait
Seward Peninsula
Yukon River
Arctic Circle
St. Lawrence Island
170W
60N
ALASKA RANGE
Mt. McKinley 20,320 ft. (6,194 m)
CANADA
Kenai Peninsula
Gulf of Alaska
Kodiak Island
Bering Sea
Aleutian Is.
PACIFIC OCEAN
160W
150W
140W
0 200 400 Miles
0 200 400 Kilometers

PACIFIC OCEAN
Ni'ihau
Kaua'i
O'ahu
Moloka'i
Hawai'ian Islands
Lāna'i
Kaho'olawe
Maui
Hawai'i
Mauna Kea 13,796 ft. (4,205 m)
20N
160W
155W
0 100 200 Miles
0 100 200 Kilometers

MEXICO

100

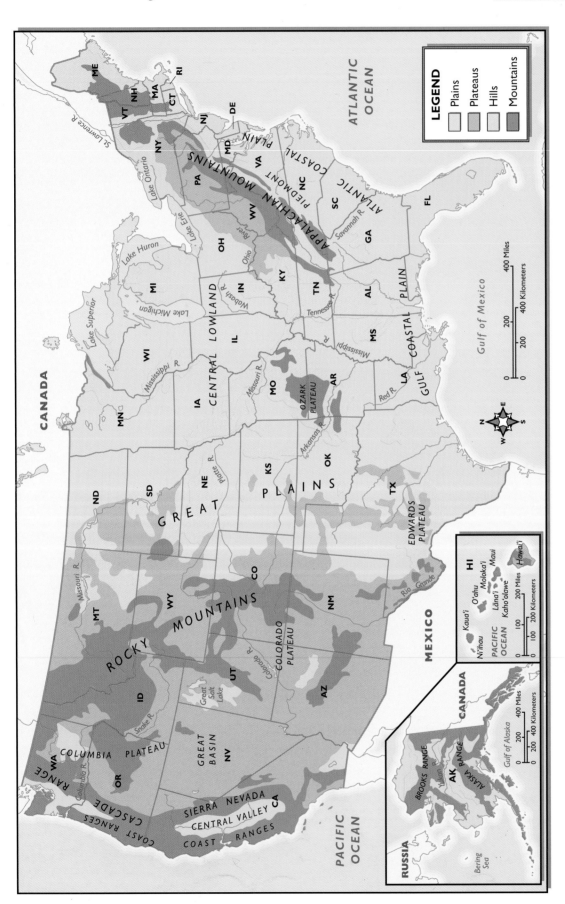

Landform Regions

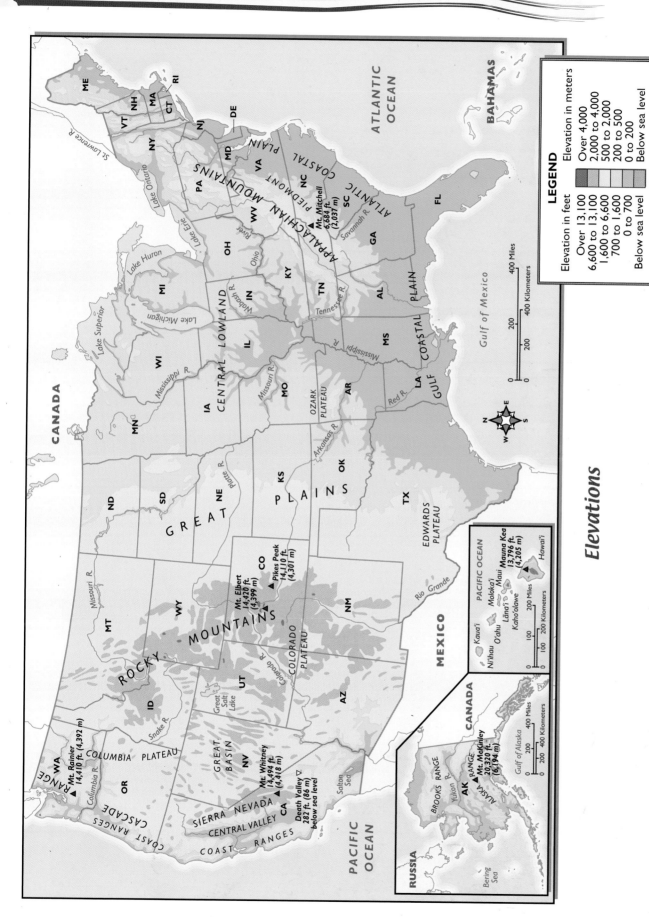

Elevations

LEGEND

Elevation in feet
- Over 13,100
- 6,600 to 13,100
- 1,600 to 6,600
- 700 to 1,600
- 0 to 700
- Below sea level

Elevation in meters
- Over 4,000
- 2,000 to 4,000
- 500 to 2,000
- 200 to 500
- 0 to 200
- Below sea level

▲ Mountain peak
▽ Lowest point

Mt. Mitchell
6,684 ft.
(2,037 m)

Pikes Peak
14,110 ft.
(4,301 m)

Mt. Elbert
14,420 ft.
(4,399 m)

Mt. Rainier
14,410 ft. (4,392 m)

Mt. Whitney
14,494 ft.
(4,418 m)

Death Valley
282 ft. (86 m)
below sea level

Mauna Kea
13,796 ft.
(4,205 m)

Mt. McKinley
20,320 ft.
(6,194 m)

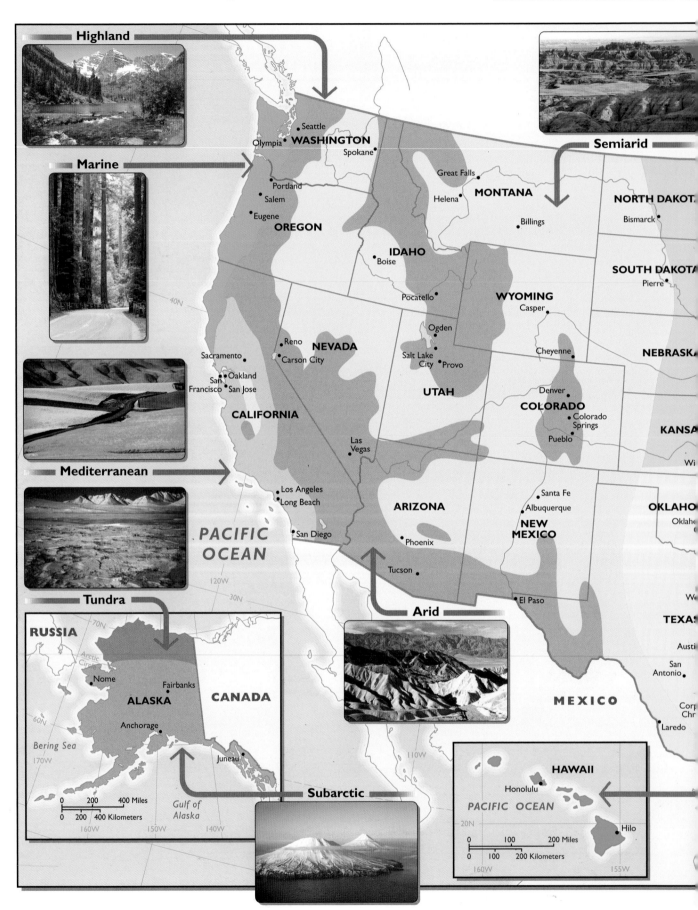

Highland

Marine

Mediterranean

Tundra

Semiarid

Arid

Subarctic

WASHINGTON
Seattle
Olympia
Spokane

Portland
Salem
Eugene
OREGON

Great Falls
Helena
MONTANA
Billings

NORTH DAKOTA
Bismarck

IDAHO
Boise

SOUTH DAKOTA
Pierre

Pocatello

WYOMING
Casper

Reno
Carson City
NEVADA

Ogden
Salt Lake City
Provo

Cheyenne

NEBRASKA

Sacramento

UTAH

Denver
COLORADO
Colorado Springs
Pueblo

KANSAS

San Francisco
Oakland
San Jose

CALIFORNIA

Las Vegas

Santa Fe
Albuquerque

OKLAHOMA
Oklahoma

Los Angeles
Long Beach

San Diego

ARIZONA
Phoenix

Tucson

NEW MEXICO

Wi

PACIFIC OCEAN

40N

120W

30N

El Paso

We

TEXAS
Austin
San Antonio

MEXICO

Corp
Chr
Laredo

RUSSIA

70N

Arctic Circle

Nome

Fairbanks
ALASKA

CANADA

Anchorage

Bering Sea

170W

60N

Juneau

Gulf of Alaska

0   200   400 Miles
0   200   400 Kilometers

160W   150W   140W

110W

HAWAII
Honolulu
PACIFIC OCEAN

Hilo

20N

0   100   200 Miles
0   100   200 Kilometers

160W   155W

CANADA

Lake Superior

Duluth

MINNESOTA

Minneapolis • St. Paul

WISCONSIN

Green Bay

MICHIGAN

Lake Michigan

Lake Huron

Madison
Milwaukee

Grand Rapids
Lansing

Detroit

Lake Erie

Humid continental

VERMONT

Burlington
Montpelier

MAINE

Augusta

Portland

Concord

NEW HAMPSHIRE
MASSACHUSETTS

NEW YORK

Albany

Lake Ontario

Boston
Providence

RHODE ISLAND
CONNECTICUT

ATLANTIC OCEAN

IOWA

Cedar Rapids
Rockford

Davenport

Omaha

Des Moines

Chicago
Gary

Fort Wayne

ILLINOIS

Peoria

Springfield

INDIANA

OHIO

Columbus

Indianapolis
Cincinnati

Toledo
Cleveland

Wheeling

PENNSYLVANIA

Harrisburg
Pittsburgh

Baltimore

Buffalo

Hartford

Newark
New York City

Trenton

NEW JERSEY

Philadelphia
Dover

DELAWARE

Annapolis

MARYLAND

WEST VIRGINIA

Charleston

Washington, D.C.

Richmond

VIRGINIA

Norfolk

Humid subtropical

MISSOURI

Kansas City

St. Louis
Jefferson City

Evansville

Frankfort
Louisville

KENTUCKY

Knoxville
Nashville

TENNESSEE

Raleigh

NORTH CAROLINA

Charlotte

Tulsa

Fort Smith

ARKANSAS

Little Rock

Memphis

Columbia

SOUTH CAROLINA

Charleston

Atlanta

Birmingham

MISSISSIPPI

ALABAMA

Montgomery

Jackson

GEORGIA

Columbus

Savannah

Shreveport

Mobile

LOUISIANA

Baton Rouge
New Orleans

Biloxi

Jacksonville

Tallahassee

FLORIDA

Orlando

Tampa

St. Petersburg

Fort Lauderdale

Miami

Gulf of Mexico

Tropic of Cancer

N
W E
S

| 0 | 200 | 400 Miles |
| 0 | 200 | 400 Kilometers |

Tropical wet

Tropical wet and dry

LEGEND

☐ Tropical wet
Hot and wet all year

☐ Tropical wet and dry
Hot all year; wet with one dry season

☐ Arid
Very dry; hot or cold depending on elevation

☐ Semiarid
Little precipitation; hot or cold depending on elevation

☐ Mediterranean
Mild, wet winter; hot, dry summer

☐ Humid subtropical
Mild to warm winter; hot summer; wet all year

☐ Marine
Mild winter; cool summer; wet all year

☐ Humid continental
Cold winter; hot summer; medium precipitation

☐ Subarctic
Very cold winter; cool summer; wet

☐ Tundra
Very cold winter; cold summer; dry

☐ Highland
High mountains; climate varies with elevation

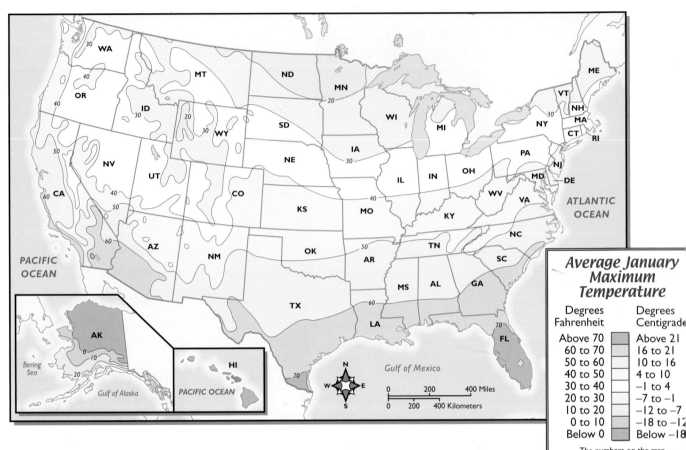

Average January Maximum Temperature

Degrees Fahrenheit	Degrees Centigrade
Above 70	Above 21
60 to 70	16 to 21
50 to 60	10 to 16
40 to 50	4 to 10
30 to 40	−1 to 4
20 to 30	−7 to −1
10 to 20	−12 to −7
0 to 10	−18 to −12
Below 0	Below −18

The numbers on the map represent degrees Fahrenheit.

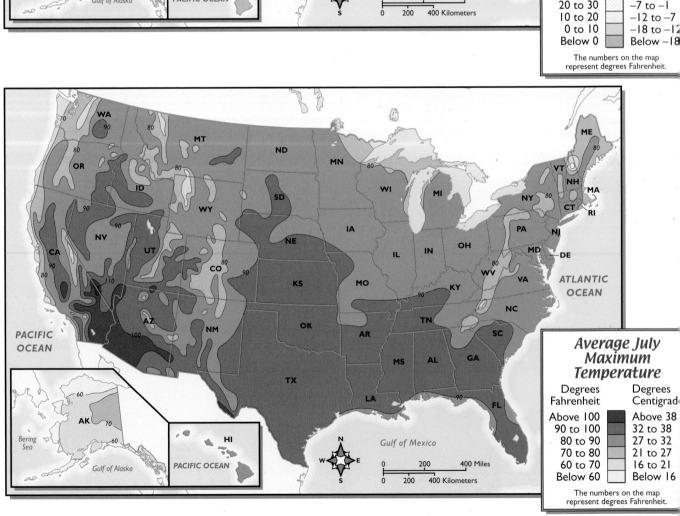

Average July Maximum Temperature

Degrees Fahrenheit	Degrees Centigrade
Above 100	Above 38
90 to 100	32 to 38
80 to 90	27 to 32
70 to 80	21 to 27
60 to 70	16 to 21
Below 60	Below 16

The numbers on the map represent degrees Fahrenheit.

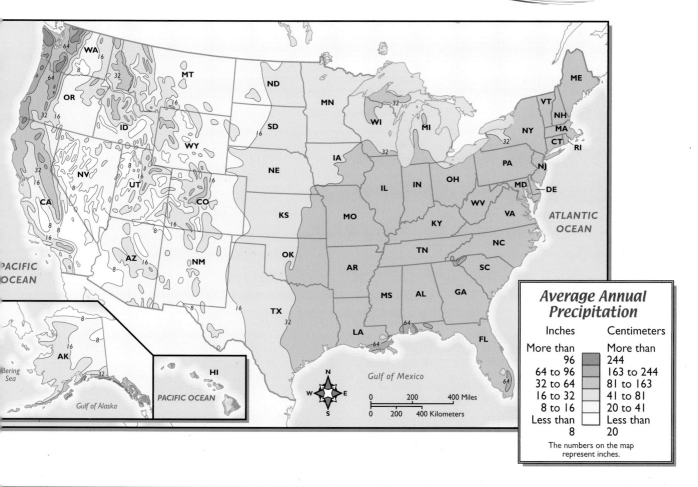

Average Annual Precipitation

Inches	Centimeters
More than 96	More than 244
64 to 96	163 to 244
32 to 64	81 to 163
16 to 32	41 to 81
8 to 16	20 to 41
Less than 8	Less than 20

The numbers on the map represent inches.

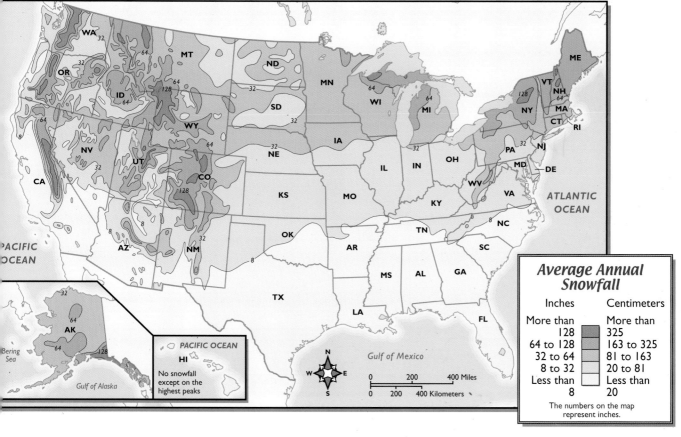

Average Annual Snowfall

Inches	Centimeters
More than 128	More than 325
64 to 128	163 to 325
32 to 64	81 to 163
8 to 32	20 to 81
Less than 8	Less than 20

The numbers on the map represent inches.

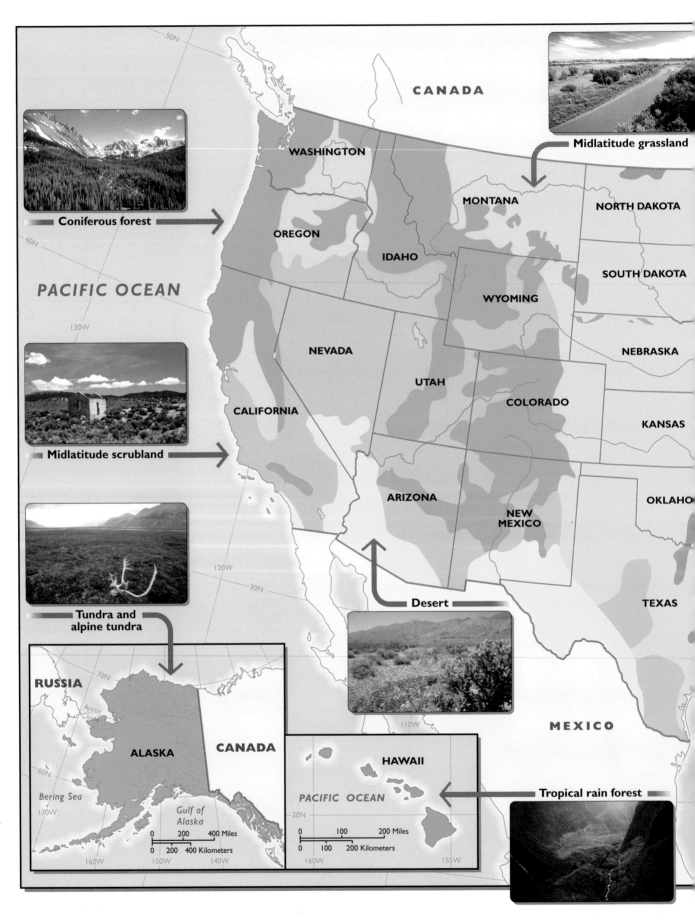

Coniferous forest

Midlatitude grassland

Midlatitude scrubland

Desert

Tundra and alpine tundra

Tropical rain forest

CANADA

WASHINGTON

OREGON

IDAHO

MONTANA

NORTH DAKOTA

SOUTH DAKOTA

WYOMING

NEBRASKA

NEVADA

UTAH

COLORADO

KANSAS

CALIFORNIA

ARIZONA

NEW MEXICO

OKLAHOMA

TEXAS

PACIFIC OCEAN

MEXICO

50N

40N

130W

120W

30N

RUSSIA

ALASKA

CANADA

Arctic Circle

70N

60N

Bering Sea

170W

160W

150W

140W

Gulf of Alaska

0   200   400 Miles

0   200   400 Kilometers

HAWAII

PACIFIC OCEAN

20N

160W

155W

0   100   200 Miles

0   100   200 Kilometers

110W

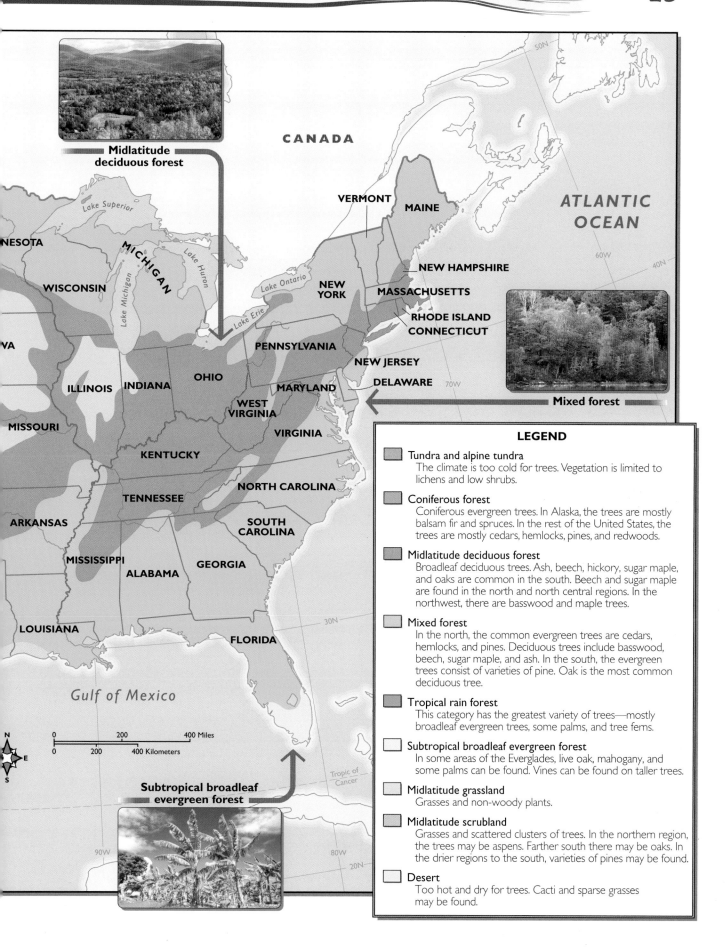

Midlatitude deciduous forest

CANADA

VERMONT

MAINE

NEW HAMPSHIRE

NEW YORK

MASSACHUSETTS

RHODE ISLAND
CONNECTICUT

ATLANTIC OCEAN

Lake Superior

MICHIGAN

Lake Michigan

Lake Huron

Lake Ontario

Lake Erie

NESOTA

WISCONSIN

VA

ILLINOIS

INDIANA

OHIO

PENNSYLVANIA

NEW JERSEY

DELAWARE

MARYLAND

WEST VIRGINIA

VIRGINIA

MISSOURI

KENTUCKY

NORTH CAROLINA

ARKANSAS

TENNESSEE

SOUTH CAROLINA

MISSISSIPPI

ALABAMA

GEORGIA

LOUISIANA

FLORIDA

Gulf of Mexico

Mixed forest

0   200   400 Miles
0   200   400 Kilometers

N
E
S

Subtropical broadleaf evergreen forest

Tropic of Cancer

50N

60W

40N

70W

30N

90W

80W

20N

LEGEND

Tundra and alpine tundra
The climate is too cold for trees. Vegetation is limited to lichens and low shrubs.

Coniferous forest
Coniferous evergreen trees. In Alaska, the trees are mostly balsam fir and spruces. In the rest of the United States, the trees are mostly cedars, hemlocks, pines, and redwoods.

Midlatitude deciduous forest
Broadleaf deciduous trees. Ash, beech, hickory, sugar maple, and oaks are common in the south. Beech and sugar maple are found in the north and north central regions. In the northwest, there are basswood and maple trees.

Mixed forest
In the north, the common evergreen trees are cedars, hemlocks, and pines. Deciduous trees include basswood, beech, sugar maple, and ash. In the south, the evergreen trees consist of varieties of pine. Oak is the most common deciduous tree.

Tropical rain forest
This category has the greatest variety of trees—mostly broadleaf evergreen trees, some palms, and tree ferns.

Subtropical broadleaf evergreen forest
In some areas of the Everglades, live oak, mahogany, and some palms can be found. Vines can be found on taller trees.

Midlatitude grassland
Grasses and non-woody plants.

Midlatitude scrubland
Grasses and scattered clusters of trees. In the northern region, the trees may be aspens. Farther south there may be oaks. In the drier regions to the south, varieties of pines may be found.

Desert
Too hot and dry for trees. Cacti and sparse grasses may be found.

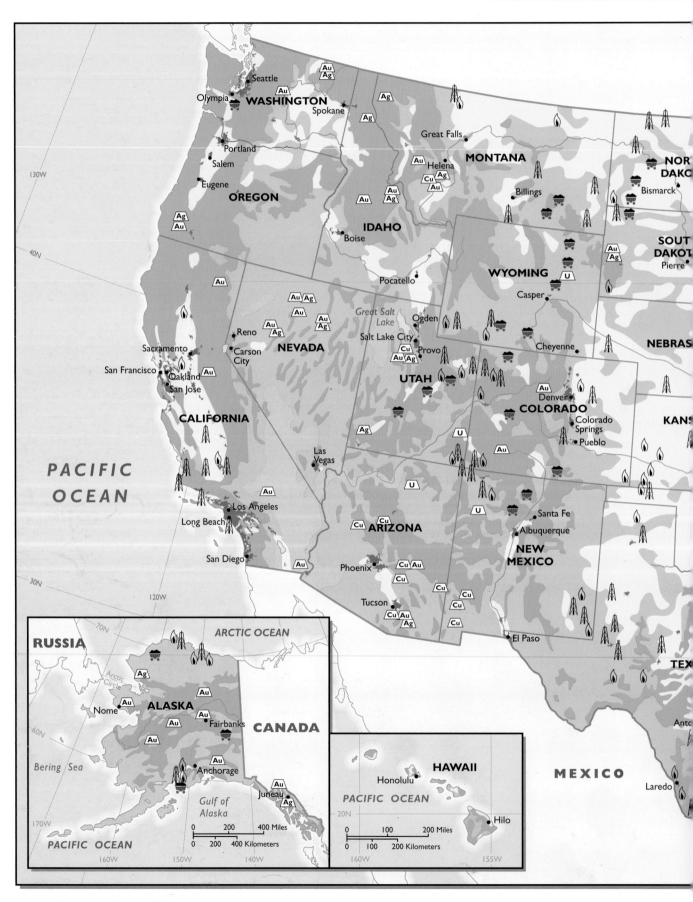

CANADA

Lake Superior

MINNESOTA

MICHIGAN

Lake Michigan

Lake Huron

WISCONSIN

IOWA

Lake Ontario

Lake Erie

NEW HAMPSHIRE
VERMONT

MAINE

Augusta

Burlington
Montpelier

Concord

Portland

NEW
YORK

MASSACHUSETTS

Boston

Albany

Providence

Hartford

RHODE ISLAND
CONNECTICUT

Buffalo

New York City

40N

ILLINOIS

INDIANA

OHIO

Cleveland

PENNSYLVANIA

Harrisburg

Pittsburgh

Trenton

NEW JERSEY

Philadelphia

Dover

DELAWARE

MARYLAND

70W

Wheeling

Columbus

Baltimore

Washington
D.C.

Annapolis

Indianapolis

Cincinnati

WEST
VIRGINIA

Charleston

MISSOURI

Jefferson
City

St.
Louis

Evansville

Frankfort

Louisville

KENTUCKY

Richmond

Norfolk

VIRGINIA

Nashville

Knoxville

Raleigh

TENNESSEE

NORTH CAROLINA

Charlotte

Memphis

Columbia

SOUTH
CAROLINA

ATLANTIC
OCEAN

Atlanta

Charleston

MISSISSIPPI

ALABAMA

Birmingham

GEORGIA

Jackson

Montgomery

Columbus

Savannah

Mobile

Tallahassee

Jacksonville

30N

New Orleans

FLORIDA

Gulf of Mexico

Orlando

Tampa

St. Petersburg

Fort
Lauderdale

Miami

Duluth

St. Paul

Minneapolis

Green
Bay

Madison

Milwaukee

Rockford

Chicago

Grand
Rapids

Lansing

Detroit

Toledo

Fort
Wayne

Gary

Cedar
Rapids

Davenport

Des
Moines

Peoria

Springfield

Kansas
City

Kansas
City

Topeka

Wichita

OKLAHOMA

Oklahoma City

Fort
Smith

ARKANSAS

Little
Rock

Tulsa

Dallas

Shreveport

LOUISIANA

Baton Rouge

Biloxi

Houston

Corpus
Christi

Omaha

N
W E
S

| 0 | | 200 | | 400 Miles |
| 0 | 200 | | 400 Kilometers |

90W   80W

LEGEND

Land Use

- Commercial agriculture
- Livestock ranching
- Primarily forest land
- Limited agricultural activity
- Urban area

Major Minerals

- Coal
- Oil
- Natural gas
- U Uranium
- Fe Iron ore
- Cu Copper
- Au Gold
- Ag Silver

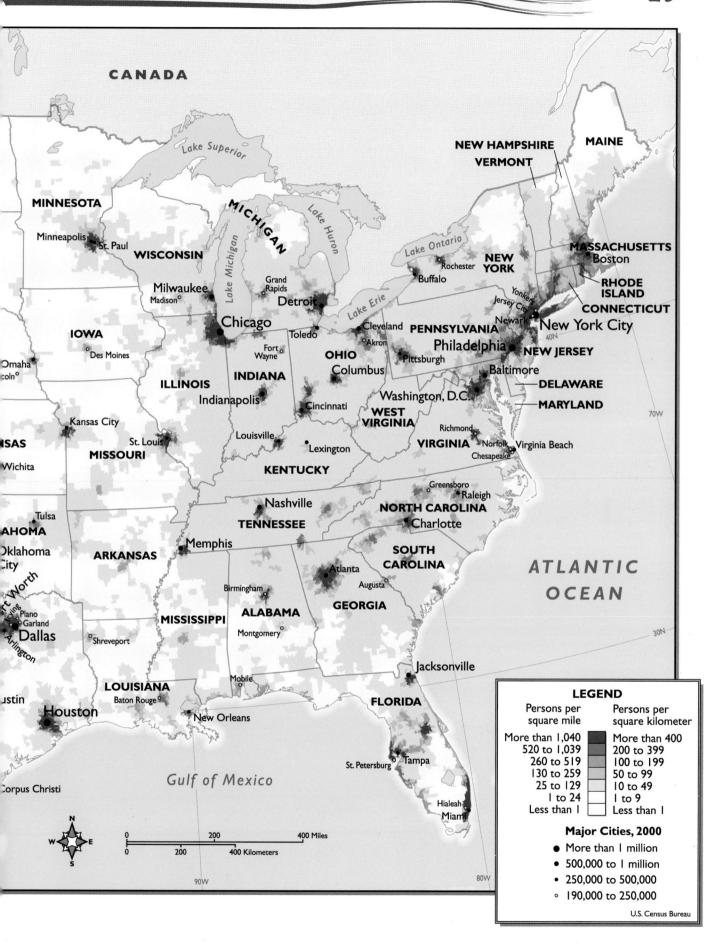

CANADA

Lake Superior

MINNESOTA

Minneapolis • St. Paul

WISCONSIN

MICHIGAN

Lake Michigan

Lake Huron

Grand
Rapids

Milwaukee
Madison°

Detroit

Lake Ontario

NEW HAMPSHIRE
VERMONT

MAINE

Rochester

NEW
YORK

MASSACHUSETTS
Boston

Buffalo

RHODE
ISLAND

CONNECTICUT

IOWA

Chicago

Lake Erie

Des Moines

Toledo

Fort
Wayne

Cleveland

PENNSYLVANIA

Akron

Yonkers
Jersey City
Newark

New York City

ILLINOIS

INDIANA

OHIO
Columbus

Pittsburgh

Philadelphia

NEW JERSEY

Baltimore

DELAWARE

Omaha

°coln

Indianapolis

Cincinnati

WEST
VIRGINIA

Washington, D.C.

MARYLAND

70W

Kansas City

Louisville

Richmond

SAS

St. Louis

Lexington

Norfolk
Chesapeake

Virginia Beach

Wichita

MISSOURI

KENTUCKY

VIRGINIA

Greensboro

Raleigh

Tulsa

Nashville

Charlotte

AHOMA

TENNESSEE

NORTH CAROLINA

Oklahoma
City

ARKANSAS

Memphis

SOUTH
CAROLINA

ATLANTIC
OCEAN

Atlanta

Augusta

Birmingham

rt Worth

MISSISSIPPI

ALABAMA

GEORGIA

Plano
Garland

Dallas

Shreveport

Montgomery°

rlington

Jacksonville

ustin

LOUISIANA

Mobile

Baton Rouge

FLORIDA

30N

Houston

New Orleans

St. Petersburg

Tampa

Gulf of Mexico

Hialeah
Miami

Corpus Christi

N
W E
S

0   200   400 Miles
0   200   400 Kilometers

90W

80W

LEGEND

Persons per square mile	Persons per square kilometer
More than 1,040	More than 400
520 to 1,039	200 to 399
260 to 519	100 to 199
130 to 259	50 to 99
25 to 129	10 to 49
1 to 24	1 to 9
Less than 1	Less than 1

Major Cities, 2000

- ● More than 1 million
- • 500,000 to 1 million
- · 250,000 to 500,000
- ° 190,000 to 250,000

U.S. Census Bureau

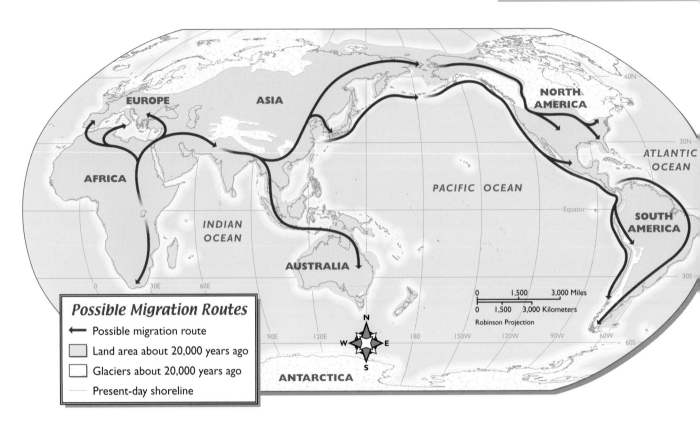

Possible Migration Routes

← Possible migration route

▢ Land area about 20,000 years ago

▢ Glaciers about 20,000 years ago

⸺ Present-day shoreline

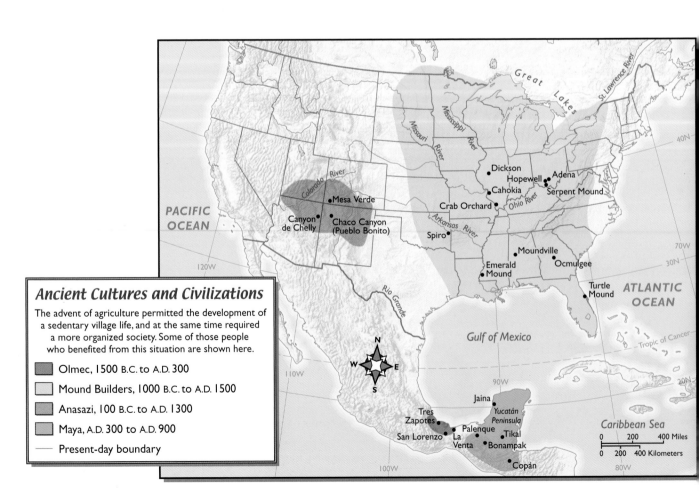

Ancient Cultures and Civilizations

The advent of agriculture permitted the development of
a sedentary village life, and at the same time required
a more organized society. Some of those people
who benefited from this situation are shown here.

▮ Olmec, 1500 B.C. to A.D. 300

▯ Mound Builders, 1000 B.C. to A.D. 1500

▮ Anasazi, 100 B.C. to A.D. 1300

▮ Maya, A.D. 300 to A.D. 900

⸺ Present-day boundary

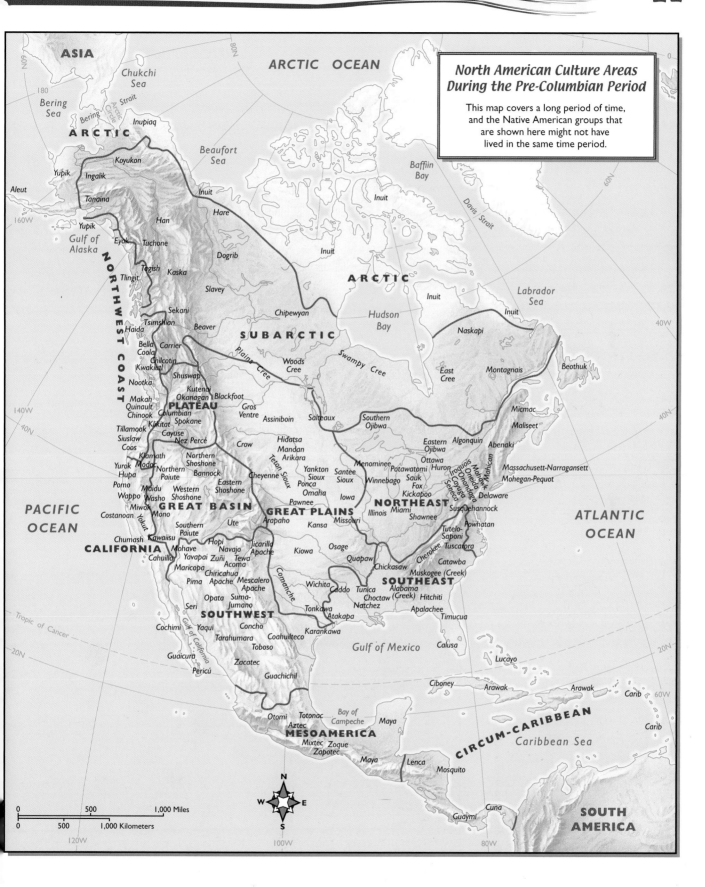

North American Culture Areas During the Pre-Columbian Period

This map covers a long period of time, and the Native American groups that are shown here might not have lived in the same time period.

ASIA
Chukchi Sea
Bering Sea
Bering Strait
Arctic Circle
ARCTIC OCEAN
Beaufort Sea
Baffin Bay
Davis Strait

ARCTIC
Inupiaq
Yupik
Koyukon
Ingalik
Aleut
Tanaina
Yupik
Eyak
Tuchone
Gulf of Alaska
Han
Inuit
Hare
Inuit
Inuit
Dogrib
Slavey
Inuit
Labrador Sea
Inuit
Naskapi
Montagnais
Beothuk

NORTHWEST COAST
Tagish
Kaska
Tlingit
Sekani
Tsimshian
Beaver
Haida
Carrier
Bella Coola
Chilcotin
Kwakiutl
Shuswap
Nootka
Okanagan
Makah
Kutenai
Quinault
Columbian
Chinook
Spokane
Blackfoot
Tillamook
Klikitat
Cayuse
Siuslaw
Nez Percé
Coos
Crow
PLATEAU
Gros Ventre
Assiniboin
Saulteaux
Southern Ojibwa

SUBARCTIC
Chipewyan
Plains Cree
Woods Cree
Swampy Cree
East Cree
Hudson Bay

Micmac
Maliseet
Eastern Ojibwa
Algonquin
Abenaki
Menominee
Huron
Iroquois
Massachusett-Narragansett
Mohawk
Oneida
Onondaga
Mohican
Mohegan-Pequot
Cayuga
Seneca
Potawatomi
Ottawa
Winnebago
Sauk
Fox
Delaware
Kickapoo
Susquehannock
NORTHEAST
Illinois
Miami
Shawnee
Powhatan
Tutelo-Saponi
Tuscarora

Klamath
Modoc
Northern Shoshone
Hidatsa
Mandan
Arikara
Yurok
Hupa
Northern Paiute
Bannock
Cheyenne
Teton Sioux
Yankton Sioux
Santee Sioux
Pomo
Maidu
Western Shoshone
Eastern Shoshone
Ponca
Omaha
Iowa
Wappo
Washo
Pawnee
GREAT BASIN
Miwok
Mono
GREAT PLAINS
Missouri

Costanoan
Yokut
Ute
Arapaho
Kansa
Southern Paiute
Kiowa
Osage
Chumash
Kawaiisu
Hopi
Jicarilla Apache
CALIFORNIA
Mohave
Navajo
Tewa
Quapaw
Chickasaw
Cherokee
Catawba
Cahuilla
Yavapai
Zuñi
Acoma
Muskogee (Creek)
Maricopa
Chiricahua
Mescalero Apache
Wichita
Tunica
SOUTHEAST
Alabama
Pima
Apache
Comanche
Caddo
Choctaw (Creek)
Hitchiti
Seri
Opata
Suma-Jumano
Tonkawa
Natchez
Apalachee
Timucua
Concho
Atakapa
SOUTHWEST
Karankawa
Cochimi
Yaqui
Coahuilteco
Calusa
Tarahumara
Toboso
Lucayo
Guaicura
Zacatec
Gulf of Mexico
Ciboney
Arawak
Arawak
Carib
Pericú
Guachichil
Carib

MESOAMERICA
Otomi
Totonac
Bay of Campeche
Maya
Aztec
Mixtec
Zoque
CIRCUM-CARIBBEAN
Zapotec
Maya
Lenca
Caribbean Sea
Mosquito
Cuna
Guaymí
SOUTH AMERICA

PACIFIC OCEAN
ATLANTIC OCEAN
Tropic of Cancer
Gulf of California

N W E S

0 500 1,000 Miles
0 500 1,000 Kilometers

180
160W
140W
120W
100W
80W
60W
40W
0
40N
20N
60N
40N
20N
60W
90N

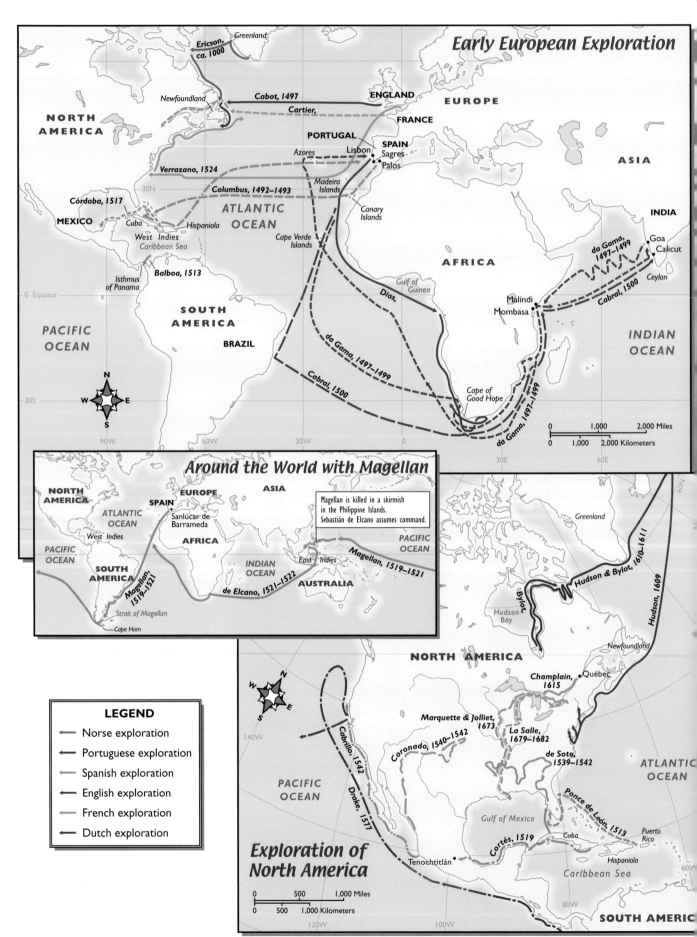

Early European Exploration

Ericson, ca. 1000
Greenland
Newfoundland
Cabot, 1497
Cartier,
ENGLAND
EUROPE
FRANCE
NORTH AMERICA
PORTUGAL
SPAIN
Azores
Lisbon
Sagres
Palos
ASIA
Verrazano, 1524
Madeira Islands
Córdoba, 1517
Columbus, 1492–1493
MEXICO
Cuba
Hispaniola
West Indies
Caribbean Sea
ATLANTIC OCEAN
Canary Islands
Cape Verde Islands
AFRICA
INDIA
Goa
Calicut
da Gama, 1497–1499
Ceylon
Isthmus of Panama
Balboa, 1513
30N
0 Equator
Dias,
Gulf of Guinea
Cabral, 1500
Malindi
Mombasa
INDIAN OCEAN
PACIFIC OCEAN
SOUTH AMERICA
BRAZIL
da Gama, 1497–1499
Cabral, 1500
Cape of Good Hope
da Gama, 1497–1499
30S
90W
60W
30W
0
30E
60E

0   1,000   2,000 Miles
0   1,000   2,000 Kilometers

Around the World with Magellan

NORTH AMERICA
EUROPE
ASIA
SPAIN
ATLANTIC OCEAN
Sanlúcar de Barrameda
AFRICA
West Indies
PACIFIC OCEAN
SOUTH AMERICA
Magellan, 1519–1521
Strait of Magellan
Cape Horn
de Elcano, 1521–1522
INDIAN OCEAN
East Indies
AUSTRALIA
Magellan, 1519–1521
PACIFIC OCEAN

Magellan is killed in a skirmish in the Philippine Islands. Sebastián de Elcano assumes command.

Greenland
Hudson & Bylot, 1610–1611
Bylot,
Hudson, 1609
Hudson Bay
Newfoundland
NORTH AMERICA
Champlain, 1615
Québec
Marquette & Jolliet, 1673
La Salle, 1679–1682
de Soto, 1539–1542
ATLANTIC OCEAN
Cabrillo, 1542
Coronado, 1540–1542
Drake, 1577
PACIFIC OCEAN
Ponce de León, 1513
Gulf of Mexico
Cortés, 1519
Cuba
Puerto Rico
Tenochtitlán
Hispaniola
Caribbean Sea
140W
120W
100W
80W
60N

LEGEND

- Norse exploration
- Portuguese exploration
- Spanish exploration
- English exploration
- French exploration
- Dutch exploration

Exploration of North America

0   500   1,000 Miles
0   500   1,000 Kilometers

SOUTH AMERIC

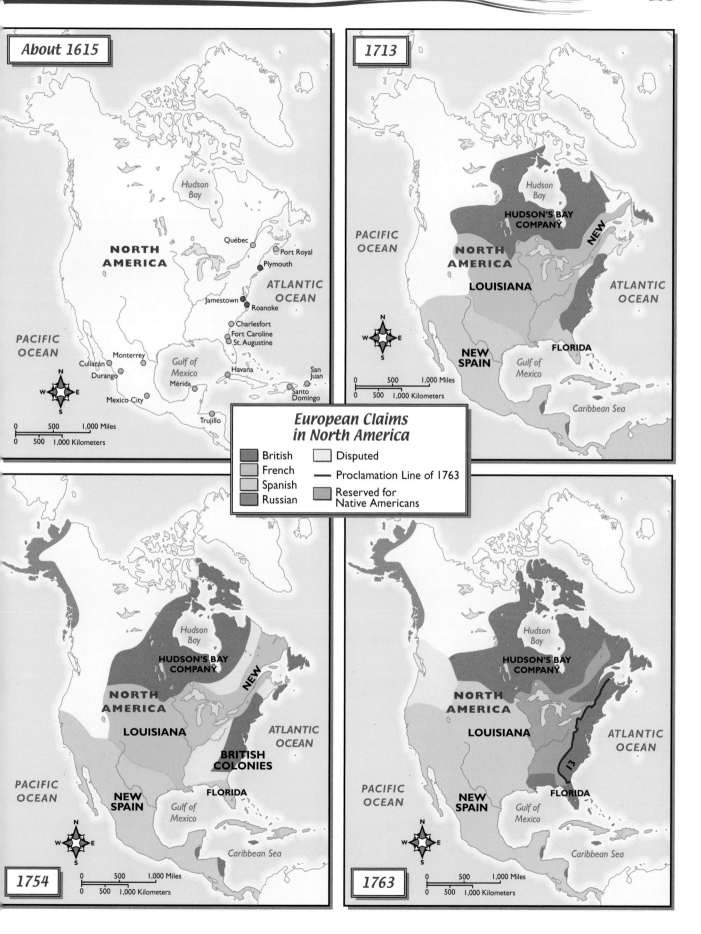

About 1615

NORTH
AMERICA

Hudson
Bay

Québec
Port Royal
Plymouth

ATLANTIC
OCEAN

Jamestown
Roanoke

Charlesfort
Fort Caroline
St. Augustine

PACIFIC
OCEAN

Culiacán
Monterrey
Durango
Mérida
Gulf of
Mexico
Havana
San
Juan

Mexico City
Santo
Domingo

Trujillo

N
W E
S

0   500   1,000 Miles
0   500   1,000 Kilometers

1713

PACIFIC
OCEAN

Hudson
Bay

HUDSON'S BAY
COMPANY

NORTH
AMERICA

NEW

LOUISIANA

ATLANTIC
OCEAN

NEW
SPAIN

FLORIDA

Gulf of
Mexico

Caribbean Sea

N
W E
S

0   500   1,000 Miles
0   500   1,000 Kilometers

European Claims
in North America

British
French
Spanish
Russian

Disputed

—— Proclamation Line of 1763

Reserved for
Native Americans

1754

Hudson
Bay

HUDSON'S BAY
COMPANY

NORTH
AMERICA

NEW

LOUISIANA

ATLANTIC
OCEAN

BRITISH
COLONIES

PACIFIC
OCEAN

NEW
SPAIN

FLORIDA

Gulf of
Mexico

Caribbean Sea

N
W E
S

0   500   1,000 Miles
0   500   1,000 Kilometers

1763

Hudson
Bay

HUDSON'S BAY
COMPANY

NORTH
AMERICA

LOUISIANA

ATLANTIC
OCEAN

13

PACIFIC
OCEAN

NEW
SPAIN

FLORIDA

Gulf of
Mexico

Caribbean Sea

N
W E
S

0   500   1,000 Miles
0   500   1,000 Kilometers

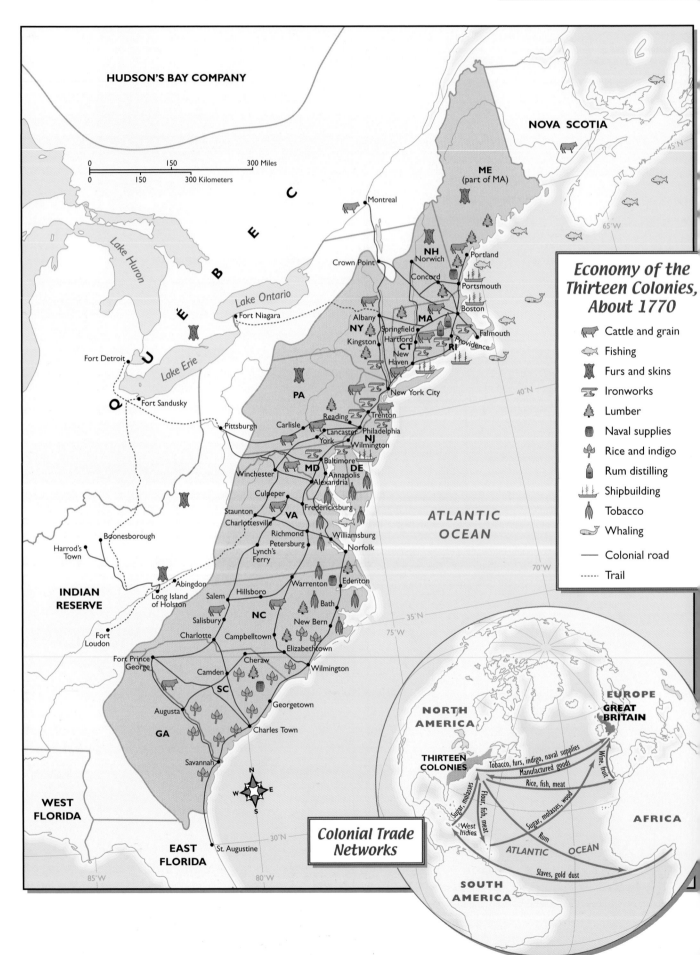

HUDSON'S BAY COMPANY

NOVA SCOTIA

ME
(part of MA)

Economy of the Thirteen Colonies, About 1770

🐂 Cattle and grain
🐟 Fishing
Furs and skins
Ironworks
🌲 Lumber
Naval supplies
Rice and indigo
Rum distilling
Shipbuilding
Tobacco
🐋 Whaling

—— Colonial road
········ Trail

0   150   300 Miles
0   150   300 Kilometers

Montreal

QUEBEC

Lake Huron

Lake Ontario

Fort Niagara

Fort Detroit

Lake Erie

Fort Sandusky

Crown Point

NH
Norwich
Concord
Portland
Portsmouth
Boston
Falmouth
Providence

Albany
NY
Springfield
Hartford
Kingston
CT
New Haven
RI

MA

Pittsburgh

PA

New York City

Carlisle
Reading
Trenton
Lancaster
York
Philadelphia
Wilmington
NJ
Baltimore
MD
DE
Annapolis
Winchester
Alexandria

ATLANTIC
OCEAN

Culpeper
Staunton
Charlottesville
VA
Fredericksburg
Richmond
Petersburg
Williamsburg
Lynch's Ferry
Norfolk

Boonesborough

Harrod's Town

Abingdon
Long Island of Holston

INDIAN RESERVE

Salem
Hillsboro
Warrenton
Edenton
Bath
NC
New Bern
Salisbury
Charlotte
Campbelltown
Elizabethtown
Wilmington

Fort Loudon

Fort Prince George
Camden
Cheraw
SC
Augusta
Georgetown
GA
Charles Town

Savannah

WEST FLORIDA

EAST FLORIDA
St. Augustine

N E S W

45°N
65°W
40°N
70°W
35°N
75°W
30°N
85°W 80°W

Colonial Trade Networks

NORTH AMERICA

EUROPE
GREAT BRITAIN

THIRTEEN COLONIES

Tobacco, furs, indigo, naval supplies
Manufactured goods
Rice, fish, meat
Wine, fruit

Sugar, molasses
Flour, fish, meat
West Indies
Sugar, molasses, wood
Rum

Slaves, gold dust

ATLANTIC OCEAN

AFRICA

SOUTH AMERICA

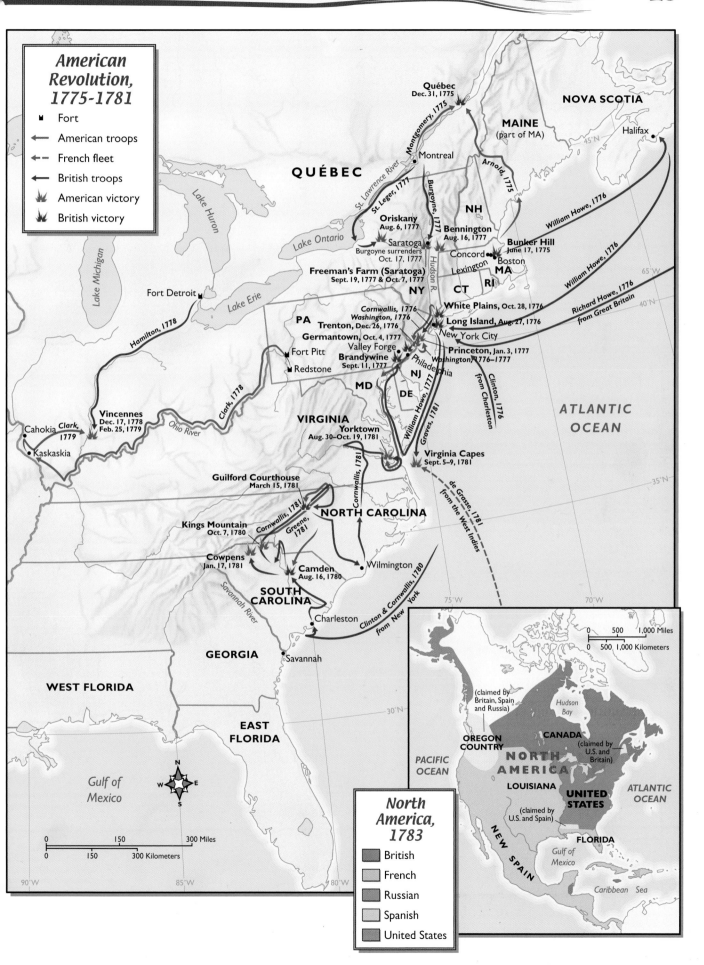

American Revolution, 1775–1781

- ■ Fort
- → American troops
- ⇠ French fleet
- → British troops
- ✴ American victory
- ✷ British victory

North America, 1783

- British
- French
- Russian
- Spanish
- United States

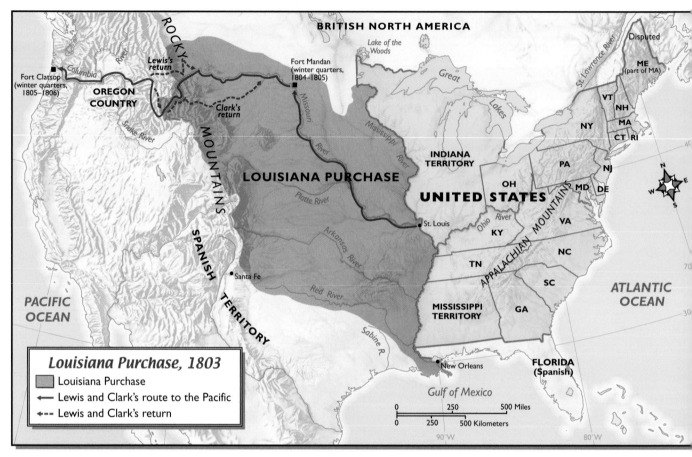

Louisiana Purchase, 1803

- Louisiana Purchase
- ← Lewis and Clark's route to the Pacific
- ←--- Lewis and Clark's return

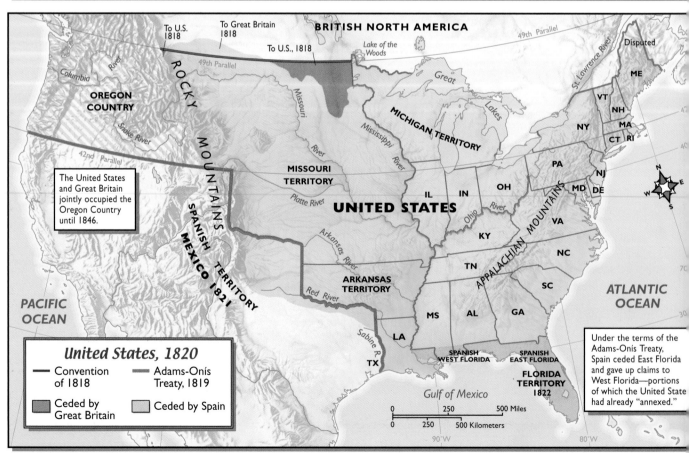

The United States and Great Britain jointly occupied the Oregon Country until 1846.

Under the terms of the Adams-Onís Treaty, Spain ceded East Florida and gave up claims to West Florida—portions of which the United State had already "annexed."

United States, 1820

- — Convention of 1818
- — Adams-Onís Treaty, 1819
- Ceded by Great Britain
- Ceded by Spain

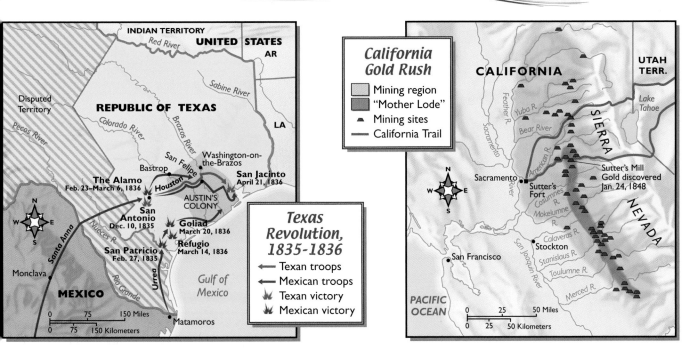

Texas Revolution, 1835-1836

INDIAN TERRITORY
UNITED STATES
AR
Red River
Sabine River
REPUBLIC OF TEXAS
LA
Disputed Territory
Pecos River
Colorado River
Brazos River
Washington-on-the-Brazos
San Felipe
Bastrop
Houston
The Alamo Feb. 23–March 6, 1836
San Jacinto April 21, 1836
AUSTIN'S COLONY
San Antonio Dec. 10, 1835
Goliad March 20, 1836
Nueces R.
Refugio March 14, 1836
San Patricio Feb. 27, 1835
Santa Anna
Monclava
Urrea
Rio Grande
MEXICO
Gulf of Mexico
Matamoros

0 75 150 Miles
0 75 150 Kilometers

Texas Revolution, 1835-1836
← Texan troops
← Mexican troops
✹ Texan victory
✹ Mexican victory

California Gold Rush
☐ Mining region
☐ "Mother Lode"
▲ Mining sites
— California Trail

CALIFORNIA
UTAH TERR.
Feather R.
Yuba R.
Bear River
Sacramento
SIERRA
Lake Tahoe
American R.
Sutter's Fort
Cosumnes R.
Mokelumne R.
NEVADA
Sutter's Mill Gold discovered Jan. 24, 1848
San Francisco
Calaveras R.
Stockton
San Joaquin River
Stanislaus R.
Toulumne R.
Merced R.
PACIFIC OCEAN

0 25 50 Miles
0 25 50 Kilometers

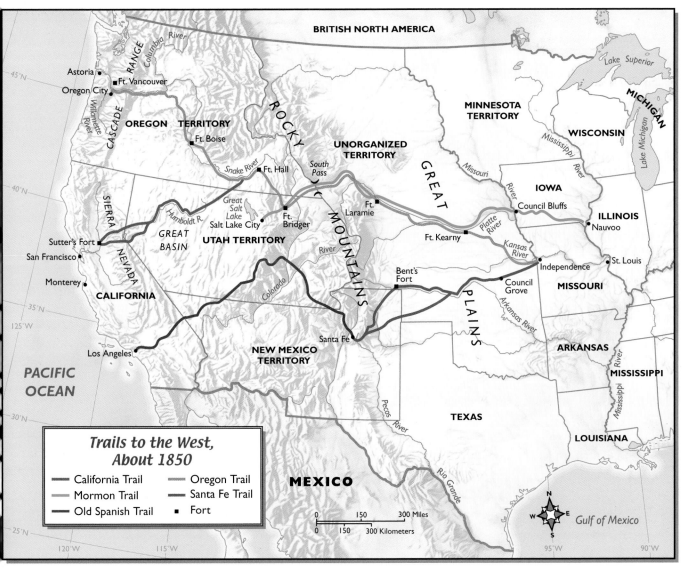

BRITISH NORTH AMERICA
Astoria
Ft. Vancouver
Oregon City
Columbia River
CASCADE RANGE
45°N
OREGON TERRITORY
Ft. Boise
Willamette River
Snake River
Ft. Hall
South Pass
ROCKY
UNORGANIZED TERRITORY
Lake Superior
MICHIGAN
MINNESOTA TERRITORY
WISCONSIN
Mississippi River
Lake Michigan
40°N
Great Salt Lake
Humboldt R.
Salt Lake City
Ft. Bridger
MOUNTAINS
Ft. Laramie
GREAT
Missouri River
IOWA
Council Bluffs
ILLINOIS
SIERRA
GREAT BASIN
UTAH TERRITORY
River
Ft. Kearny
Platte River
Nauvoo
Sutter's Fort
NEVADA
Kansas River
Independence
St. Louis
San Francisco
Colorado
Bent's Fort
Council Grove
MISSOURI
Monterey
CALIFORNIA
PLAINS
Arkansas River
125°W
Santa Fe
ARKANSAS
Los Angeles
NEW MEXICO TERRITORY
Mississippi River
35°N
MISSISSIPPI
PACIFIC OCEAN
Pecos River
TEXAS
LOUISIANA
30°N
Rio Grande
MEXICO
Gulf of Mexico
25°N
120°W   115°W   95°W   90°W

Trails to the West, About 1850
— California Trail   — Oregon Trail
— Mormon Trail   — Santa Fe Trail
— Old Spanish Trail   ■ Fort

0 150 300 Miles
0 150 300 Kilometers

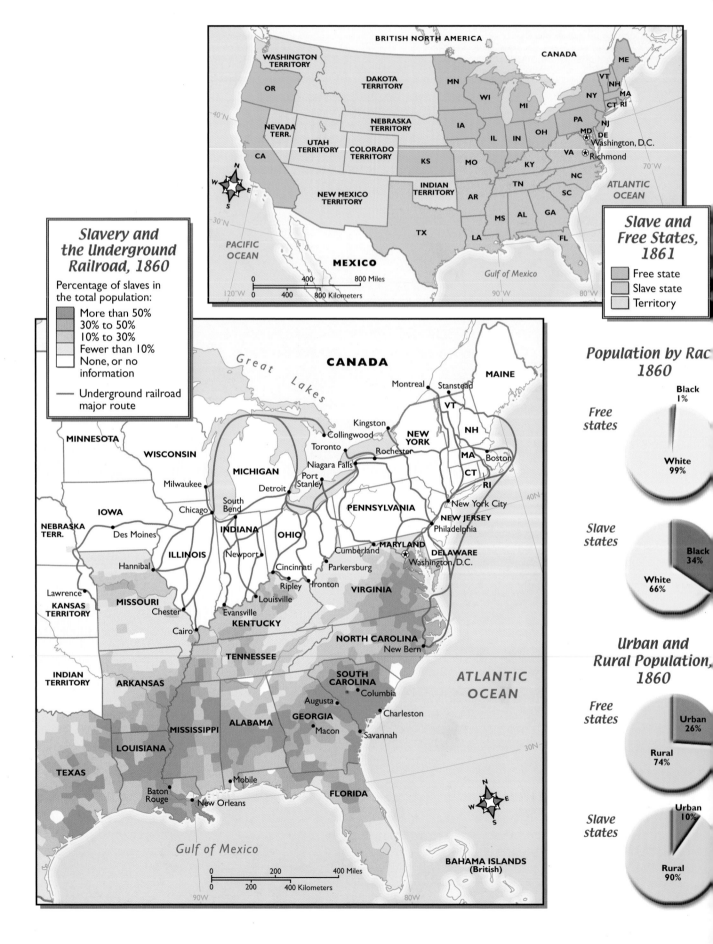

Slavery and the Underground Railroad, 1860

Percentage of slaves in the total population:

- More than 50%
- 30% to 50%
- 10% to 30%
- Fewer than 10%
- None, or no information

— Underground railroad major route

Slave and Free States, 1861

- Free state
- Slave state
- Territory

Population by Race, 1860

Free states
- Black 1%
- White 99%

Slave states
- Black 34%
- White 66%

Urban and Rural Population, 1860

Free states
- Urban 26%
- Rural 74%

Slave states
- Urban 10%
- Rural 90%

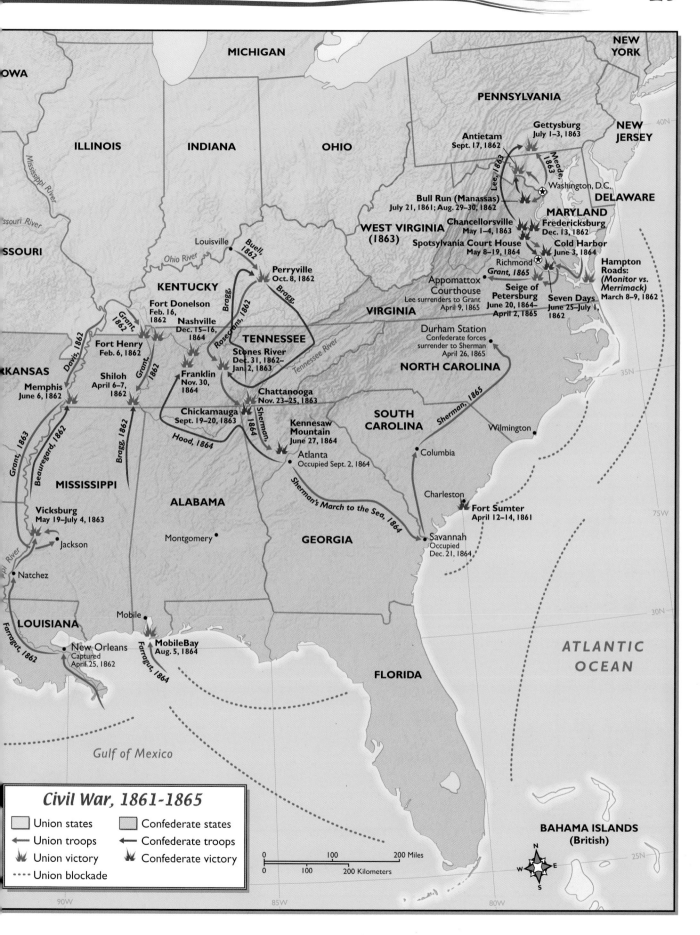

MICHIGAN

OWA

ILLINOIS   INDIANA   OHIO

PENNSYLVANIA

NEW YORK

NEW JERSEY

Mississippi River

Missouri River

SSOURI

Louisville

Ohio River

KENTUCKY

Buell, 1862

Perryville
Oct. 8, 1862

Bragg, 1862

Bragg

Antietam
Sept. 17, 1862

Gettysburg
July 1–3, 1863

Lee, 1863

Meade, 1863

Washington, D.C.

DELAWARE

WEST VIRGINIA
(1863)

Bull Run (Manassas)
July 21, 1861; Aug. 29–30, 1862

Chancellorsville
May 1–4, 1863

MARYLAND

Fredericksburg
Dec. 13, 1862

Spotsylvania Court House
May 8–19, 1864

Cold Harbor
June 3, 1864

Grant, 1862

Fort Donelson
Feb. 16, 1862

Nashville
Dec. 15–16, 1864

Rosecrans, 1862

Fort Henry
Feb. 6, 1862

Davis, 1862

Grant, 1862

TENNESSEE

Stones River
Dec. 31, 1862–
Jan. 2, 1863

Richmond

Grant, 1865

VIRGINIA

Tennessee River

Appomattox
Courthouse
Lee surrenders to Grant
April 9, 1865

Seige of
Petersburg
June 20, 1864–
April 2, 1865

Seven Days
June 25–July 1,
1862

Hampton
Roads:
(Monitor vs.
Merrimack)
March 8–9, 1862

ARKANSAS

Memphis
June 6, 1862

Shiloh
April 6–7,
1862

Bragg, 1862

Franklin
Nov. 30,
1864

Chickamauga
Sept. 19–20, 1863

Hood, 1864

Chattanooga
Nov. 23–25, 1863

Sherman, 1864

Durham Station
Confederate forces
surrender to Sherman
April 26, 1865

NORTH CAROLINA

Sherman, 1865

SOUTH
CAROLINA

Wilmington

Grant, 1863

Beauregard, 1862

Bragg, 1862

Kennesaw
Mountain
June 27, 1864

Sherman's March to the Sea, 1864

Atlanta
Occupied Sept. 2, 1864

Columbia

MISSISSIPPI

Vicksburg
May 19–July 4, 1863

ALABAMA

Montgomery

GEORGIA

Charleston

Fort Sumter
April 12–14, 1861

Jackson

pi River

Natchez

Savannah
Occupied
Dec. 21, 1864

LOUISIANA

Mobile

Farragut, 1862

New Orleans
Captured
April 25, 1862

Farragut, 1864

MobileBay
Aug. 5, 1864

FLORIDA

ATLANTIC
OCEAN

40N

75W

35N

30N

Gulf of Mexico

BAHAMA ISLANDS
(British)

25N

Civil War, 1861-1865

- ☐ Union states
- ☐ Confederate states
- ← Union troops
- ← Confederate troops
- ✹ Union victory
- ✹ Confederate victory
- ···· Union blockade

0   100   200 Miles

0   100   200 Kilometers

N
W E
S

90W   85W   80W

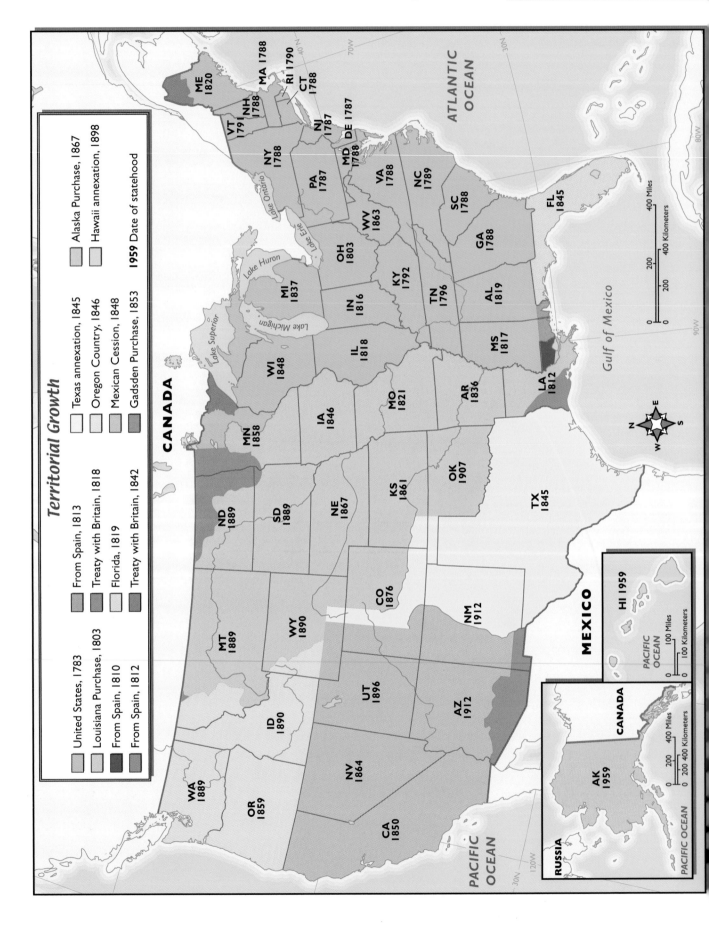

Territorial Growth

United States, 1783

Louisiana Purchase, 1803

From Spain, 1810

From Spain, 1812

From Spain, 1813

Treaty with Britain, 1818

Florida, 1819

Treaty with Britain, 1842

Texas annexation, 1845

Oregon Country, 1846

Mexican Cession, 1848

Gadsden Purchase, 1853

Alaska Purchase, 1867

Hawaii annexation, 1898

1959 Date of statehood

ME 1820 · MA 1788 · RI 1790 · CT 1788 · NH 1788 · VT 1791 · NY 1788 · NJ 1787 · DE 1787 · MD 1788 · VA 1788 · NC 1789 · PA 1787 · WV 1863 · SC 1788 · OH 1803 · GA 1788 · KY 1792 · TN 1796 · AL 1819 · MI 1837 · IN 1816 · MS 1817 · IL 1818 · AR 1836 · LA 1812 · WI 1848 · MO 1821 · IA 1846 · MN 1858 · OK 1907 · KS 1861 · TX 1845 · ND 1889 · SD 1889 · NE 1867 · CO 1876 · NM 1912 · MT 1889 · WY 1890 · UT 1896 · AZ 1912 · ID 1890 · NV 1864 · CA 1850 · WA 1889 · OR 1859 · FL 1845 · HI 1959 · AK 1959

CANADA · MEXICO · RUSSIA

ATLANTIC OCEAN · PACIFIC OCEAN · Gulf of Mexico

Lake Ontario · Lake Erie · Lake Huron · Lake Michigan · Lake Superior

400 Miles · 400 Kilometers · 100 Miles · 100 Kilometers

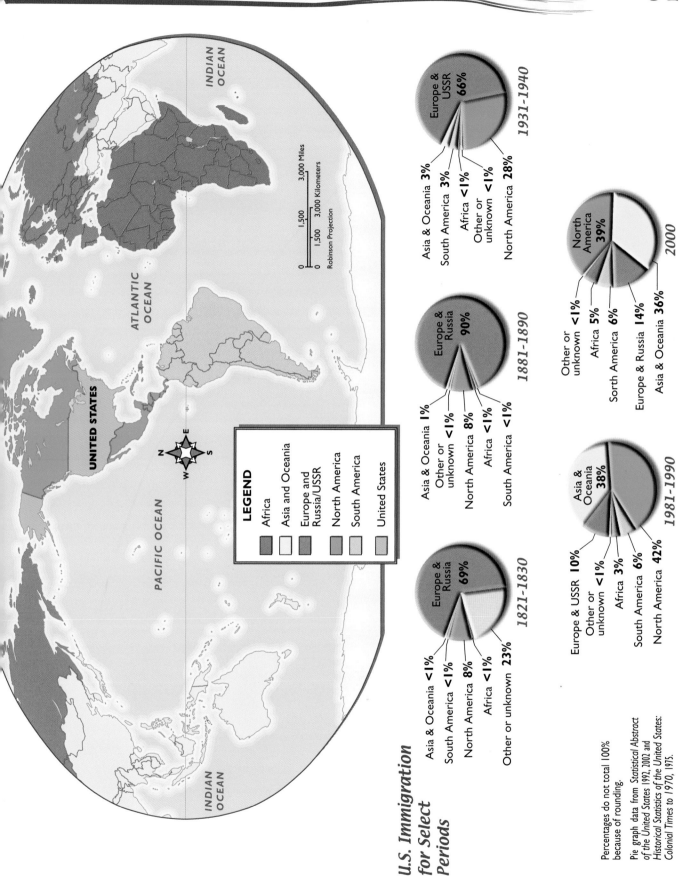

U.S. Immigration for Select Periods

LEGEND

- Africa
- Asia and Oceania
- Europe and Russia/USSR
- North America
- South America
- United States

1931–1940

- Europe & USSR **66%**
- Asia & Oceania **3%**
- South America **3%**
- Africa **<1%**
- Other or unknown **<1%**
- North America **28%**

1881–1890

- Europe & Russia **90%**
- Asia & Oceania **1%**
- Other or unknown **<1%**
- North America **8%**
- Africa **<1%**
- South America **<1%**

1821–1830

- Europe & Russia **69%**
- Asia & Oceania **<1%**
- South America **<1%**
- North America **8%**
- Africa **<1%**
- Other or unknown **23%**

2000

- North America **39%**
- Other or unknown **<1%**
- Africa **5%**
- South America **6%**
- Europe & Russia **14%**
- Asia & Oceania **36%**

1981–1990

- Asia & Oceania **38%**
- Europe & USSR **10%**
- Other or unknown **<1%**
- Africa **3%**
- South America **6%**
- North America **42%**

Percentages do not total 100% because of rounding.

Pie graph data from *Statistical Abstract of the United States 1992, 2002* and *Historical Statistics of the United States: Colonial Times to 1970, 1975.*

U.S. International Trade in Goods and Services

Billions of dollars

Imports

Trade Balance

Exports

**January 2003
TRADE BALANCE
–$41.1 Billion**

January 2001 · January 2002 · January 2003

Foreign Trade Statistics, U.S. Census Bureau

This graph indicates that the U.S. spends more money purchasing foreign products than it receives from selling domestic products abroad.

World Trade Organizations

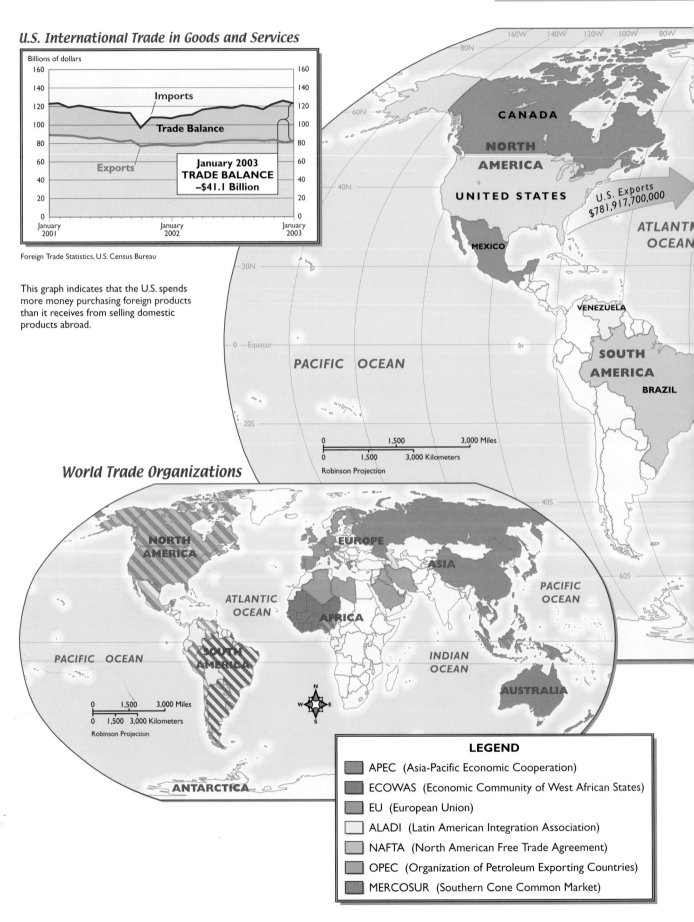

LEGEND

- APEC (Asia-Pacific Economic Cooperation)
- ECOWAS (Economic Community of West African States)
- EU (European Union)
- ALADI (Latin American Integration Association)
- NAFTA (North American Free Trade Agreement)
- OPEC (Organization of Petroleum Exporting Countries)
- MERCOSUR (Southern Cone Common Market)

U.S. Exports $781,917,700,000

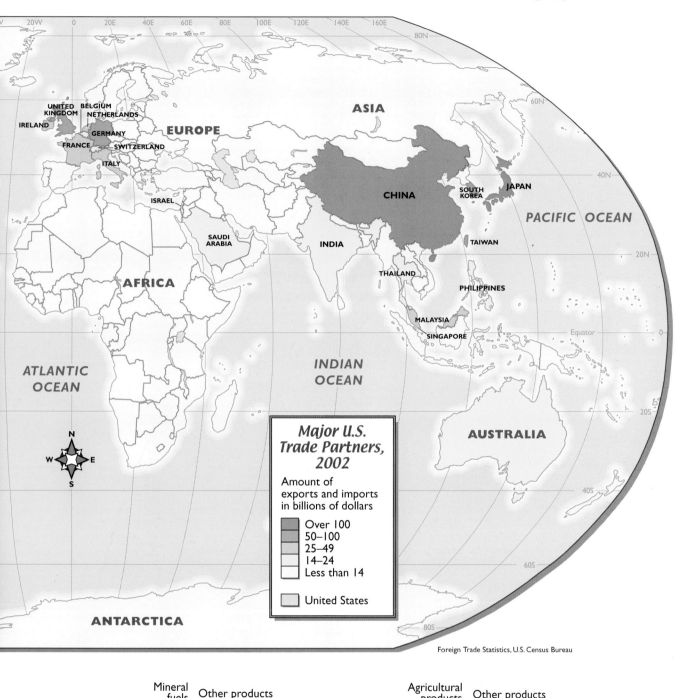

20W   0   20E   40E   60E   80E   100E   120E   140E   160E   80N

ASIA   60N

UNITED BELGIUM
KINGDOM NETHERLANDS
IRELAND   EUROPE   40N
GERMANY
FRANCE SWITZERLAND   CHINA   SOUTH   JAPAN
ITALY   KOREA
ISRAEL   PACIFIC OCEAN
SAUDI   TAIWAN   20N
ARABIA   INDIA
AFRICA   THAILAND
PHILIPPINES
MALAYSIA
SINGAPORE   Equator   0

ATLANTIC   INDIAN
OCEAN   OCEAN   20S

AUSTRALIA

N
W   E   40S
S

Less than 14

ANTARCTICA   80S

Major U.S. Trade Partners, 2002

Amount of exports and imports in billions of dollars

- Over 100
- 50–100
- 25–49
- 14–24
- Less than 14

United States

Foreign Trade Statistics, U.S. Census Bureau

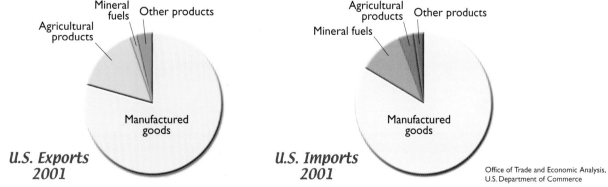

Mineral fuels   Other products
Agricultural products

Manufactured goods

U.S. Exports 2001

Agricultural products   Other products
Mineral fuels

Manufactured goods

U.S. Imports 2001

Office of Trade and Economic Analysis, U.S. Department of Commerce

CANADA

WASHINGTON
- Seattle
- Olympia
- Spokane

OREGON
- Portland
- Salem
- Eugene

IDAHO
- Boise
- Pocatello

MONTANA
- Great Falls
- Helena
- Billings

WYOMING
- Casper

NEVADA
- Reno
- Carson City

NORTH DAKOTA
- Bismarck
- Grand Forks
- Fargo

MINNESO
- Minneapolis

SOUTH DAKOTA
- Pierre
- Sioux Falls

IOV
- Des Moines

NEBRASKA
- Omaha
- Lincoln

UTAH
- Salt Lake City
- Ogden
- Provo

CALIFORNIA
- Sacramento
- San Francisco
- Oakland
- San Jose
- Las Vegas
- Los Angeles
- Long Beach
- San Diego

COLORADO
- Denver
- Colorado Springs
- Pueblo
- Cheyenne

KANSAS
- Wichita
- Topeka

Kansas City
Kans
City

MISSO

ARIZONA
- Phoenix
- Tucson

NEW MEXICO
- Santa Fe
- Albuquerque
- El Paso

OKLAHOMA
- Tulsa
- Oklahoma City

For
Sm

ARKAN

TEXAS
- Fort Worth
- Dallas
- Shreveport
- Austin
- San Antonio
- Houston
- Laredo
- Corpus Christi

PACIFIC OCEAN

MEXICO

130W
40N
30N
120W

RUSSIA

ALASKA
- Nome
- Fairbanks
- Anchorage
- Juneau

CANADA

Arctic Circle

Bering Sea

Gulf of Alaska

70N
60N
170W
160W
150W
140W

N E W S

0   200   400 Miles
0   200   400 Kilometers

HAWAII
- Honolulu
- Hilo

PACIFIC OCEAN

N E W S

0   100   200 Miles
0   100   200 Kilometers

20N
160W
155W

N E W S

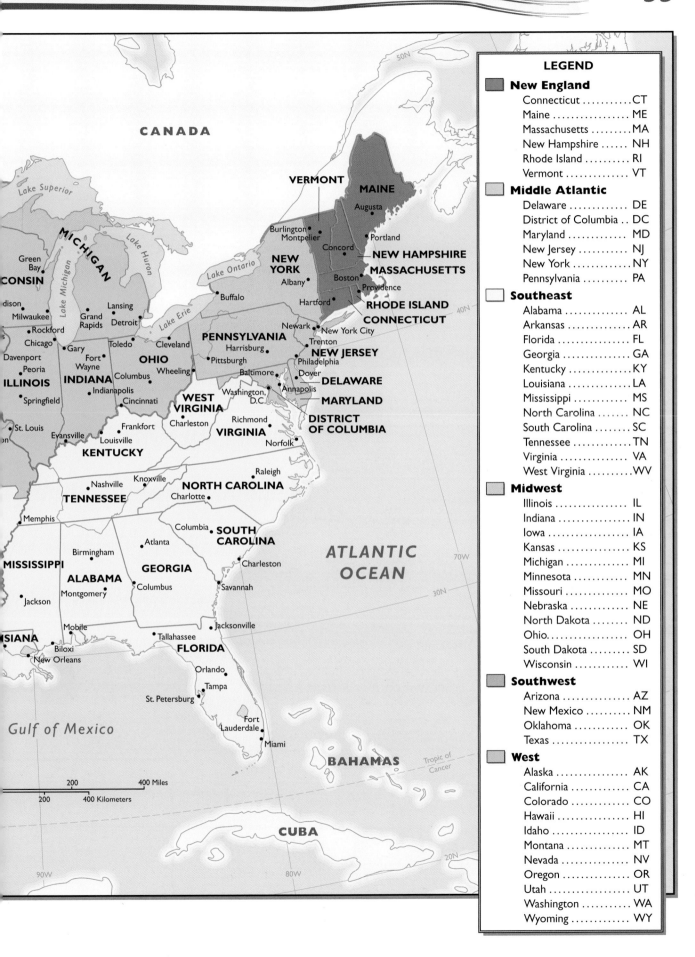

TENNESSEE

MISSISSIPPI

GEORGIA

FLORIDA

Chattanooga

LEGEND
★ State capital
• City
SHELBY County
▲ Mountain peak
National or other park
Urban area

Pickwick Lake   LAUDERDALE
Florence
LIMESTONE
• Athens
Wheeler Lake   MADISON
• Muscle Shoals
COLBERT
LAWRENCE
• Russellville
FRANKLIN
• Decatur
MORGAN
Huntsville
• Scottsboro
JACKSON
Tennessee River
DE KALB
Fort Payne
Guntersville Lake   MARSHALL
• Guntersville
Weiss Lake
CHEROKEE
ETOWAH
Gadsden

MARION
• Hamilton
WINSTON
CULLMAN
• Cullman
BLOUNT
ST. CLAIR
CALHOUN
• Jacksonville
CLEBURNE
Atlanta ★

LAMAR
FAYETTE
Lewis Smith Lake
WALKER
• Jasper
JEFFERSON
Birmingham
Bessemer • • Hoover
▲ Cheaha Mtn. 2,405 ft. (733 m)
• Anniston
• Talladega
TALLADEGA
CLAY
RANDOLPH
Roanoke

PICKENS
TUSCALOOSA
Black Warrior R.
SHELBY
• Tuscaloosa
BIBB
• Sylacauga
West Point Lake
CHAMBERS

GREENE
HALE
CHILTON
• Clanton
• Alexander City
COOSA
Tallapoosa R.
TALLAPOOSA
Lake Martin
• Opelika
• Auburn
LEE
• Columbus

SUMTER
Tombigbee River
PERRY
• Marion
AUTAUGA
ELMORE
Coosa River
MACON
• Tuskegee
Phenix City
RUSSELL

• Demopolis
MARENGO
DALLAS
• Selma
Alabama River
LOWNDES
★ Montgomery
MONTGOMERY
BULLOCK

CHOCTAW
WILCOX
William "Bill" Dannelly Reservoir
BUTLER
• Greenville
CRENSHAW
• Troy
PIKE
BARBOUR
• Eufaula
Walter F. George Reservoir
Pea River

CLARKE
MONROE
• Jackson
• Monroeville
CONECUH
COFFEE
• Andalusia
• Opp
COVINGTON
• Enterprise
DALE
• Ozark
HENRY
Chattahoochee River

WASHINGTON
Alabama River
ESCAMBIA
• Brewton
Conecuh River
• Atmore
GENEVA
HOUSTON
Dothan
Flint River

MOBILE
• Bay Minette
BALDWIN
Escambia River
Choctawhatchee River

• Prichard
Mobile
Mobile Bay

• Gulfport

• Pensacola
GULF ISLANDS NATL. SEASHORE
Gulf of Mexico

0   25   50 Miles
0   25   50 Kilometers

SOUTHEAST

ALABAMA

88W   86W   34N   32N   88W   86W

he shapes of Alabama and its neighbor Mississippi could most be called mirror images of each other. However, at description must be used cautiously because Alabama unique. The northern portion of the state includes hills d the southernmost ranges of the Appalachian ountains. The Tennessee River, dammed for flood control d electric power, crosses this part of the state. Central d southern Alabama is primarily flat and is home to the st agricultural land. The state has a small segment of oastline along the Gulf of Mexico. Birmingham makes steel well as a variety of other manufactured goods. All the ements used to make steel can be found within the state. ecause of its industries, Alabama attracted immigrants 100 ars ago, unlike the other southern states. High-tech, aero- pace-related businesses can be found in Huntsville, while obile is an important seaport.

Did You Know?

Alabama honored an insect pest with a statue because it forced farmers to switch from cotton to more profitable crops:

Boll Weevil Monument in Enterprise

Alabama Almanac

Nicknames	Heart of Dixie, Camellia State
State capital	Montgomery
Date of statehood	Dec. 14, 1819; 22nd state
State bird	Yellowhammer
State flower	Camellia
State tree	Southern longleaf pine
State motto	We Dare Defend Our Rights
Total population & rank	4,464,356 (in 2001); 23rd
Population density	88 per sq. mile (34 per sq. km)
Population distribution	55% urban, 45% rural
Largest cities	Birmingham, Montgomery, Mobile, Huntsville
Highest elevation	Cheaha Mountain, 2,405 ft. (733 m)
Lowest elevation	sea level
Land area & rank	50,744 sq. miles (131,427 sq. km); 28th
Average January temperature	45°F (7°C)
Average July temperature	80°F (27°C)
Average yearly precipitation	56 inches (142 cm)
Major industries	pulp and paper, chemicals, electronics, apparel, textiles
Places to visit	Alabama Space and Rocket Center (Huntsville), Carver Museum (Tuskegee), Civil Rights Memorial (Montgomery)
Web site	www.alabama.gov

Economy – Chief Products

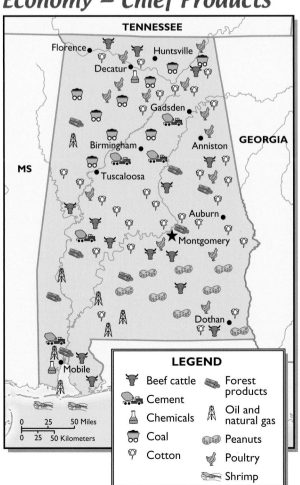

LEGEND

- 🐂 Beef cattle
- 🚚 Cement
- ⚗️ Chemicals
- Coal
- 🌸 Cotton
- Forest products
- Oil and natural gas
- Peanuts
- 🐓 Poultry
- 🦐 Shrimp

Physical

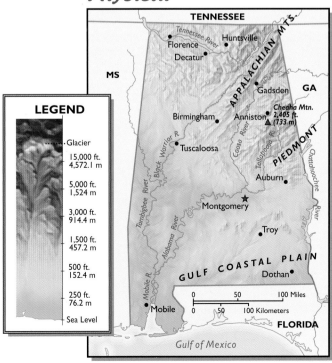

Map

Chukchi Sea

Pt. Barrow
Barrow

70N
180
170W
160W
150W
140W
130W

Beaufort Sea

Arctic Circle

RUSSIA

NORTHWEST TERRITORIES

Inuvik

Kotzebue

KOBUK VALLEY N.P.

GATES OF THE ARCTIC N.P. AND PRESERVE

Colville River

Sagavaniktok R.

Kotzebue Sound

Kobuk River

SEWARD PENINSULA

Koyukuk River

Porcupine River

Yukon River

LEGEND

★ State capital
• City
▲ Mountain peak
▬ National park

Nome

Norton Sound

Yukon River

College • Fairbanks

YUKON TERRITORY

St. Lawrence Island

Yukon Delta

Tanana River

DENALI N.P. AND PRESERVE

CANADA

St. Matthew Island

60N

Kuskokwim River

Mt. McKinley
20,320 ft
(6,194 m) ▲

Mt. Blackburn
16,390 ft (4,996 m) ▲

Whitehorse

Bethel

Wasilla • Palmer

Anchorage

Valdez

WRANGELL-ST. ELIAS N.P. AND PRESERVE

Mt. St. Elias
18,008 ft
(5,489 m) ▲

BRITISH COLUMBIA

Nunivak Island

Kuskokwim Bay

LAKE CLARK N.P. & PRES.

Nikiski
Kenai • Soldotna
KENAI PENINSULA
Seward

Prince William Sound

GLACIER BAY N.P. & PRES.

★ Juneau

Bering Sea

Nushagak R.

Lake Clark

Iliamna Lake

Homer

KENAI FJORDS NATL. PARK

Chichagof I.

Sitka

Pribilof Islands

170W

KATMAI N.P. & PRES.

Afognak Island

Gulf of Alaska

Baranof I.

Petersburg

130W

Becharof Lake

Shelikof Strait

Kodiak

Ketchikan

Bristol Bay

Kodiak Island

Prince of Wales I.

0   200   400 Miles
0   200   400 Kilometers

150W
140W

Alexander Archipelago

Dixon Entrance

Prince Rupert

Aleutian Islands

ALASKA PENINSULA

Unimak Island

PACIFIC OCEAN

Unalaska

Umnak Island

Unalaska Island

For continuation of map, see inset at right

160W

Aleutian Islands inset

Attu I.

Bering Sea

Umnak I.

Agattu I.

52N

Aleutian Islands

Kiska I.

Semisopochnoi I.

Kanaga I.
Atka I.

Seguam I.
Yunaska I.

52N

Amchitka I.

Adak I. **PACIFIC OCEAN**
Tanaga I.

Amlia I.

180
170W

ALASKA

WEST

Twice the size of Texas, Alaska is the largest U.S. state. Sitting in the extreme northwest portion of North America, it is also the coldest. Above the Arctic Circle, winter means six months without sun, though in the summer the sun never sets. Many mountains here are very high: Mt. McKinley is the highest in North America. Many feel that the first people to settle North America may have come through Alaska from Asia many thousands of years ago. Alaska was settled on a large scale during and after the Gold Rush of the late 1890s, after it had become part of the United States. Today, most people earn a living by fishing, mining, oil extraction, transportation, and the service industry. Though almost 70% are of European descent, Native Alaskans still form about 16% of the population and actively maintain their heritage. Regardless of their origin, most people choose to live in Alaska rather than end up here by chance.

Alaska Almanac

Nickname	The Last Frontier	**Lowest elevation**	sea level
State capital	Juneau	**Land area & rank**	571,951 sq. miles (1,481,353 sq. km); 1st
Date of statehood	Jan. 3, 1959; 49th state		
State bird	Willow ptarmigan	**Average January temperature**	10°F (−12°C)
State flower	Forget-me-not		
State tree	Sitka spruce	**Average July temperature**	54°F (12°C)
State motto	North to the Future		
Total population & rank	634,892 (in 2001); 47th	**Average yearly precipitation**	22 inches (56 cm)
Population density	1.1 per sq. mile (0.4 per sq. km)	**Major industries**	petroleum, tourism, fishing, mining, forestry
Population distribution	66% urban, 34% rural		
Largest cities	Anchorage, Juneau, Fairbanks	**Places to visit**	Glacier Bay National Park, Denali National Park, Inside Passage, Mendenhall Glacier, Skagway
Highest elevation	Mt. McKinley, 20,320 ft. (6,194 m)		
		Web site	www.state.ak.us

Economy – Chief Products

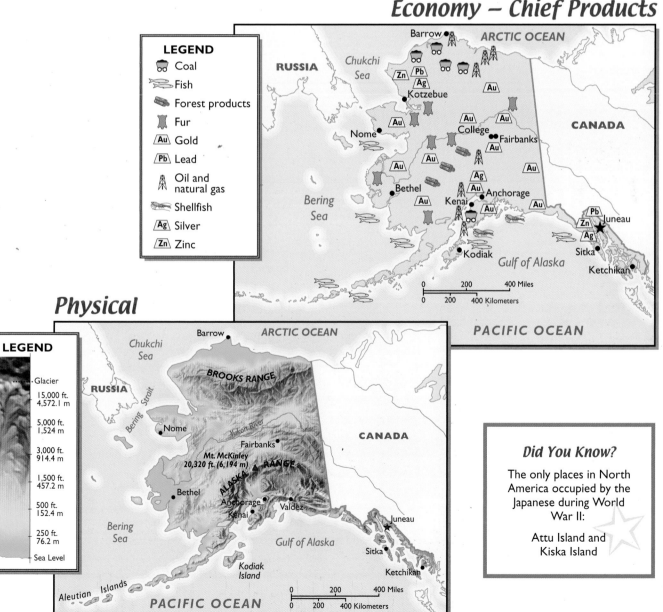

LEGEND
- Coal
- Fish
- Forest products
- Fur
- Au Gold
- Pb Lead
- Oil and natural gas
- Shellfish
- Ag Silver
- Zn Zinc

Physical

LEGEND

- Glacier
- 15,000 ft. / 4,572.1 m
- 5,000 ft. / 1,524 m
- 3,000 ft. / 914.4 m
- 1,500 ft. / 457.2 m
- 500 ft. / 152.4 m
- 250 ft. / 76.2 m
- Sea Level

Did You Know?

The only places in North America occupied by the Japanese during World War II:

Attu Island and Kiska Island

LEGEND

★ State capital
• City
PIMA County
▲ Mountain peak
National or other park
Urban area

50 Miles　100 Miles
50 Kilometers　100 Kilometers

UTAH

NEVADA

CO

CALIFORNIA

NM

MEXICO

St. George

Las Vegas

Grand Canyon

VERMILION CLIFFS NATL. MON.

Page

Lake Powell

NAVAJO NATL. MON.

Kayenta

Chinle

CANYON DE CHELLY NATL. MON.

GRAND CANYON-PARASHANT NATL. MONUMENT

Lake Mead

GRAND CANYON NATL. PARK

LAKE MEAD NATL. REC. AREA

MOHAVE

COCONINO

Tuba City

GLEN CANYON NATL. REC. AREA

Lake Mohave

Kingman

Bullhead City

▲ Hualapai Pk. 8,417 ft. (2,566 m)

WUPATKI NATL. MON.

SUNSET CRATER VOLCANO NATL. MON.

Humphreys Pk. 12,633 ft. (3,851 m) ▲

Flagstaff

WALNUT CANYON NATL. MON.

NAVAJO

APACHE

Puerco River

Winslow

Holbrook

PETRIFIED FOREST NATL. PARK

Lake Havasu

Lake Havasu City

Chino Valley

Sedona

Cottonwood

YAVAPAI

Prescott Valley

Prescott

Camp Verde

Verde River

St. Johns

Show Low

▲ Mt. Baldy 11,403 ft. (3,476 m)

Bill Williams River

AGUA FRIA NATL. MON.

Payson

Wickenburg

LA PAZ

Theodore Roosevelt Lake

GILA

Salt River

Colorado River

Glendale

Phoenix ★

Scottsdale

Mesa

Tempe

Chandler

Globe

San Carlos Reservoir

GREENLEE

MARICOPA

YUMA

Gila River

Gila Bend

SONORAN DESERT NATL. MON.

Florence

PINAL

Casa Grande

Eloy

Gila River

San Pedro River

GRAHAM

Safford

Yuma

San Luis

Ajo

IRONWOOD FOREST NATL. MON.

Santa Cruz River

Tucson

SAGUARO NATL. PARK

SAGUARO NATL. PARK

PIMA

CHIRICAHUA NATL. MON.

COCHISE

Green Valley

▲ Mt. Wrightson 9,453 ft. (2,881 m)

Tombstone

▲ Chiricahua Pk. 9,798 ft. (2,986 m)

Sierra Vista

Bisbee

Douglas

SANTA CRUZ

Nogales

Nogales

Gulf of California

ARIZONA

SOUTHWEST

114W　2　112W　3　4　110W　5

36N　34N　32N

While many think of Arizona as a dry, desert state, it also has many rivers and high, forested mountains. In the north, the raging Colorado River winds its way at the bottom of the spectacular Grand Canyon—which is as much as 1 mile (1.6 km) deep—before entering Lake Mead. Farther south, the land turns into a hot, dry desert with tall saguaro cacti dotting the landscape, and summertime high temperatures often top 110°F (43°C). Even though Arizona became a state only in 1912, Spanish explorers searching for gold were already here by 1539. Today, the people of Arizona are as mixed as the landscape. Mexican, Native American, European, and other cultures are all represented. Mining and ranching are common in the countryside, but services, tourism, and retail trade form the backbone of Arizona's economy. The sprawling capital city of Phoenix also has a vibrant high-technology industry, while the warm climate invites many to retire here.

Did You Know?

Pluto, the most distant planet from the sun, was discovered at this observatory: Lowell Observatory in Flagstaff

Arizona Almanac

Nickname	Grand Canyon State
State capital	Phoenix
Date of statehood	Feb. 14, 1912; 48th state
State bird	Cactus wren
State flower	Blossom of the Saguaro cactus
State tree	Paloverde
State motto	*Ditat Deus* (God Enriches)
Total population & rank	5,307,331 (in 2001); 20th
Population density	47 per sq. mile (18 per sq. km)
Population distribution	88% urban, 12% rural
Largest cities	Phoenix, Tucson, Mesa, Glendale, Scottsdale, Chandler
Highest elevation	Humphreys Peak, 12,633 ft. (3,851 m)
Lowest elevation	Colorado River in Yuma Co., 70 ft. (21 m)
Land area & rank	113,635 sq. miles (294,315 sq. km); 6th
Average January temperature	44°F (7°C)
Average July temperature	83°F (28°C)
Average yearly precipitation	13 inches (33 cm)
Major industries	manufacturing, construction, tourism, mining, agriculture
Places to visit	Grand Canyon, Painted Desert, Petrified Forest, Navajo National Monument, Meteor Crater
Web site	www.state.az.gov

Economy – Chief Products

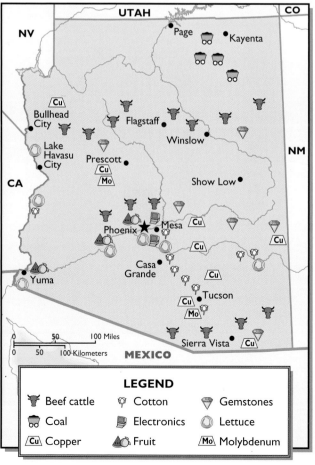

LEGEND

- 🐂 Beef cattle
- Coal
- Cu Copper
- 🌸 Cotton
- Electronics
- Fruit
- Gemstones
- Lettuce
- Mo Molybdenum

Physical

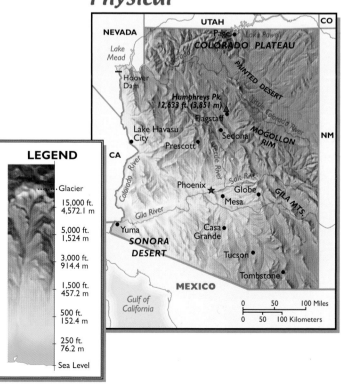

LEGEND

Glacier	
15,000 ft. 4,572.1 m	
5,000 ft. 1,524 m	
3,000 ft. 914.4 m	
1,500 ft. 457.2 m	
500 ft. 152.4 m	
250 ft. 76.2 m	
Sea Level	

ARKANSAS

LEGEND

★ State capital
• City
GRANT County
▲ Mountain peak

National or other park
Urban area

MISSOURI

N W E S

Joplin
Springfield

Grand Lake O' The Cherokees
Table Rock Lake
Bull Shoals Lake
Norfolk Lake

BENTON
Bentonville
Rogers
Springdale
Fayetteville

Beaver Lake
CARROLL
BOONE
Harrison
MARION
BAXTER
Mountain Home

FULTON
RANDOLPH
Pocahontas
CLAY

Black River
GREENE
Paragould

36N

WASHINGTON
MADISON
NEWTON
BUFFALO NATL. RIVER
Buffalo River
SEARCY
STONE
Mountain View

IZARD
SHARP
LAWRENCE

White River

CRAIGHEAD
Jonesboro
Blytheville
MISSISSIPPI
Osceola

OKLAHOMA

CRAWFORD
FRANKLIN
JOHNSON
Clarksville
POPE
Lake Dardanelle
Russellville
CONWAY

VAN BUREN
CLEBURNE
Greers Ferry Lake
Heber Springs
Little Red River

Batesville
INDEPENDENCE
JACKSON
Newport
POINSETT
Trumann

CROSS
St. Francis River
Wynne

TENNESSEE

Van Buren
Fort Smith
SEBASTIAN
Magazine Mtn. ▲
2,753 ft. (839 m)
LOGAN
Arkansas River
YELL

Morrilton
FAULKNER
Conway

WHITE
Searcy

WOODRUFF
ST. FRANCIS
Forrest City

CRITTENDEN
West Memphis
Memphis

SCOTT
Fourche La Fave River
PERRY

PULASKI
North Little Rock
Little Rock

PRAIRIE
LONOKE
MONROE

Bayou De View
White River

LEE
Marianna

West Helena
Helena
PHILLIPS

Mena
POLK
MONTGOMERY
Lake Ouachita
GARLAND
HOT SPRINGS NATL. PARK
Hot Springs
SALINE

JEFFERSON
Stuttgart
ARKANSAS

MISSISSIPPI

34N

Malvern
HOT SPRING
GRANT
Pine Bluff

De Queen
SEVIER
HOWARD
PIKE
Murfreesboro
Arkadelphia
CLARK
DALLAS
CLEVELAND
LINCOLN

Dumas
DESHA

Saline River

LITTLE RIVER
Red River
Ashdown
HEMPSTEAD
Hope
NEVADA
OUACHITA
Camden
CALHOUN
Warren
DREW
BRADLEY
Monticello

Texarkana
Texarkana
MILLER
Magnolia
LAFAYETTE
COLUMBIA
UNION
El Dorado
ASHLEY
Crossett
CHICOT

Mississippi River

TEXAS

ARKANSAS
SOUTHEAST

LOUISIANA

Longview
Shreveport
Monroe
Vicksburg
Jackson

0 25 50 Miles
0 25 50 Kilometers

94W 92W 90W

Imagine a box with its right side beginning to tip out at the top, and you'll have the outline of Arkansas. The slanted eastern side is formed by the Mississippi River, a stream that looks as twisted and coiled as a phone cord. Crossing the state from west to southeast is the Arkansas River. Its valley divides the state's mountains. Year-round comfortable weather plus scenic beauty provided by forests, rivers, and lakes attract many visitors and residents to the mountains, especially to the northern portion known as the Ozarks. The southern portion features Hot Springs National Park, the country's oldest national park. Rivers flowing from the mountains cross a wide and flat plain on their way to the Mississippi. This is the state's prime farmland, used to raise a great variety of crops. Elsewhere in Arkansas, chickens, timber, and minerals are valuable, joined by important manufacturing and service businesses. The world headquarters of Wal-Mart is located near Bentonville.

Economy – Chief Products

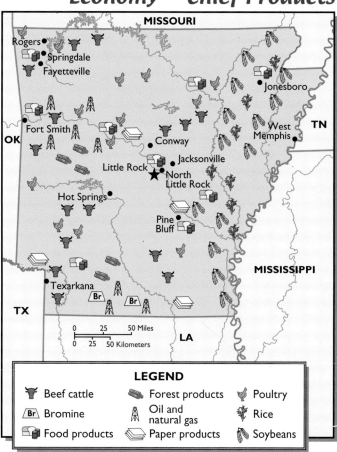

LEGEND

Beef cattle	Forest products	Poultry
Bromine	Oil and natural gas	Rice
Food products	Paper products	Soybeans

Physical

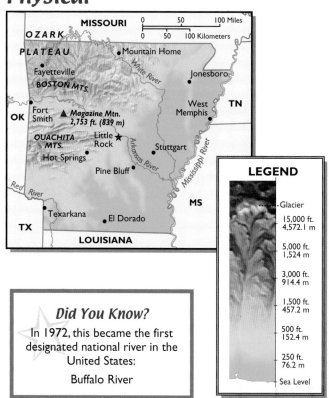

LEGEND

Glacier
15,000 ft. 4,572.1 m
5,000 ft. 1,524 m
3,000 ft. 914.4 m
1,500 ft. 457.2 m
500 ft. 152.4 m
250 ft. 76.2 m
Sea Level

Arkansas Almanac

Nicknames	Natural State, Razorback State
State capital	Little Rock
Date of statehood	June 15, 1836; 25th state
State bird	Mockingbird
State flower	Apple blossom
State tree	Pine
State motto	*Regnat Populus* (The People Rule)
Total population & rank	2,692,090 (in 2001); 33rd
Population density	52 per sq. mile (20 per sq. km)
Population distribution	52% urban, 48% rural
Largest cities	Little Rock, Fort Smith, North Little Rock, Fayetteville
Highest elevation	Magazine Mountain, 2,753 ft. (839 m)
Lowest elevation	Ouachita River, in Ashley & Union Counties, 55 ft. (17 m)
Land area & rank	52,068 sq. miles (134,856 sq. km); 27th
Average January temperature	40°F (4°C)
Average July temperature	80°F (27°C)
Average yearly precipitation	50 inches (127 cm)
Major industries	manufacturing, agriculture, tourism, forestry
Places to visit	Hot Springs National Park, Ozark Folk Center and Blanchard Springs Cavern (Mountain View), Crater of Diamonds (Murfreesboro)
Web site	www.state.ar.us

Did You Know?

In 1972, this became the first designated national river in the United States:

Buffalo River

CALIFORNIA REPUBLIC

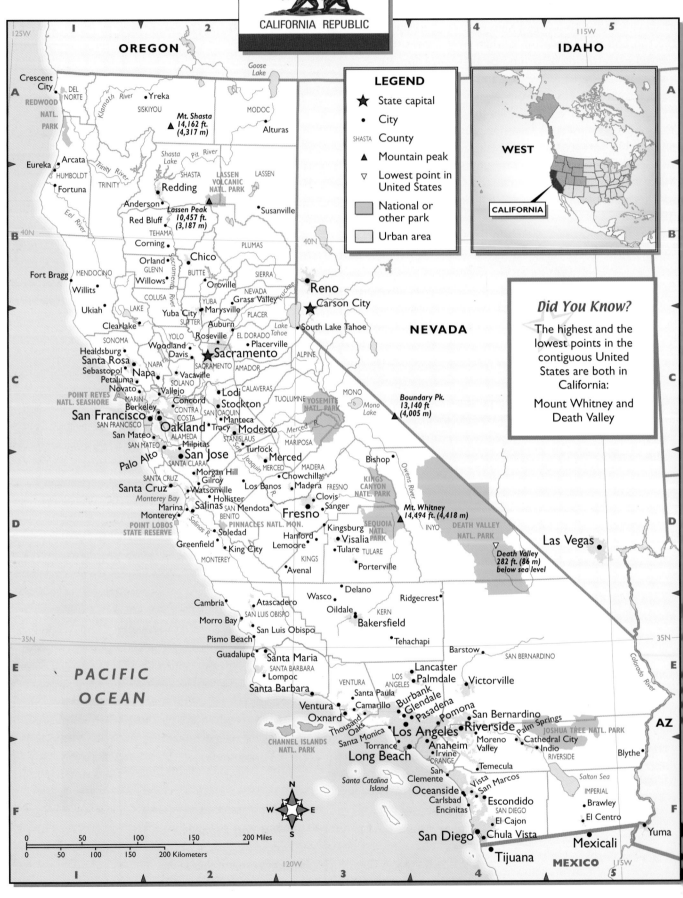

OREGON

IDAHO

LEGEND

★ State capital
• City
SHASTA County
▲ Mountain peak
▽ Lowest point in United States
National or other park
Urban area

WEST

CALIFORNIA

Did You Know?

The highest and the lowest points in the contiguous United States are both in California:

Mount Whitney and Death Valley

NEVADA

Crescent City
REDWOOD NATL. PARK
DEL NORTE
•Yreka
SISKIYOU
MODOC
▲ Mt. Shasta 14,162 ft. (4,317 m)
•Alturas
Klamath River

Eureka
Arcata
HUMBOLDT
Fortuna
Trinity River
Shasta Lake
Pit River
SHASTA
LASSEN VOLCANIC NATL. PARK
LASSEN
Goose Lake

40N
Fort Bragg
MENDOCINO
Willits
Ukiah
Clearlake
LAKE
Redding
Anderson
Red Bluff
▲ Lassen Peak 10,457 ft. (3,187 m)
Corning
TEHAMA
PLUMAS
Susanville
40N

Eel River

Chico
GLENN
Orland
Willows
COLUSA
Sacramento River
BUTTE
•Oroville
YUBA
Grass Valley
NEVADA
Reno
Carson City
•Marysville
PLACER
Yuba City
SUTTER
Auburn
South Lake Tahoe
Lake Tahoe
EL DORADO

NEVADA

Healdsburg
Santa Rosa
SONOMA
Sebastopol
Petaluma
Novato
Napa
NAPA
Vacaville
SOLANO
Woodland
Davis
YOLO
★ Sacramento
SACRAMENTO
Placerville
AMADOR
ALPINE

POINT REYES NATL. SEASHORE
MARIN
Vallejo
Berkeley
CONTRA COSTA
Concord
Lodi
CALAVERAS
Stockton
SAN JOAQUIN
TUOLUMNE
YOSEMITE NATL. PARK
MONO
Mono Lake
Boundary Pk. 13,140 ft (4,005 m)

San Francisco
SAN FRANCISCO
Oakland
ALAMEDA
SAN MATEO
San Mateo
Milpitas
Manteca
Tracy
Modesto
STANISLAUS
Merced R.
MARIPOSA
Bishop
Owens River
Las Vegas

Palo Alto
San Jose
SANTA CLARA
Morgan Hill
Gilroy
Turlock
MERCED
Merced
MADERA
SANTA CRUZ
Santa Cruz
Watsonville
Hollister
Los Banos
Chowchilla
Madera
KINGS CANYON NATL. PARK
Monterey Bay
Marina
Salinas
SAN BENITO
San Mendota
Clovis
FRESNO
Fresno
Sanger
Mt. Whitney 14,494 ft. (4,418 m)
DEATH VALLEY NATL. PARK
Monterey
PINNACLES NATL. MON.
Soledad
Mendota
INYO
POINT LOBOS STATE RESERVE
Kingsburg
SEQUOIA NATL. PARK
Greenfield
Salinas R.
Hanford
Visalia
Death Valley 282 ft. (86 m) below sea level
King City
Lemoore
Tulare
TULARE
MONTEREY
KINGS
Porterville
Avenal

Cambria
Atascadero
Delano
Wasco
Oildale
Ridgecrest
Morro Bay
San Luis Obispo
Bakersfield
KERN
San Luis Obispo
SAN LUIS OBISPO
Pismo Beach
35N
Tehachapi
Barstow
SAN BERNARDINO
35N

PACIFIC OCEAN

Guadalupe
Santa Maria
SANTA BARBARA
Lompoc
Santa Barbara
VENTURA
Santa Paula
Camarillo
Ventura
Oxnard
Thousand Oaks
LOS ANGELES
Lancaster
Palmdale
Victorville
Burbank
Glendale
Pasadena
Pomona
San Bernardino
Riverside
Palm Springs
JOSHUA TREE NATL. PARK
AZ

CHANNEL ISLANDS NATL. PARK
Santa Monica
Los Angeles
Moreno Valley
Cathedral City
Indio
RIVERSIDE
Blythe
Torrance
Anaheim
Irvine
ORANGE
Long Beach
Temecula
Santa Catalina Island
San Clemente
San Marcos
Vista
Salton Sea
IMPERIAL
Oceanside
Escondido
Brawley
Carlsbad
Encinitas
SAN DIEGO
El Cajon
El Centro
San Diego
Chula Vista
Mexicali
Tijuana
MEXICO
Yuma
Colorado River

0   50   100   150   200 Miles
0   50   100   150   200 Kilometers

N W E S

120W
115W

With its 840-mile (1,352-km) coastline, California is probably the easiest western state to find on a map. California also has the largest population of any state in the United States. With its large size and population, California has many geographical features and many different kinds of people. It has hot, dry deserts and rich, green farmland; rolling foothills and rocky coastal regions; the nation's deepest valley and the highest mountain in the lower 48 states; and a variety of national parks and monuments. People have come to California from nearly every place on Earth, especially Asia and Latin America. Many come to live permanently, but many also come as tourists. For years, California has been famous as the home of movies and television. Many people work in these and other industries, including agriculture, tourism, and high-tech businesses.

California Almanac

Nickname	Golden State
State capital	Sacramento
Date of statehood	Sept. 9, 1850; 31st state
State bird	California valley quail
State flower	Golden poppy
State tree	California redwood
State motto	*Eureka* (I Have Found It)
Total population & rank	34,501,130 (in 2001); 1st
Population density	221 per sq. mile (85 per sq. km)
Population distribution	94% urban, 6% rural
Largest cities	Los Angeles, San Diego, San Jose, San Francisco, Long Beach
Highest elevation	Mt. Whitney, 14,494 ft. (4,418 m)
Lowest elevation	Death Valley, 282 ft. (86 m) below sea level
Land area & rank	155,959 sq. miles (403,934 sq. km); 3rd
Average January temperature	43°F (6°C)
Average July temperature	72°F (22°C)
Average yearly precipitation	22 inches (56 cm)
Major industries	agriculture, tourism, apparel, electronics, telecommunications, entertainment
Places to visit	Yosemite National Park, Lake Tahoe, Disneyland (Anaheim), San Diego Zoo, Hollywood, Sequoia Natl. Park, Pt. Lobos State Reserve
Web site	www.state.ca.us

Economy—Chief Products

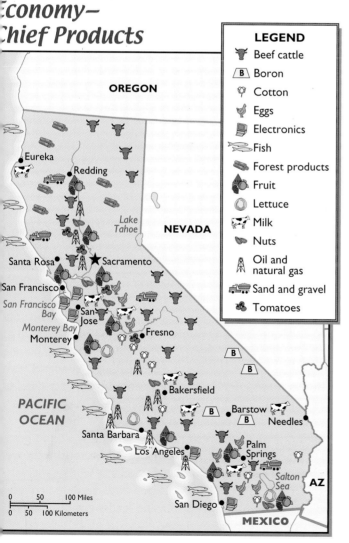

LEGEND

- Beef cattle
- B Boron
- Cotton
- Eggs
- Electronics
- Fish
- Forest products
- Fruit
- Lettuce
- Milk
- Nuts
- Oil and natural gas
- Sand and gravel
- Tomatoes

Physical

LEGEND

Glacier	
	15,000 ft. 4,572.1 m
	5,000 ft. 1,524 m
	3,000 ft. 914.4 m
	1,500 ft. 457.2 m
	500 ft. 152.4 m
	250 ft. 76.2 m
	Sea Level

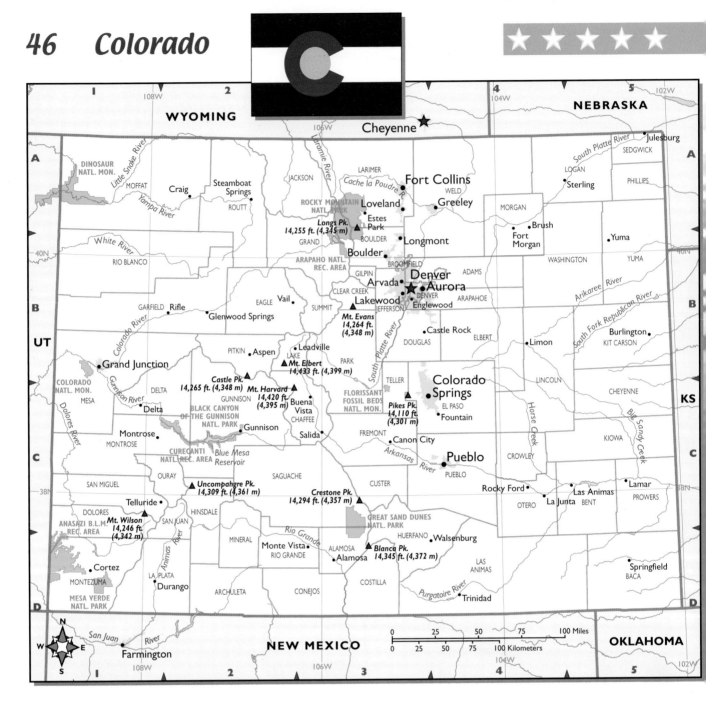

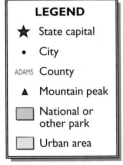

LEGEND

⭐ State capital

• City

ADAMS County

▲ Mountain peak

National or other park

Urban area

WEST

COLORADO

For many people, Colorado means the tall, snow-capped peaks of the Rocky Mountains and ski resorts. The state has more peaks over 14,000 feet (4,267 m)—known as "fourteeners"—than any of the lower 48 states. Having this scenery so close to the Front Range cities of Denver, Boulder, and Fort Collins causes even many city-dwellers to maintain an active outdoor lifestyle. The spectacular beauty of the mountains in the center of the state is balanced by dry, rugged ranchland in the west and prairie farmland in the east. Arid canyons in the southwest were once inhabited by Anasazi cliff dwellers, whose ancient structures can still be seen. Soon after settlers arrived in the 19th century, gold, silver, and lead were discovered and the population exploded. Today, a more diverse economy supplies a livelihood as ranching, farming, mining, tourism, and high technology all play major roles.

Colorado Almanac

Nickname	Centennial State
State capital	Denver
Date of statehood	Aug. 1, 1876; 38th state
State bird	Lark bunting
State flower	Rocky Mountain columbine
State tree	Colorado blue spruce
State motto	Nil Sine Numine (Nothing Without Providence)
Total population & rank	4,417,714 (in 2001); 24th
Population density	43 per sq. mile (17 per sq. km)
Population distribution	84% urban, 16% rural
Largest cities	Denver, Colorado Springs, Aurora, Lakewood
Highest elevation	Mt. Elbert, 14,433 ft. (4,399 m)
Lowest elevation	Arikaree River in Yuma Co., 3,315 ft. (1,010 m)

Land area & rank	103,718 sq. miles (268,630 sq. km); 8th
Average January temperature	23°F (−5°C)
Average July temperature	68°F (20°C)
Average yearly precipitation	15 inches (38 cm)
Major industries	manufacturing, construction, government, tourism, agriculture, aerospace, electronics equipment
Places to visit	Rocky Mountain National Park, Mesa Verde National Park, Dinosaur National Monument, Pikes Peak, Central City
Web site	www.colorado.gov

Physical

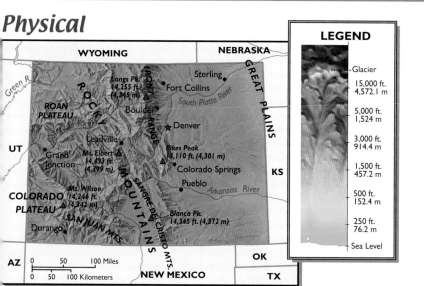

Did You Know?

The famous song "America the Beautiful" was inspired by the view from here:

Pikes Peak

Economy— Chief Products

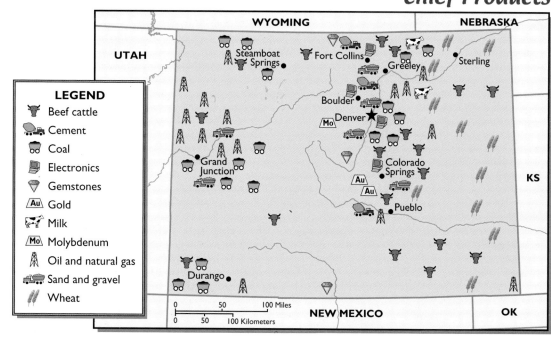

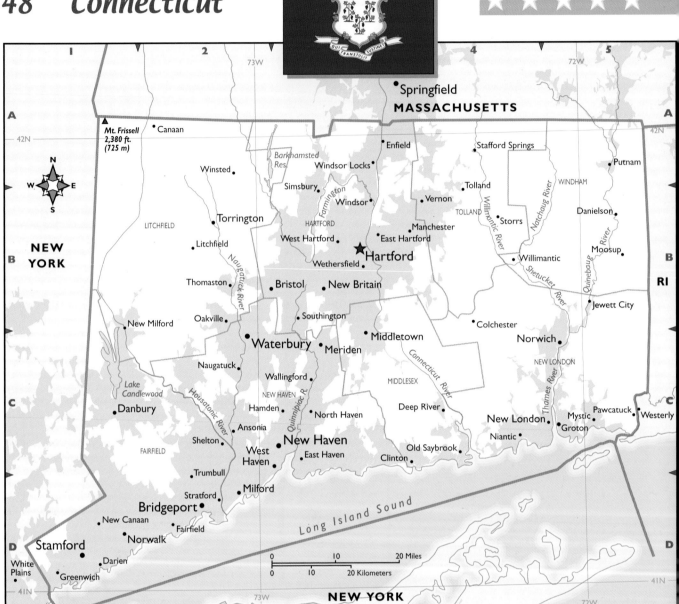

MASSACHUSETTS

Springfield

Mt. Frissell
2,380 ft.
(725 m)

Canaan

42N

LITCHFIELD

NEW YORK

Winsted

Barkhamsted Res.

Enfield

Stafford Springs

Putnam

Windsor Locks

Simsbury

Tolland

WINDHAM

Torrington

Windsor

Vernon

Danielson

Litchfield

West Hartford

Manchester

East Hartford

Storrs

Moosup

Hartford

Willimantic

Thomaston

Wethersfield

Bristol

New Britain

Jewett City

New Milford

Oakville

Southington

Colchester

Norwich

Waterbury

Meriden

Middletown

NEW LONDON

Naugatuck

Wallingford

MIDDLESEX

Lake Candlewood

NEW HAVEN

Danbury

Hamden

North Haven

Deep River

New London

Mystic

Pawcatuck

Westerly

Ansonia

Niantic

Groton

Shelton

New Haven

FAIRFIELD

West Haven

East Haven

Old Saybrook

Clinton

Trumbull

Milford

Stratford

Bridgeport

New Canaan

Fairfield

Stamford

Norwalk

Long Island Sound

Darien

White Plains

Greenwich

41N

NEW YORK

0   10   20 Miles
0   10   20 Kilometers

RI

LEGEND

★ State capital   FAIRFIELD County   Urban area

• City   ▲ Mountain peak

CONNECTICUT

NEW ENGLAND

New England's southernmost state is also the nation's third smallest state. The northwest and northeast portions are full of mountains and hills while the southern lowlands of the Atlantic coastal plain and the Connecticut River Valley, which bisects the state, are home to most of the state's population. The people of this state are mainly descendants of Western European immigrants who came to Connecticut in the 1800s. African Americans, Asians, and Latinos complete the make-up of this slow-growing state. Connecticut is rich in history, contributing the first state constitution based on the free consent of the people — the beginning of U.S. democracy. Most of the people in the state have jobs in the service industry (such as hotels), and finance industry (insurance, banking, and real estate). Because Connecticut has the highest percentage of workers with college degrees, high-tech manufacturing companies that make submarines, helicopters, and airplanes can find the qualified workers they need. Connecticut's beautiful coastline and charming New England towns attract many tourists.

Connecticut Almanac

Nicknames	Constitution State, Nutmeg State	**Lowest elevation**	sea level
State capital	Hartford	**Land area & rank**	4,845 sq. miles (12,549 sq. km); 48th
Date of statehood	Jan. 9, 1788; 5th state	**Average January temperature**	26°F (–3°C)
State bird	American robin		
State flower	Mountain laurel	**Average July temperature**	71°F (22°C)
State tree	White oak		
State motto	*Qui Transtulit Sustinet* (He Who Transplanted Still Sustains)	**Average yearly precipitation**	47 inches (119 cm)
Total population & rank	3,425,074 (in 2001); 29th	**Major industries**	manufacturing, retail trade, government, services, finance, insurance
Population density	707 per sq. mile (273 per sq. km)		
Population distribution	88% urban, 12% rural	**Places to visit**	Mystic Seaport, Marine Life Aquarium (Mystic), P.T. Barnum Museum (Bridgeport), Peabody Museum (New Haven)
Largest cities	Bridgeport, New Haven, Hartford, Stamford, Waterbury		
Highest elevation	south slope of Mt. Frissell, 2,380 ft. (725 m)		
		Web site	www.state.ct.us

Physical

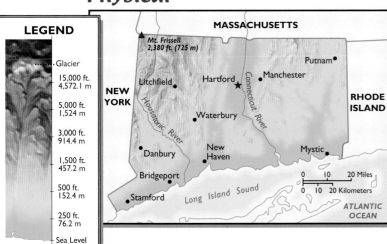

LEGEND

- Glacier
- 15,000 ft. / 4,572.1 m
- 5,000 ft. / 1,524 m
- 3,000 ft. / 914.4 m
- 1,500 ft. / 457.2 m
- 500 ft. / 152.4 m
- 250 ft. / 76.2 m
- Sea Level

Did You Know?

The inspiration for that popular toy, the flying disk, was a baking company in Bridgeport:

Frisbee Baking Company

Economy— Chief Products

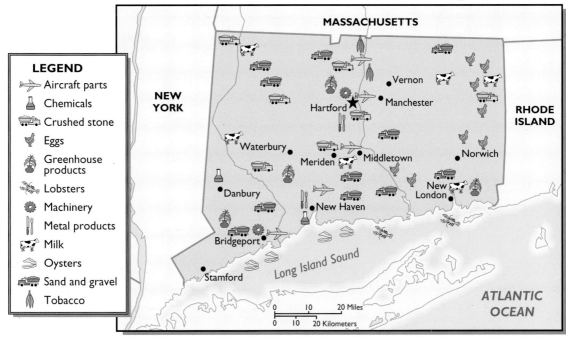

LEGEND

- ✈ Aircraft parts
- Chemicals
- 🚚 Crushed stone
- 🐔 Eggs
- Greenhouse products
- 🦞 Lobsters
- ⚙ Machinery
- Metal products
- 🐄 Milk
- Oysters
- 🚚 Sand and gravel
- Tobacco

DECEMBER 7, 1787

PENNSYLVANIA

Brandywine Creek

Delaware River

Claymont

Elsmere

Wilmington

Newark

New Castle

DELAWARE

MIDATLANTIC

Delaware City

NEW CASTLE

Odessa

Middletown

NEW JERSEY

Millville

MARYLAND

Chesapeake Bay

Smyrna River

Clayton

Smyrna

N
W · E
S

Dover

Wyoming

Camden

KENT

Bowers Beach

Delaware Bay

LEGEND

★ State capital

• City

KENT County

Urban area

Felton

Frederica

Harrington

Mispillion River

Milford

Cape Henlopen

Did You Know?

One of the most important and famous synthetic products was invented by Delaware's DuPont Company:

Nylon

Ellendale

Milton

Lewes

Bridgeville

Rehoboth Beach

Georgetown

Dewey Beach

Rehoboth Bay

SUSSEX

ATLANTIC OCEAN

Seaford

Nanticoke River

Indian River Bay

Millsboro

Laurel

Bethany Beach

Frankford

Delmar

Selbyville

0   5   10 Miles

0   5   10 Kilometers

Delaware is the second smallest state. Most of the wedge-shaped state is on the Delmarva Peninsula with the Atlantic Ocean and its beautiful white sand beaches on the east. Delaware is the flattest state and also the state with the overall lowest elevation. Most of the population of Delaware is in the north where E.I. du Pont established a gunpowder plant in 1802 that became one of the world's largest chemical companies. Since then, Delaware's taxes have favored corporations, encouraging many large banking, insurance, and real estate companies to open offices in the state's northern cities. These companies have made Delaware one of the wealthiest states. Southern Delaware has many farms. Poultry is the most important agricultural product in the state. In the last 20 years, tourism has grown because of the fine beach resorts, excellent museums, and the historic sites in colonial towns like New Castle and Lewes.

Economy – Chief Products

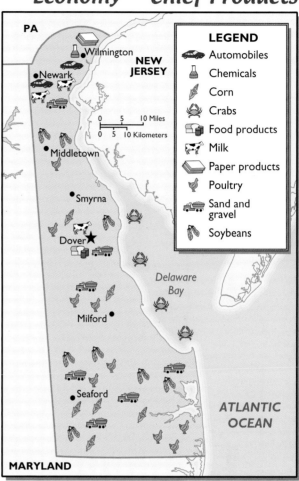

Physical

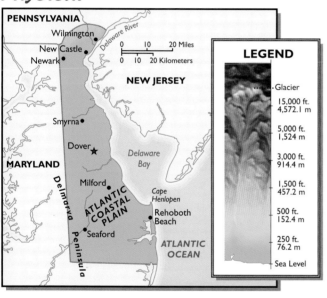

Delaware Almanac

Nicknames	First State, Diamond State	**Lowest elevation**	sea level
State capital	Dover	**Land area & rank**	1,954 sq. miles (5,061 sq. km); 49th
Date of statehood	Dec. 7, 1787; 1st state		
State bird	Blue hen chicken	**Average January temperature**	34°F (1°C)
State flower	Peach blossom		
State tree	American holly	**Average July temperature**	76°F (24°C)
State motto	Liberty and Independence		
Total population & rank	796,165 (in 2001); 45th	**Average yearly precipitation**	45 inches (114 cm)
Population density	408 per sq. mile (158 per sq. km)	**Major industries**	chemicals, agriculture, finance, poultry, shellfish, tourism
Population distribution	80% urban, 20% rural		
Largest cities	Wilmington, Dover, Newark	**Places to visit**	Wilmington: Winterthur Museum and Hagley Museum, Rehoboth Beach, New Castle
Highest elevation	Ebright Road in New Castle Co., 448 ft. (137 m)		
		Web site	www.delaware.gov

GEORGIA

LEGEND

★ State capital
• City
HENDRY County
National or other park
Swamp
Urban area

Lake Seminole
Marianna
JACKSON
GADSDEN
CALHOUN
LIBERTY
Ochlockonee River
84W
2
Tallahassee
LEON
MADISON
JEFFERSON
HAMILTON
COLUMBIA
BAKER
Suwannee River
WAKULLA
Aucilla River
Perry
TAYLOR
SUWANNEE
LAFAYETTE
UNION
BRADFORD
CLAY
GILCHRIST
ALACHUA
DIXIE
Gainesville
PUTNAM
FLAGLER
St. Marys River
82W
NASSAU
Fernandina Beach
Amelia Island
DUVAL
Jacksonville
Lake City
ST. JOHNS
St. Augustine
Palm Coast
80W

Apalachicola River
GULF
FRANKLIN
Apalachee Bay
St. George Island
30N
For continuation of map, see inset below

Gulf of Mexico

Waccasassa Bay
LEVY
MARION
Ocala
Lake George
Withlacoochee River
CITRUS
Inverness
SUMTER
Spring Hill
HERNANDO
PASCO
New Port Richey
Tarpon Springs
Clearwater
PINELLAS
St. Petersburg
Tampa Bay
Tampa
HILLSBOROUGH
Lakeland
POLK
MANATEE
Bradenton
Sarasota
SARASOTA
Venice
DE SOTO
Charlotte Harbor
CHARLOTTE
Port Charlotte

Lake Apopka
SEMINOLE
Sanford
Deltona
VOLUSIA
Daytona Beach
Port Orange
ATLANTIC OCEAN
CANAVERAL NATL. SEASHORE
Orlando
ORANGE
Titusville
BREVARD
Cape Canaveral
Merritt Island
Kissimmee
OSCEOLA
Melbourne
Palm Bay
Lake Kissimmee
INDIAN RIVER
Vero Beach
Fort Pierce
ST. LUCIE
Port St. Lucie
Sebring
HIGHLANDS
Lake Istokpoga
HARDEE
GLADES
OKEECHOBEE
Kissimmee River
Lake Okeechobee
MARTIN
Jupiter
West Palm Beach
PALM BEACH
Belle Glade
Delray Beach
Boca Raton
Pompano Beach
BROWARD
Coral Springs
Fort Lauderdale
Hollywood
Hialeah
Miami Beach
Miami
Coral Gables
Biscayne Bay
MIAMI-DADE
BISCAYNE NATL. PARK
Homestead

30N
28N
26N

Peace River
Fort Myers
LEE
Cape Coral
Sanibel Island
Immokalee
HENDRY
Caloosahatchee River
COLLIER
Naples
Tamiami Canal
Marco Island
EVERGLADES NATIONAL PARK
Whitewater Bay
MONROE
Cape Sable
Florida Bay
Key Largo
Keys
Florida Keys
Marathon
Key West
DRY TORTUGAS NATL. PARK

N
W   E
S

SOUTHEAST
FLORIDA

ALABAMA
Conecuh R.
Dothan
ESCAMBIA
SANTA ROSA
Escambia R.
OKALOOSA
Crestview
WALTON
HOLMES
Choctawhatchee R.
JACKSON
Marianna
WASHINGTON
Niceville
Pensacola
GULF ISLANDS NATL. SEASHORE
Fort Walton Beach
BAY
CALHOUN
Panama City
GULF
Gulf of Mexico
86W
84W

0   25   50 Miles
0   25   50 Kilometers

1   2   3   4   5

Economy – Chief Products

orida is located in the southeastern orner of the United States. It has a arrow extension called the Panhandle hat curves south to become a wide, flat eninsula separating the Gulf of Mexico d the Atlantic Ocean. Tropical ummertime heat discouraged year-ound residents before air conditioning as common. Now the state has the ourth-largest population in the United tates, boosted by senior citizens and nmigrants from nearby Caribbean and entral American nations. Florida is well nown for its oranges and orange juice, ut other leading farm products include egetables and sugar cane. The space xploration facilities at Cape Canaveral ve birth to ever-growing electronic and igh-tech businesses. Yet Florida is best nown as a vacation destination, from the orld famous attractions in Orlando to e mile after mile of beaches urrounding the state like a sandy skin.

LEGEND

- Aircraft parts
- Beef cattle
- Citrus fruit
- Electronics
- Fish and shellfish
- Forest products
- Oil
- Phosphate rock
- Potted plants
- Sugar cane
- Tomatoes
- Vegetables

Did You Know?

In 1564, the French established a colony on the St. Johns River. The following year, Spaniards killed the French and founded their own settlement, now the oldest permanent settlement in the United States:

St. Augustine

hysical

LEGEND

- Glacier
- 15,000 ft. / 4,572.1 m
- 5,000 ft. / 1,524 m
- 3,000 ft. / 914.4 m
- 1,500 ft. / 457.2 m
- 500 ft. / 152.4 m
- 250 ft. / 76.2 m
- Sea Level

Florida Almanac

Nickname	Sunshine State
State capital	Tallahassee
Date of statehood	March 3, 1845; 27th state
State bird	Mockingbird
State flower	Orange blossom
State tree	Sabal palmetto palm
State motto	In God We Trust
Total population & rank	16,396,515 (in 2001); 4th
Population density	304 per sq. mile (117 per sq. km)
Population distribution	89% urban, 11% rural
Largest cities	Jacksonville, Miami, Tampa, St. Petersburg, Hialeah
Highest elevation	Sec. 30, T.6N, R.20W in Walton Co., 345 ft. (105 m)
Lowest elevation	sea level
Land area & rank	53,927 sq. miles (139,671 sq. km); 26th
Average January temperature	61°F (16°C)
Average July temperature	82°F (28°C)
Average yearly precipitation	54 inches (137 cm)
Major industries	tourism, agriculture, manufacturing, construction
Places to visit	Busch Gardens (Tampa), Spaceport USA at Kennedy Space Center, Everglades Natl. Park, St. Augustine, Orlando: Walt Disney World, Universal Studios
Web site	www.myflorida.com

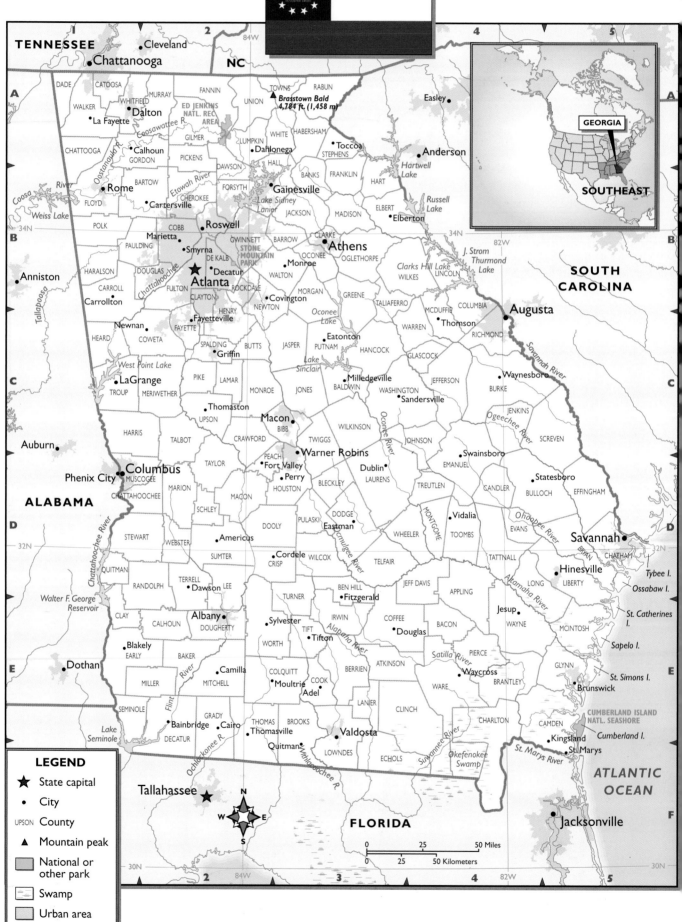

The largest state east of the Mississippi River, Georgia sits at the turning point where the column of Atlantic Coast states bends to become the row of Gulf Coast states. Since 1990, Georgia has been among the fastest growing states. This growth rate has been elevated by new residents moving into the state, particularly people looking for a comfortable place to retire. The southern half of the state is a coastal plain: flat and primarily farmland. The southeastern corner contains the wet-and-wild Okefenokee Swamp. The northern half of the state rises from rolling hills to the peaks of the Appalachian Mountains. Many of the rivers within the mountains are popular for whitewater rafting. Georgia is well known for its farm products, especially peanuts, peaches, and chickens, but manufacturing and services are even more important. Many of these businesses are located in metropolitan Atlanta.

Did You Know?

Most people have heard about California's Gold Rush, but the first U.S. gold rush was near this town in the late 1820s:

Dahlonega

Georgia Almanac

Nicknames	Empire State of the South, Peach State
State capital	Atlanta
Date of statehood	Jan, 2, 1788; 4th state
State bird	Brown thrasher
State flower	Cherokee rose
State tree	Live oak
State motto	Wisdom, Justice and Moderation
Total population & rank	8,383,915 (in 2001); 10th
Population density	145 per sq. mile (56 per sq. km)
Population distribution	72% urban, 28% rural
Largest cities	Atlanta, Augusta, Columbus, Savannah, Athens
Highest elevation	Brasstown Bald, 4,784 ft. (1,458 m)
Lowest elevation	sea level
Land area & rank	57,906 sq. miles (149,977 sq. km); 21st
Average January temperature	46°F (8°C)
Average July temperature	80°F (27°C)
Average yearly precipitation	50 inches (127 cm)
Major industries	services, manufacturing, retail trade
Places to visit	Stone Mountain Park, Historic Savannah, Okefenokee Swamp, Atlanta: Six Flags Over Georgia, Martin Luther King, Jr. National Historic Site;
Web site	www.georgia.gov

Economy – Chief Products

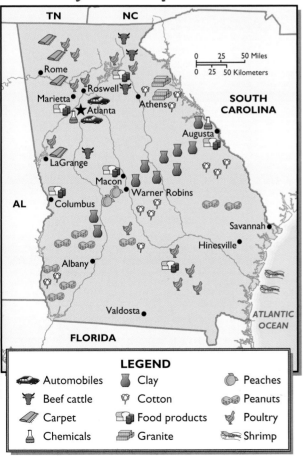

LEGEND

Automobiles		Clay		Peaches	
Beef cattle		Cotton		Peanuts	
Carpet		Food products		Poultry	
Chemicals		Granite		Shrimp	

Physical

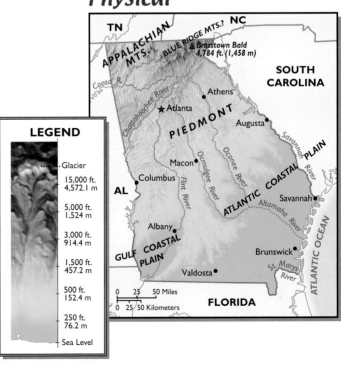

Inset map (WEST/North America)

WEST

HAWAII

LEGEND

★ State capital
• City
KAUAI County
▲ Mountain peak
National or other park
Urban area

Main map (Hawaiian Islands overview)

PACIFIC OCEAN

KAUAI COUNTY
Lehua
Niihau
Kauai
Kaula
Kauai Channel
Oahu
HONOLULU COUNTY
Honolulu
Kawi Channel
KALAWAO COUNTY
MAUI COUNTY
Molokai
Lānai
Maui
Kahoolawe
Alenuihāhā Channel

Hawaii
HAWAII COUNTY

21N
20N
19N
160W 159W 158W 157W 156W 155W

N E S W

0   50   100 Miles
0   50   100 Kilometers

Oahu

Kahuku Pt.
Waimea Bay
PACIFIC OCEAN
Kauai Channel
Anahulu R.
Kaena Pt.
Mt. Kaala 4,030 ft. (1,228 m)
Oahu
Wahiawā
Mākaha Beach
Mililani Town
Kāneohe Bay
Mōkapu Peninsula
Pearl City
Kailua Bay
Waipahu
Kāneohe
Kailua
Pearl Harbor
Hālawa R.
Waimānalo Bay
Barbers Pt.
Ewa Beach
Honolulu
Māmala Bay
Maunalua Bay
Makapuu Pt.
Koko Head
Kaiwi Channel

2130'N
21N
158W

0   5   10 Miles
0   5   10 Kilometers

Kauai

2230'N
PACIFIC OCEAN
Kauai
Hanalei Bay
Mt. Waialeale 5,148 ft. (1,569 m)
Kawaikini Peak 5,243 ft. (1,598 m)
Kapaa
Hanamaulu
Kekaha
Lihue
Kaulakahi Channel
Kalaheo
22N

0   10   20 Miles
0   10   20 Kilometers

160W 15930'W 159W

Molokai, Lānai, Maui, Kahoolawe

Kaiwi Channel
PACIFIC OCEAN
KALAUPAPA NATL. HIST. PARK
Pailolo Channel
Molokai
Kaunakakai
Kalohi Channel
Auau Channel
Kahului Bay
Wailuku
Kahului
Makawao
Maui
Lahaina
Lānai
Pukalani
Hāna Bay
Maalaea Bay
Kīhei
Kealaikahiki Channel
Puuulaula (Red Hill) 10,023 ft. (3,055 m)
HALEAKALĀ NATIONAL PARK
'Alalākeiki Channel
Kahoolawe
'Alenuihāhā Channel

21N
2030'N

0   10   20 Miles
0   10   20 Kilometers

157W 15630'W 156W

Hawaii (Big Island)

2030'N
'Alenuihāʻā Channel
Upolu Pt.
PACIFIC OCEAN
Kawaihae Bay
Waimea (Kamuela)
Keahole Pt.
Kalaoa
Mauna Kea 13,796 ft. (4,205 m)
Hilo Bay
Kailua-Kona
Mt. Hualālai 8,271 ft. (2,521 m)
Hilo
Holualoa
Hawaii
Mountain View
Captain Cook
1930'N
Cape Kumukahi
Kealakekua Bay
Mauna Loa 13,677 ft. (4,169 m)
HAWAI'I VOLCANOES NATIONAL PARK
Kaunā Pt.
20N
19N
Kalae (South Pt.)

0   10   20 Miles
0   10   20 Kilometers

156W 15530'W 155W

Hawaii is often thought of as a tropical paradise, and it is that. Magnificent sun-drenched beaches stretch for miles on the state's many islands, and along the coast the temperature hovers around 85°F (29°C) every day. However, snow falls on Mauna Kea, which soars almost 14,000 feet (4,267 m) above the sea. Molokai has the highest sea cliffs in the world at 3,300 feet (1,006 m). On the island of Hawaii, Kilauea Volcano began erupting in 1983 with spectacular fountains of molten rock and is still active. Polynesians first settled on the islands around A.D. 300. In 1898, Hawaii was annexed by the United States, and it became the 50th state to enter the Union in 1959. The tourist industry has boomed, drawing visitors from around the globe and forming the mainstay of Hawaii's economy. Pineapple and sugar growing have declined in importance, while the military and service sectors are strong. Residents share a mix of cultures, with Hawaiian, European, and Japanese being most prominent.

Did You Know?

The channel between Lānai and Kahoolawe may indicate from where early Hawaiians came:

Kealaikahiki—The Route to Tahiti

Economy – Chief Products

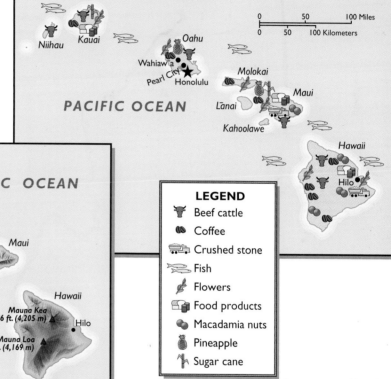

LEGEND

- 🐂 Beef cattle
- ☕ Coffee
- 🚚 Crushed stone
- 🐟 Fish
- 🌺 Flowers
- 📦 Food products
- 🥜 Macadamia nuts
- 🍍 Pineapple
- 🌾 Sugar cane

Physical

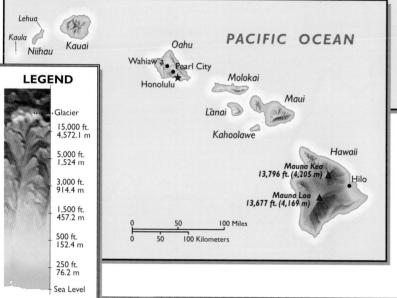

LEGEND

- Glacier
- 15,000 ft. 4,572.1 m
- 5,000 ft. 1,524 m
- 3,000 ft. 914.4 m
- 1,500 ft. 457.2 m
- 500 ft. 152.4 m
- 250 ft. 76.2 m
- Sea Level

Hawaii Almanac

Nickname	Aloha State	**Lowest elevation**	sea level
State capital	Honolulu	**Land area & rank**	6,423 sq. miles (16,636 sq. km); 47th
Date of statehood	Aug. 21, 1959; 50th state		
State bird	Nēnē (Hawaiian goose)	**Average January temperature**	68°F (20°C)
State flower	Yellow hibiscus		
State tree	Kukui (candlenut)	**Average July temperature**	74°F (23°C)
State motto	Ua mau ke ea o ka aina i ka pono (The Life of the Land Is Perpetuated in Righteousness)	**Average yearly precipitation**	67 inches (170 cm)
		Major industries	tourism, defense, agriculture
Total population & rank	1,224,398 (in 2001); 42nd	**Places to visit**	Hawaii Volcanoes National Park, Haleakalā National Park, Pearl Harbor and U.S.S. Arizona Memorial
Population density	191 per sq. mile (74 per sq. km)		
Population distribution	92% urban, 8% rural		
Largest cities	Honolulu, Hilo, Kailua, Kāneohe		
Highest elevation	Mauna Kea, 13,796 ft. (4,205 m)	**Web site**	www.hawaii.gov

LEGEND

★ State capital

• City

LEMHI County

▲ Mountain peak

National or other park

Urban area

IDAHO

WEST

BRITISH COLUMBIA

ALBERTA   **CANADA**

118W   116W   114W   112W   110W

48N   48N

BOUNDARY

Priest Lake

Bonners Ferry

Kootenai

Pend Oreille River

Columbia River

BONNER

Sandpoint

Lake Pend Oreille

Clark Fork

KOOTENAI

Post Falls

Spokane

Coeur d'Alene

Coeur d'Alene Lake

Kellogg

WASHINGTON

St. Maries

St. Joe River

BENEWAH

SHOSHONE

LATAH

Dworshak Reservoir

Pot Mtn. 7,175 ft. (2,187 m) ▲

Snake River

Moscow

CLEARWATER

Clearwater R.

Orofino

Missoula

Lewiston

NEZ PERCE

LEWIS

LEWIS

44N

Grangeville

IDAHO

Selway River

46N

Did You Know?

This horse, believed to have been bred by the Nez Percé Indians from horses originally brought by the Spanish, is now the state horse of Idaho:

The Appaloosa

MONTANA

HELLS CANYON NATL. REC. AREA

Salmon River

Salmon

0   25   50   75   100 Miles
0   25   50   75   50 Kilometers

ADAMS

McCall

VALLEY

CUSTER

LEMHI

OREGON

Snake River

WASHINGTON

Weiser

North Fork Payette

Payette

PAYETTE

44N

GEM

Payette River

CANYON

Boise R.

SAWTOOTH NATL. REC. AREA

Borah Pk. ▲ 12,662 ft. (3,859 m)

Big Lost R.

CLARK

FREMONT

St. Anthony

YELLOWSTONE NATL. PARK

Yellowstone Lake

44N

Caldwell

Nampa

Boise ★

Meridian

ADA

BOISE

South Fork Boise R.

Ketchum

Sun Valley

BUTTE

Arco

JEFFERSON

MADISON

Rexburg

TETON

Idaho Falls

BONNEVILLE

Snake River

GRAND TETON NATL. PARK

WYOMING

CAMAS

Hailey

BLAINE

ELMORE

Mountain Home

GOODING

Gooding

LINCOLN

CRATERS OF THE MOON NATL. MON. & PRES.

BINGHAM

American Falls Res.

Blackfoot

Grays Lake

Pocatello

CARIBOU

Soda Springs

Jerome

JEROME

MINIDOKA

Rupert

American Falls

POWER

BANNOCK

Bear R.

Twin Falls

Burley

CASSIA

ONEIDA

FRANKLIN

BEAR LAKE

Montpelier

Bear Lake

OWYHEE

Owyhee River

TWIN FALLS

Cache Pk. ▲ 10,339 ft. (3,151 m)

42N   42N

N

W   E

S

NEVADA   **UTAH**

Logan

118W   116W   114W   112W   110W

1   2   3   4   5

The shape of Idaho is notable for its narrowing, northern extension called the Panhandle. This creates an outline that looks a little like a triangle but also could be described as a factory building with a tall chimney. Idaho is one of the Rocky Mountain States whose population growth has been greater than the U.S. average. Many of the cities in the state have grown to be twice the size they were in 1990. People are coming to Idaho to work in high-tech businesses and because they expect to be more comfortable in a state with a small population and an attractive environment. Making a large, U-shaped curve across the widest part of the state is the Snake River. The flat plain surrounding the river is where most of the people live and where most of the farming is done. Idaho is famous for growing potatoes. Potatoes are even mentioned on its automobile license plates. The rugged mountains north of the plain are the home of alpine lakes, dense forests, and roadless wilderness areas.

Idaho Almanac

Nickname	Gem State
State capital	Boise
Date of statehood	July 3, 1890; 43rd state
State bird	Mountain bluebird
State flower	Syringa
State tree	White pine
State motto	Esto Perpetua (It Is Perpetual)
Total population & rank	1,321,006 (in 2001); 39th
Population density	16 per sq. mile (6 per sq. km)
Population distribution	66% urban, 34% rural
Largest cities	Boise, Nampa, Pocatello
Highest elevation	Borah Peak, 12,662 ft. (3,859 m)
Lowest elevation	Snake River in Nez Perce Co., 710 ft. (216 m)
Land area & rank	82,747 sq. miles (214,315 sq. km); 11th
Average January temperature	24°F (–4°C)
Average July temperature	68°F (20°C)
Average yearly precipitation	19 inches (48 cm)
Major industries	manufacturing, agriculture, tourism, lumber, mining
Places to visit	Sun Valley, Hells Canyon, Craters of the Moon National Monument, World Center for Birds of Prey (Boise), Old Fort Hall (Pocatello)
Web site	www.state.id.us

Economy– Chief Products

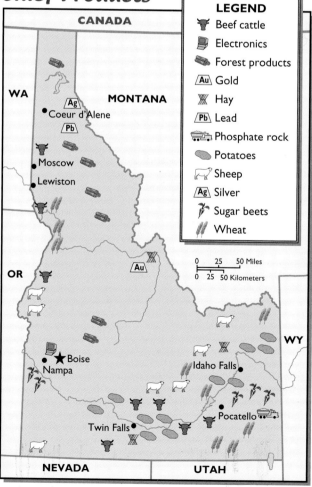

LEGEND
- 🐂 Beef cattle
- 💻 Electronics
- 🪵 Forest products
- Au Gold
- ✳ Hay
- Pb Lead
- 🚚 Phosphate rock
- Potatoes
- 🐑 Sheep
- Ag Silver
- 🌱 Sugar beets
- 🌾 Wheat

Physical

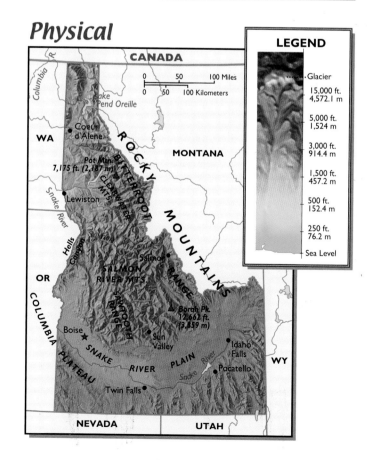

LEGEND
- Glacier
- 15,000 ft. 4,572.1 m
- 5,000 ft. 1,524 m
- 3,000 ft. 914.4 m
- 1,500 ft. 457.2 m
- 500 ft. 152.4 m
- 250 ft. 76.2 m
- Sea Level

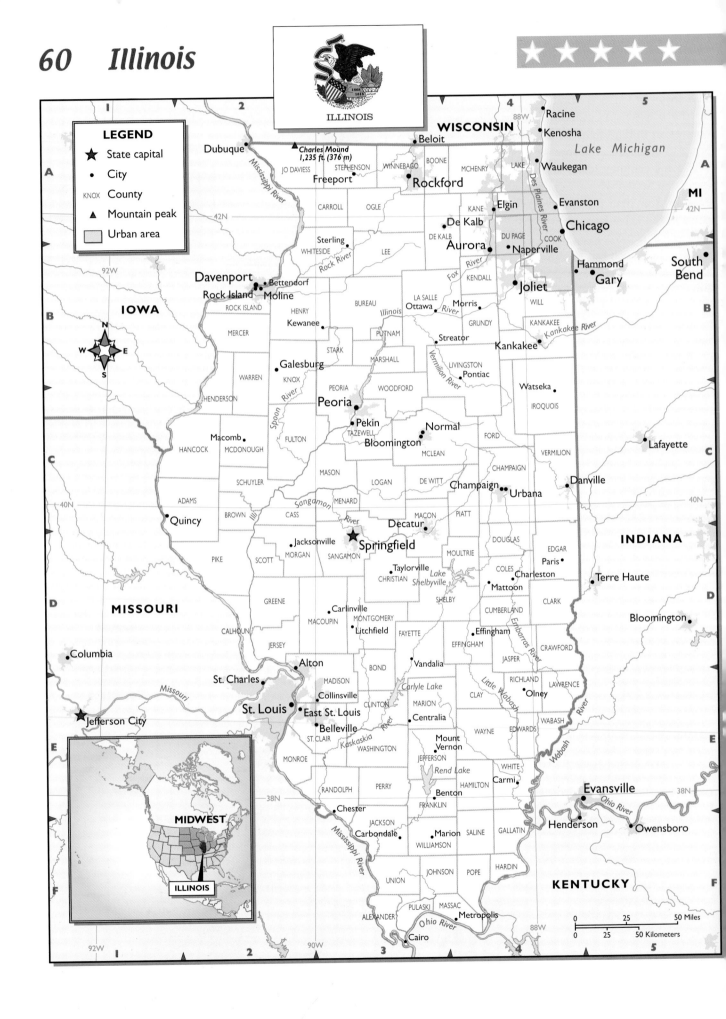

ILLINOIS

LEGEND
★ State capital
• City
KNOX County
▲ Mountain peak
▢ Urban area

WISCONSIN

Lake Michigan

IOWA

MISSOURI

INDIANA

KENTUCKY

MI

Charles Mound
1,235 ft. (376 m)

Dubuque
Beloit
Racine
Kenosha
Waukegan
Freeport
Rockford
Elgin
Evanston
De Kalb
Chicago
Aurora
Naperville
Hammond
Gary
South Bend
Davenport
Bettendorf
Rock Island
Moline
Joliet
Kewanee
Ottawa
Morris
Streator
Kankakee
Galesburg
Pontiac
Watseka
Peoria
Pekin
Normal
Bloomington
Lafayette
Macomb
Champaign
Urbana
Danville
Quincy
Decatur
Jacksonville
Springfield
Paris
Terre Haute
Taylorville
Charleston
Mattoon
Bloomington
Carlinville
Effingham
Litchfield
Vandalia
Columbia
Olney
Alton
St. Charles
Collinsville
Centralia
St. Louis
East St. Louis
Belleville
Mount
Vernon
Carmi
Jefferson City
Benton
Evansville
Chester
Henderson
Owensboro
Carbondale
Marion
Metropolis
Cairo

Des Plaines River
Mississippi River
Rock River
Fox River
Illinois River
Kankakee River
Spoon River
Vermilion River
Sangamon River
Lake Shelbyville
Embarras River
Little Wabash
Carlyle Lake
Kaskaskia River
Rend Lake
Wabash River
Ohio River
Missouri River

JO DAVIESS
STEPHENSON
WINNEBAGO
BOONE
MCHENRY
LAKE
CARROLL
OGLE
KANE
DE KALB
DU PAGE
COOK
WHITESIDE
LEE
ROCK ISLAND
HENRY
BUREAU
LA SALLE
KENDALL
WILL
MERCER
STARK
PUTNAM
GRUNDY
KANKAKEE
MARSHALL
LIVINGSTON
IROQUOIS
WARREN
KNOX
PEORIA
WOODFORD
HENDERSON
FULTON
TAZEWELL
MCLEAN
FORD
VERMILION
HANCOCK
MCDONOUGH
SCHUYLER
MASON
LOGAN
DE WITT
CHAMPAIGN
ADAMS
BROWN
CASS
MENARD
PIATT
MACON
EDGAR
PIKE
SCOTT
MORGAN
SANGAMON
CHRISTIAN
MOULTRIE
DOUGLAS
COLES
CLARK
GREENE
SHELBY
CUMBERLAND
CALHOUN
MACOUPIN
MONTGOMERY
FAYETTE
EFFINGHAM
JASPER
CRAWFORD
JERSEY
BOND
CLINTON
MARION
CLAY
RICHLAND
LAWRENCE
MADISON
WAYNE
EDWARDS
WABASH
ST. CLAIR
WASHINGTON
JEFFERSON
WHITE
MONROE
RANDOLPH
PERRY
FRANKLIN
HAMILTON
SALINE
GALLATIN
JACKSON
WILLIAMSON
JOHNSON
POPE
HARDIN
UNION
ALEXANDER
PULASKI
MASSAC

88W
92W
90W
88W
42N
40N
38N

1 2 3 4 5

N
W E
S

MIDWEST

ILLINOIS

0   25   50 Miles
0 25 50 Kilometers

Illinois is a tall and narrow state—tall like Abraham Lincoln, who lived there for many years, and tall like a skyscraper, which was a type of building invented in Chicago. The protruding western edge is formed by the Mississippi River. Illinois has more miles of Mississippi River boundary than any other state. Although the southern tip of the state has some modest, forest-covered hills, about 80% of the land is used for farming. Illinois farmers typically raise corn, soybeans, and livestock. The most valuable products of Illinois come from its cities, particularly Chicago. More than a transportation hub, food processing center, and corporate headquarters, Chicago has made many contributions to the state, the United States, and even the world. These contributions have involved art, music, literature, and architecture, as well as social welfare and the rights of workers.

Economy – Chief Products

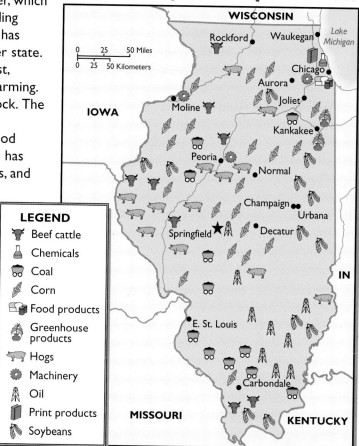

LEGEND
- Beef cattle
- Chemicals
- Coal
- Corn
- Food products
- Greenhouse products
- Hogs
- Machinery
- Oil
- Print products
- Soybeans

Physical

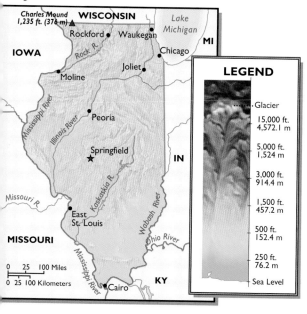

LEGEND
- Glacier
- 15,000 ft. 4,572.1 m
- 5,000 ft. 1,524 m
- 3,000 ft. 914.4 m
- 1,500 ft. 457.2 m
- 500 ft. 152.4 m
- 250 ft. 76.2 m
- Sea Level

Did You Know?

This southern Illinois region got its nickname because it supplied corn to other parts of the state during the severe winter of 1830–1831:

Little Egypt

Illinois Almanac

Nickname	Prairie State	**Lowest elevation**	Mississippi River in Alexander Co., 279 ft. (85 m)
State capital	Springfield	**Land area & rank**	55,584 sq. miles (143,963 sq. km); 24th
Date of statehood	Dec. 3, 1818; 21st state		
State bird	Cardinal	**Average January temperature**	26°F (−3°C)
State flower	Native violet		
State tree	White oak	**Average July temperature**	76°F (24°C)
State motto	State Sovereignty, National Union		
Total population & rank	12,482,301 (in 2001); 5th	**Average yearly precipitation**	38 inches (97 cm)
Population density	225 per sq. mile (87 per sq. km)	**Major industries**	services, manufacturing, travel, wholesale and retail trade, finance, insurance, real estate
Population distribution	88% urban, 12% rural		
Largest cities	Chicago, Rockford, Aurora, Naperville, Peoria	**Places to visit**	Chicago museums and parks, Lincoln shrines in Springfield, Cahokia Mounds (Collinsville)
Highest elevation	Charles Mound, 1,235 ft. (376 m)	**Web site**	www.state.il.us

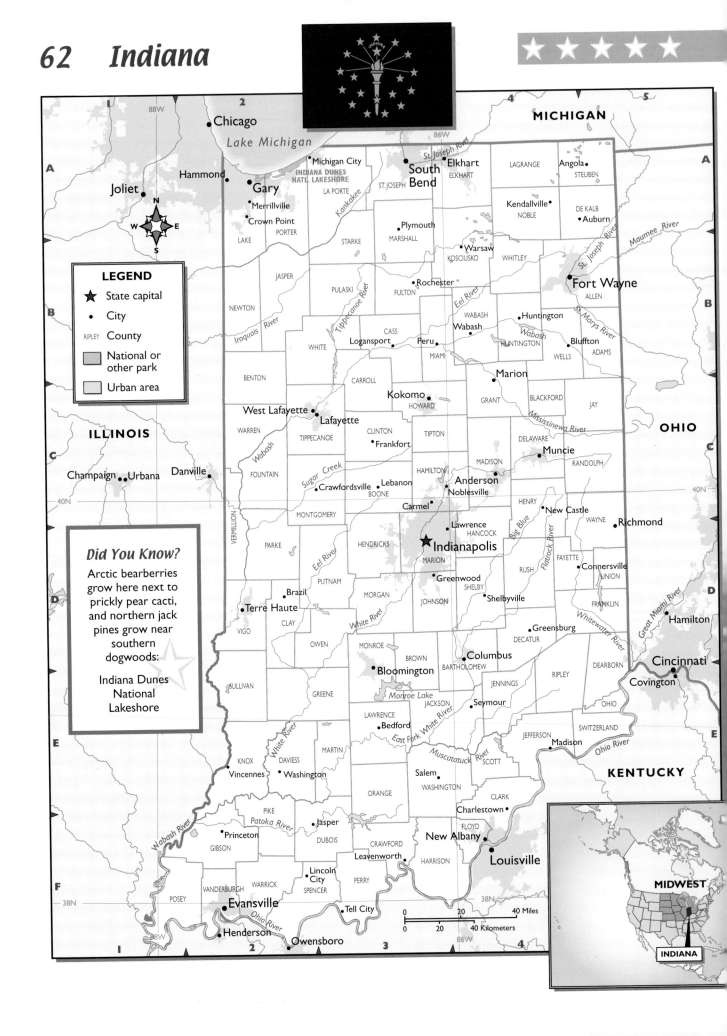

LEGEND

★ State capital

• City

RIPLEY County

National or other park

Urban area

Did You Know?

Arctic bearberries grow here next to prickly pear cacti, and northern jack pines grow near southern dogwoods:

Indiana Dunes National Lakeshore

ILLINOIS

OHIO

KENTUCKY

MICHIGAN

Chicago

Lake Michigan

Joliet

Hammond

Gary

Merrillville

Crown Point

Michigan City

INDIANA DUNES NATL. LAKESHORE

LA PORTE

South Bend

ST. JOSEPH

Elkhart

ELKHART

LAGRANGE

Angola

STEUBEN

NOBLE

Kendallville

DE KALB

Auburn

LAKE

PORTER

STARKE

Plymouth

MARSHALL

Warsaw

KOSCIUSKO

WHITLEY

St. Joseph River

ALLEN

Fort Wayne

Maumee River

JASPER

NEWTON

PULASKI

FULTON

Rochester

Eel River

WABASH

Huntington

HUNTINGTON

Wabash

St. Marys River

Bluffton

WELLS

ADAMS

Iroquois River

Tippecanoe River

WHITE

CASS

Logansport

Peru

MIAMI

Mississinewa River

Marion

GRANT

BLACKFORD

JAY

BENTON

CARROLL

Kokomo

HOWARD

WARREN

West Lafayette

Lafayette

TIPPECANOE

CLINTON

Frankfort

TIPTON

HAMILTON

MADISON

Muncie

DELAWARE

RANDOLPH

FOUNTAIN

Sugar Creek

Crawfordsville

BOONE

Lebanon

Carmel

Noblesville

Anderson

HENRY

New Castle

WAYNE

Richmond

Champaign

Urbana

Danville

Wabash

MONTGOMERY

PARKE

Eel River

PUTNAM

HENDRICKS

Lawrence

Indianapolis

MARION

HANCOCK

Big Blue

Flatrock River

FAYETTE

Connersville

UNION

FRANKLIN

Whitewater River

Great Miami River

Hamilton

Brazil

Terre Haute

VIGO

CLAY

OWEN

White River

MORGAN

JOHNSON

Greenwood

SHELBY

Shelbyville

RUSH

DECATUR

Greensburg

RIPLEY

DEARBORN

Cincinnati

Covington

SULLIVAN

GREENE

MONROE

Monroe Lake

BROWN

Columbus

BARTHOLOMEW

Bloomington

JACKSON

East Fork White River

Seymour

JENNINGS

OHIO

SWITZERLAND

LAWRENCE

Bedford

Muscatatuck River

SCOTT

JEFFERSON

Madison

Ohio River

KNOX

DAVIESS

MARTIN

Vincennes

Washington

Salem

WASHINGTON

CLARK

Charlestown

ORANGE

CRAWFORD

PIKE

Patoka River

Jasper

DUBOIS

Princeton

GIBSON

Leavenworth

HARRISON

FLOYD

New Albany

Louisville

Lincoln City

SPENCER

PERRY

VANDERBURGH

WARRICK

POSEY

Evansville

Tell City

Ohio River

Henderson

Owensboro

Wabash River

MIDWEST

INDIANA

0   20   40 Miles

0   20   40 Kilometers

The shape of Indiana resembles the letter "J" drawn by a very thick crayon. The southernmost quarter, curving west to a point, is bordered by the Ohio River and the Wabash River. Nearly all of the state's rivers flow south, even those in areas very close to Lake Michigan. Indiana calls itself the Crossroads of America, a reference to the spider web of interstate highways interlinked within the state and to its central location among the major cities of the central and northeastern United States. The initial occupation by settlers from Kentucky continues to influence the personality of the state. Indiana's southern hills contain most of the forested land and can be quite steep. Other portions of the state are flat and are used for farming. Massive industrial plants on the shores of Lake Michigan allow Indiana to lead all states in the production of steel. Indianapolis is the most important city and attracts visitors to its museums, historic sites, and sports facilities.

Indiana Almanac

Nickname	Hoosier State
State capital	Indianapolis
Date of statehood	Dec. 11, 1816; 19th state
State bird	Cardinal
State flower	Peony
State tree	Tulip poplar
State motto	The Crossroads of America
Total population & rank	6,114,745 (in 2001); 14th
Population density	170 per sq. mile (66 per sq. km)
Population distribution	71% urban, 29% rural
Largest cities	Indianapolis, Fort Wayne, Evansville, South Bend, Gary
Highest elevation	Franklin Township in Wayne Co., 1,257 ft. (383 m)
Lowest elevation	Ohio River in Posey Co., 320 ft. (98 m)
Land area & rank	35,867 sq. miles (92,896 sq. km); 38th
Average January temperature	27°F (−3°C)
Average July temperature	75°F (24°C)
Average yearly precipitation	40 inches (102 cm)
Major industries	manufacturing, services, agriculture, government, wholesale and retail trade
Places to visit	Connor Prairie Pioneer Settlement (Noblesville), Childrens Museum (Indianapolis), Indiana Dunes National Lakeshore, Lincoln Boyhood National Memorial (Lincoln City), Wyandotte Cave (Leavenworth)
Web site	www.ai.org

Economy – Chief Products

Physical

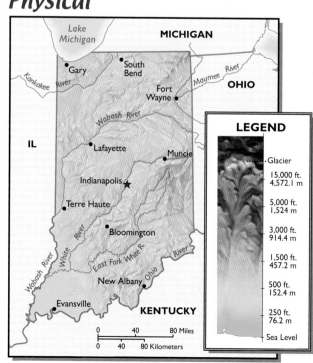

LEGEND

⭐ State capital

• City

PAGE County

▨ Urban area

MIDWEST

IOWA

Some people point out a human profile on the eastern si of Iowa, with the sweeping curves of the Mississippi Rive forming the forehead, nose, and chin. Another famous riv lies on its western edge. The Missouri River was a pathw of exploration and commerce, and for many years the gateway to the disputed Native American lands of the frontier. Though bridging east and west, Iowa has always been unified by its fundamental physical geography and it people. This is a land with dependable water, a long grow season, and dark prairie topsoil extending down for man feet. No other state grows as much corn as Iowa or rais as many hogs. Few other states produce as much beef or have as many people living and working on farms. Manufacturing has historically been connected to farming and food, but the well-educated population has been attracting an increasing variety of businesses, including publishing, banking, and insurance.

Iowa Almanac

Nickname	Hawkeye State	**Lowest elevation**	Mississippi River in Lee Co., 480 ft, (146 m)
State capital	Des Moines	**Land area & rank**	55,869 sq. miles (144,701 sq. km); 23rd
Date of statehood	Dec. 28, 1846; 29th state	**Average January temperature**	18°F (–8°C)
State bird	Eastern goldfinch	**Average July temperature**	74°F (23°C)
State flower	Wild rose	**Average yearly precipitation**	33 inches (84 cm)
State tree	Oak	**Major industries**	agriculture, communications, construction, finance, insurance, trade, services, manufacturing
State motto	Our Liberties We Prize, and Our Rights We Will Maintain		
Total population & rank	2,923,179 (in 2001); 30th	**Places to visit**	Effigy Mounds National Monument (Marquette), Living History Farms (Des Moines), Amana Colonies
Population density	52 per sq. mile (20 per sq. km)		
Population distribution	61% urban, 39% rural		
Largest cities	Des Moines, Cedar Rapids, Davenport, Sioux City	**Web site**	www.state.ia.us
Highest elevation	Sec. 29, T.100N, R.41W in Osceola Co., 1,670 ft. (509 m)		

Physical

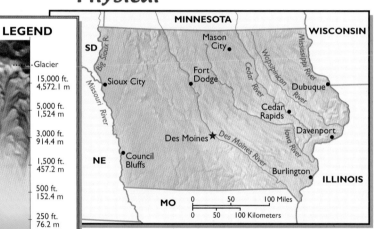

Did You Know?

The number of Iowans who fought in the Civil War—measured as a percent of total residents—was greater than any other Union state:

About 12% or 80,000

Economy–Chief Products

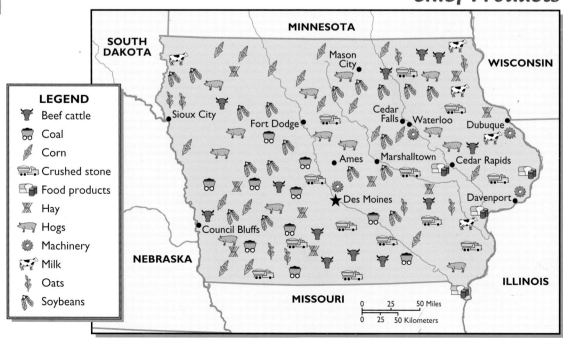

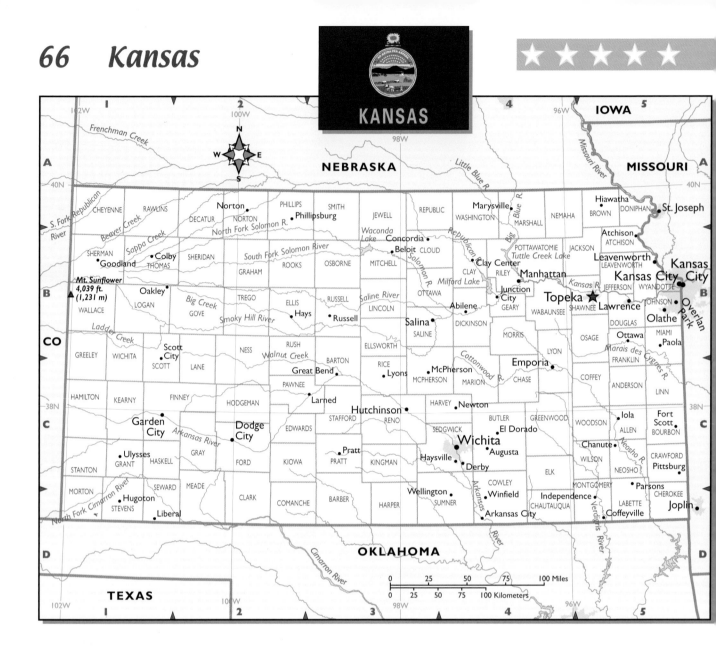

KANSAS

NEBRASKA

IOWA

MISSOURI

CHEYENNE | RAWLINS | DECATUR | NORTON
Norton | PHILLIPS | Phillipsburg | SMITH | JEWELL | REPUBLIC | Marysville | WASHINGTON | MARSHALL | NEMAHA | BROWN | DONIPHAN | Hiawatha | St. Joseph

Frenchman Creek

S. Fork Republican River

Beaver Creek

Sappa Creek

North Fork Solomon R.

Waconda Lake

Concordia
Beloit
CLOUD

Republican R.

Big Blue R.

Little Blue R.

Missouri River

Atchison
ATCHISON

Leavenworth
LEAVENWORTH

Kansas City

SHERMAN | Goodland | Colby | THOMAS | SHERIDAN
GRAHAM | ROOKS | OSBORNE | MITCHELL | Clay Center | RILEY | Manhattan | POTTAWATOMIE | JACKSON | Tuttle Creek Lake | Topeka | Lawrence | JOHNSON | Olathe | Overland Park

South Fork Solomon River

Mt. Sunflower
4,039 ft.
(1,231 m)
Oakley
LOGAN
WALLACE

Big Creek
TREGO

Hays
ELLIS
RUSSELL
Russell

Smoky Hill River

Saline River

LINCOLN

Abilene
DICKINSON

Salina
SALINE

CLAY

Milford Lake

OTTAWA

GEARY

Junction City

WABAUNSEE

SHAWNEE

Kansas R.

JEFFERSON | WYANDOTTE

DOUGLAS

Ottawa
MIAMI
Paola

Ladder Creek

GREELEY | WICHITA | Scott City | SCOTT | LANE | NESS | RUSH | BARTON | RICE | McPherson | MCPHERSON | MARION | CHASE | LYON | Emporia | COFFEY | ANDERSON | LINN | FRANKLIN

Marais des Cygnes R.

Walnut Creek

Great Bend

Lyons

Cottonwood R.

HAMILTON | KEARNY | FINNEY | HODGEMAN | PAWNEE | Larned | STAFFORD | Hutchinson | RENO | HARVEY | Newton | BUTLER | GREENWOOD | WOODSON | ALLEN | Iola | Fort Scott | BOURBON

Garden City
GRAY

Dodge City
FORD

EDWARDS

Arkansas River

SEDGWICK

Wichita

El Dorado
Augusta

CRAWFORD
Pittsburg

Chanute
Neosho R.
WILSON
NEOSHO

STANTON | GRANT | HASKELL | MEADE | CLARK | COMANCHE | BARBER | HARPER | KINGMAN | SUMNER | COWLEY | ELK | CHAUTAUQUA | MONTGOMERY | LABETTE | CHEROKEE

Ulysses

MORTON | STEVENS | SEWARD
Hugoton
Liberal

North Fork Cimarron River

Pratt
PRATT

Haysville
Derby

Wellington
Winfield
SUMNER

Arkansas City

Independence

Parsons

Coffeyville
Verdigris River

Joplin

OKLAHOMA

TEXAS

Cimarron River

0 25 50 75 100 Miles
0 25 50 75 100 Kilometers

LEGEND

★ State capital
● City
SCOTT County

▲ Mountain peak
▢ Urban area

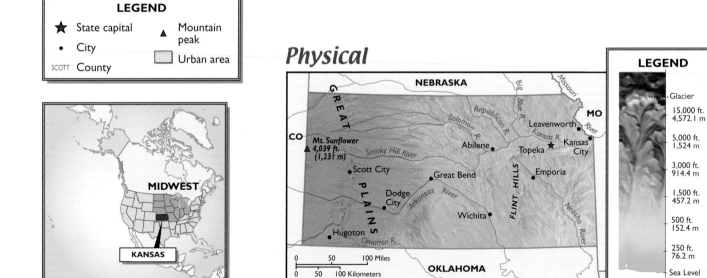

MIDWEST

KANSAS

Physical

NEBRASKA

GREAT PLAINS

CO

Mt. Sunflower
4,039 ft.
(1,231 m)

Smoky Hill River

Solomon R.

Republican R.

Big Blue R.

Missouri River

MO

Leavenworth

Abilene

Topeka

Kansas R.

Kansas City

Scott City

Great Bend

Arkansas River

Dodge City

FLINT HILLS

Emporia

Wichita

Neosho River

Hugoton

Cimarron R.

0 50 100 Miles
0 50 100 Kilometers

OKLAHOMA

LEGEND

Glacier
15,000 ft.
4,572.1 m
5,000 ft.
1,524 m
3,000 ft.
914.4 m
1,500 ft.
457.2 m
500 ft.
152.4 m
250 ft.
76.2 m
Sea Level

If you guessed that Kansas is in the exact center of the United States, you'd be partly right. The geographical center of the lower 48 states is in Smith County, Kansas. The state just barely avoids having four straight sides. A short portion of its northeastern boundary lies along the Missouri River. A large amount of Kansas farmland is devoted to growing wheat. It produces more wheat than any other state. Corn and other grains are also important crops. The western part of Kansas is dry, but farmers obtain water from deep wells. Although much of the state is relatively flat, the Flint Hills are steep, and the land is still covered in grass and used for cattle ranching. Tourists in Kansas often visit famous Old West towns like Dodge City, where large herds of cattle driven north from Texas reached the railroad and cowboys confronted lawmen. Food processing is an important business, but Wichita is home to a unique industry. More than two out of every three private airplanes sold in the world are manufactured and tested there.

Did You Know?

Clashes between pro-slavery and anti-slavery groups before the Civil War earned Kansas a scary but temporary nickname:

Bleeding Kansas

Kansas Almanac

Nickname	Sunflower State
State capital	Topeka
Date of statehood	Jan. 29, 1861; 34th state
State bird	Western meadowlark
State flower	Native sunflower
State tree	Cottonwood
State motto	*Ad Astra per Aspera* (To the Stars Through Difficulties)
Total population & rank	2,694,641 (in 2001); 32nd
Population density	33 per sq. mile (13 per sq. km)
Population distribution	71% urban, 29% rural
Largest cities	Wichita, Overland Park, Kansas City, Topeka
Highest elevation	Mt. Sunflower, 4,039 ft. (1,231 m)
Lowest elevation	Verdigris River in Montgomery Co., 679 ft. (207 m)
Land area & rank	81,815 sq. miles (211,901 sq. km); 13th
Average January temperature	29°F (–2°C)
Average July temperature	79°F (26°C)
Average yearly precipitation	28 inches (71 cm)
Major industries	manufacturing, finance, insurance, real estate, services
Places to visit (Larned), Kansas Cosmosphere and Space Discovery Center (Hutchinson), Dodge City, Eisenhower Center (Abilene)	Fort Larned Natl. Historic Site
Web site	www.accesskansas.org

Economy – Chief Products

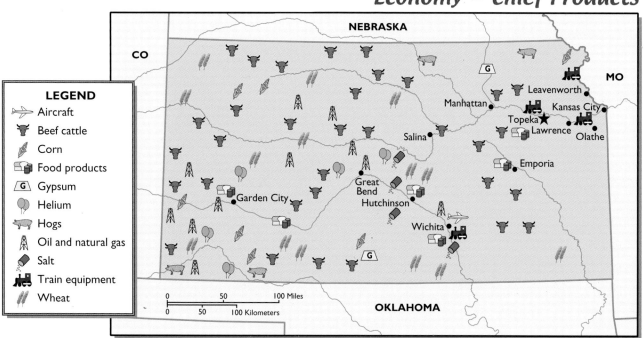

LEGEND
- ✈ Aircraft
- 🐂 Beef cattle
- 🌽 Corn
- 🥫 Food products
- Ⓖ Gypsum
- 🎈 Helium
- 🐖 Hogs
- 🛢 Oil and natural gas
- 🧂 Salt
- 🚂 Train equipment
- 🌾 Wheat

Kentucky Almanac

Nickname	Bluegrass State	**Land area & rank**	39,728 sq. miles (102,896 sq. km); 36th
State capital	Frankfort	**Average January temperature**	34°F (1°C)
Date of statehood	June 1, 1792; 15th state	**Average July temperature**	76°F (24°C)
State bird	Cardinal		
State flower	Goldenrod	**Average yearly precipitation**	47 inches (119 cm)
State tree	Tulip poplar		
State motto	United We Stand, Divided We Fall	**Major industries**	manufacturing, services, finance, insurance and real estate
Total population & rank	4,065,556 (in 2001); 25th		
Population density	102 per sq. mile (39 per sq. km)	**Places to visit**	Mammoth Cave National Park, Lincoln's Birthplace (Hodgenville), Cumberland Gap National Historical Park
Population distribution	56% urban, 44% rural		
Largest cities	Lexington, Louisville, Owensboro		
Highest elevation	Black Mountain, 4,145 ft. (1,263 m)	**Web site**	www.kydirect.net
Lowest elevation	Mississippi River in Fulton Co., 257 ft. (78 m)		

With its nearly-flat bottom and its bulging, irregular top, the profile of Kentucky might be compared to a submarine cruising on calm surface waters: that bumpy top is the Ohio River, squirming its way downstream. Kentucky has more miles of Ohio River boundary than any other state. Kentucky was one of the first areas across the Appalachians to be settled, and it is one of the oldest noncolonial states. Isolated areas in the mountains retain the character of early American life. Coal has been widely mined in the mountains, although the environment has suffered. The most famous part of the state is the Bluegrass Region, where immaculate horse farms raise some of the best thoroughbred race horses in the world. The most valuable farm crop is tobacco, while car manufacturing is an important industry. Louisville attracts many visitors who enjoy its Southern manners and hospitality.

Did You Know?

Kentucky is home to the longest—about 350 miles (563 km)—known cave system in the world:

Mammoth Cave

Physical

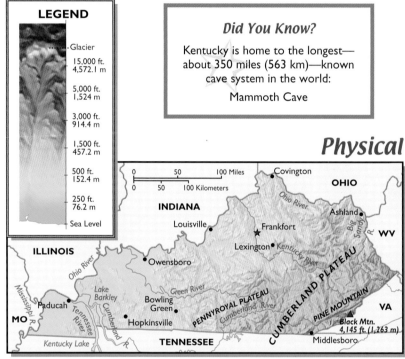

Economy—Chief Products

LEGEND

- Automobiles
- Beef cattle
- Chemicals
- Coal
- Corn
- Horses
- Limestone
- Natural gas
- Tobacco

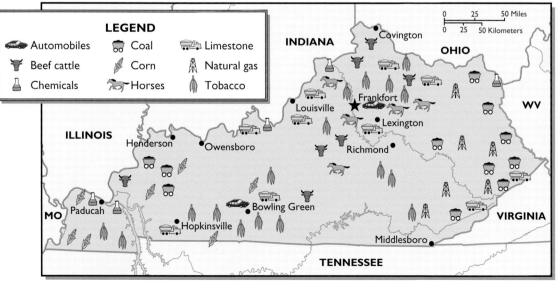

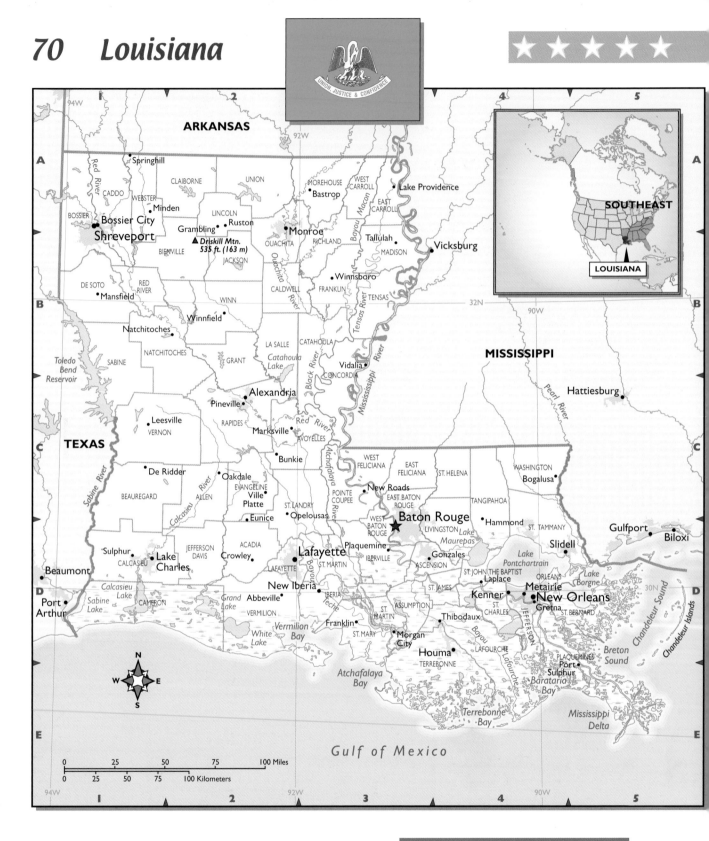

ARKANSAS

Springhill

CADDO
CLAIBORNE
UNION
MOREHOUSE
WEST CARROLL
Lake Providence

WEBSTER
Minden
Bossier City
BOSSIER
Shreveport

LINCOLN
Grambling
Ruston
Bastrop

▲ Driskill Mtn.
535 ft. (163 m)

BIENVILLE
JACKSON

OUACHITA
Monroe
RICHLAND
EAST CARROLL
Tallulah
MADISON
Vicksburg

DE SOTO
RED RIVER
Mansfield

WINN
Winnfield
CALDWELL
FRANKLIN
Winnsboro

Natchitoches

NATCHITOCHES
SABINE
GRANT
Catahoula Lake
LA SALLE
CATAHOULA
Black River
CONCORDIA
Vidalia

MISSISSIPPI

Toledo Bend Reservoir

Hattiesburg
Pearl River

32N
90W

TEXAS

Leesville
VERNON
RAPIDES
Alexandria
Pineville

Red River
Marksville
AVOYELLES
Bunkie

De Ridder
BEAUREGARD
Calcasieu River
ALLEN
Oakdale
EVANGELINE
Ville Platte
ST. LANDRY
Eunice
Opelousas

Atchafalaya River
POINTE COUPEE
New Roads
WEST FELICIANA
EAST FELICIANA
ST. HELENA
WASHINGTON
Bogalusa

EAST BATON ROUGE
Baton Rouge
WEST BATON ROUGE
LIVINGSTON
Lake Maurepas
TANGIPAHOA
Hammond
ST. TAMMANY

Gulfport
Biloxi

Sabine River

Sulphur
CALCASIEU
Lake Charles
JEFFERSON DAVIS
ACADIA
Crowley
LAFAYETTE
Lafayette
ST. MARTIN
Plaquemine
IBERVILLE
Gonzales
ASCENSION

Slidell
Lake Pontchartrain

Beaumont

Calcasieu Lake
CAMERON
Sabine Lake
Abbeville
IBERIA
New Iberia
Bayou Teche
VERMILION

ST. JOHN THE BAPTIST
Laplace
ORLEANS
Lake Borgne

Kenner
Metairie
Gretna
New Orleans

ST. JAMES
ASSUMPTION
ST. CHARLES
ST. BERNARD

Port Arthur

Grand Lake
Vermilion Bay
White Lake
Franklin
ST. MARTIN
ST. MARY
Morgan City
Thibodaux
JEFFERSON

30N

Chandeleur Sound
Chandeleur Islands

N
W E
S

Houma
TERREBONNE
Bayou Lafourche
LAFOURCHE
Port Sulphur
PLAQUEMINES
Barataria Bay

Breton Sound

Atchafalaya Bay
Terrebonne Bay
Mississippi Delta

Gulf of Mexico

| 0 | 25 | 50 | 75 | 100 Miles |
| 0 | 25 | 50 | 75 | 100 Kilometers |

94W
1
92W
2
3
90W
4
5

SOUTHEAST

LOUISIANA

UNION, JUSTICE & CONFIDENCE

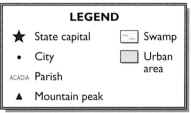

LEGEND

★ State capital
• City
ACADIA Parish
▲ Mountain peak

Swamp
Urban area

Did You Know?

British troops were crushed in the final battle of the War of 1812, but it actually occurred after a peace treaty had been signed in Europe:

The Battle of New Orleans

Boot-shaped Louisiana, the state standing prominently at the center of the Gulf Coast, is a shadow of its former self. In 1803, the territory of Louisiana stretched all the way to the present state of Montana. In a sense, the Mississippi River is its parent. Much of the land within the state is the result of the mud carried south and dumped at the edge of the Gulf of Mexico by the river. Southern Louisiana is the home of the Cajuns, the descendants of French Canadians who were transported to the area 250 years ago. The Creole culture, a mix of Spanish and French traditions, began to form at about the same time. African-American traditions influenced music and laid foundations for the development of jazz and the blues. Louisiana's Gulf Coast is a supermarket of resources, providing shrimp, oysters, and crawfish as well as salt, sulphur, and natural gas. New Orleans is an immensely popular tourist destination. Visitors come for jazz and Cajun music, its famous regional cooking, and the multi-day festival and street party called Mardi Gras, usually held in February.

Economy— Chief Products

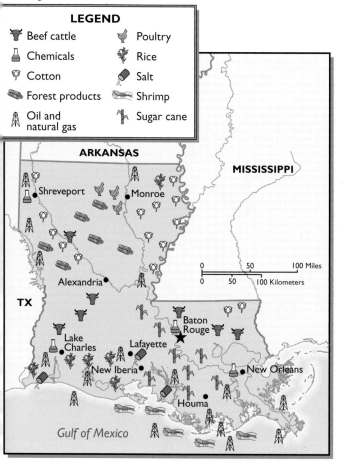

LEGEND

- Beef cattle
- Chemicals
- Cotton
- Forest products
- Oil and natural gas
- Poultry
- Rice
- Salt
- Shrimp
- Sugar cane

Louisiana Almanac

Nickname	Pelican State
State capital	Baton Rouge
Date of statehood	April 30, 1812; 18th state
State bird	Eastern brown pelican
State flower	Magnolia
State tree	Cypress
State motto	Union, Justice and Confidence
Total population & rank	4,465,430 (in 2001); 22nd
Population density	103 per sq. mile (40 per sq. km)
Population distribution	73% urban, 27% rural
Largest cities	New Orleans, Baton Rouge, Shreveport, Metairie
Highest elevation	Driskill Mountain, 535 ft. (163 m)
Lowest elevation	New Orleans, 8 ft. (2.4 m) below sea level
Land area & rank	43,562 sq. miles (112,826 sq. km); 33rd
Average January temperature	49°F (9°C)
Average July temperature	82°F (28°C)
Average yearly precipitation	58 inches (147 cm)
Major industries	wholesale and retail trade, tourism, manufacturing, construction, transportation
Places to visit	Natchitoches, New Orleans: Aquarium of the Americas, Audubon Zoo and Gardens, French Quarter, Jackson Square, Confederate Museum
Web site	www.state.la.us

★ ★ ★ ★ ★

LEGEND

★ State capital
• City
KNOX County
▲ Mountain peak
National or other park
Urban area

Did You Know?

The winters are cold in Maine, and this wintertime accessory was invented here:

Earmuffs

QUÉBEC

CANADA

NEW BRUNSWICK

CANADA

Madawaska
Fort Kent
Van Buren
Caribou
AROOSTOOK
Presque Isle
Houlton

St. Lawrence River
St. John River
Allagash River
St. John River

N W E S

Eagle Lake

Chesuncook Lake

BAXTER STATE PARK

▲ Mt. Katahdin
5,267 ft. (1,605 m)

Moosehead Lake
PISCATAQUIS
Pemadumcook Lake
Millinocket

SOMERSET

PENOBSCOT
Lincoln

West Grand Lake

St. Croix River

Flagstaff Lake

Dover-Foxcroft
Piscataquis River

Big Lake

Calais

Kennebago R.

FRANKLIN
Mooselookmeguntic Lake

Penobscot River

WASHINGTON

Eastport

Connecticut River

OXFORD

Skowhegan

Bangor
Orono

HANCOCK

Machias

Farmington

Rumford

Androscoggin River

Waterville

KENNEBEC

Kennebec River

WALDO

Belfast

Ellsworth

Bar Harbor

ACADIA NATL. PARK

★ Augusta
• Gardiner

ANDROSCOGGIN

Auburn Lewiston

LINCOLN

KNOX

Penobscot Bay

Rockland

NEW HAMPSHIRE

44N

SAGADAHOC

Sebago Lake
Brunswick Bath Boothbay

CUMBERLAND

ACADIA NATL. PARK

ATLANTIC OCEAN

Westbrook
Portland
South Portland

YORK

Saco
Sanford
Biddeford

Kennebunkport

Lake Winnipesaukee

★ Concord

Kittery

Manchester Portsmouth

MAINE

NEW ENGLAND

0   25   50 Miles
0   25   50 Kilometers

46N

68W

70W

Maine, the easternmost state and the largest of the New England states, is wedged between the Canadian provinces of New Brunswick and Quebec. Maine is most famous for the rugged beauty of its 228-mile (367 km) rocky coast. There are many port cities and fishing villages along the coast, where tourism, fishing, and ship-building prosper. Maine's lobster catch is the largest of any state. Lobster is its most well-known product and the Maine Lobster Festival one of its outstanding annual events. Forests cover about 90% of the state— more woodland area than any other state. These forests are a beautiful wilderness area for hiking and other outdoor sports as well as the natural resource for Maine's largest industry—lumber, wood, and paper products. The people here, descendants of English, French, French-Canadian, Irish, and German immigrants, are noted for their tough independent spirit. Because Maine's economy relies on its natural resources, the state's residents take conservation very seriously.

Maine Almanac

Nickname	Pine Tree State
State capital	Augusta
Date of statehood	March 15, 1820; 23rd state
State bird	Chickadee
State flower	White pine cone and tassel
State tree	Eastern white pine
State motto	*Dirigo* (I Direct)
Total population & rank	1,286,670 (in 2001); 40th
Population density	42 per sq. mile (16 per sq. km)
Population distribution	40% urban, 60% rural
Largest cities	Portland, Lewiston, Bangor
Highest elevation	Mt. Katahdin, 5,267 ft. (1,605 m)
Lowest elevation	sea level
Land area & rank	30,862 sq. miles (79,933 sq. km); 39th
Average January temperature	17°F (−8°C)
Average July temperature	67°F (19°C)
Average yearly precipitation	41 inches (104 cm)
Major industries	manufacturing, agriculture, fishing, services, trade
Places to visit	Acadia National Park, Portland Head Lighthouse, Boothbay Railway Museum
Web site	www.state.me.us

Economy – Chief Products

LEGEND

- Blueberries
- Eggs
- Fish
- Gemstones
- Milk
- Oats
- Paper products
- Potatoes
- Sand and gravel
- Shellfish

Physical

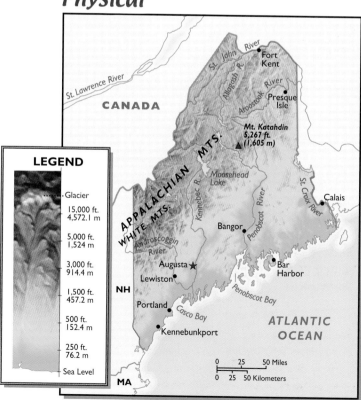

LEGEND

- Glacier
- 15,000 ft. 4,572.1 m
- 5,000 ft. 1,524 m
- 3,000 ft. 914.4 m
- 1,500 ft. 457.2 m
- 500 ft. 152.4 m
- 250 ft. 76.2 m
- Sea Level

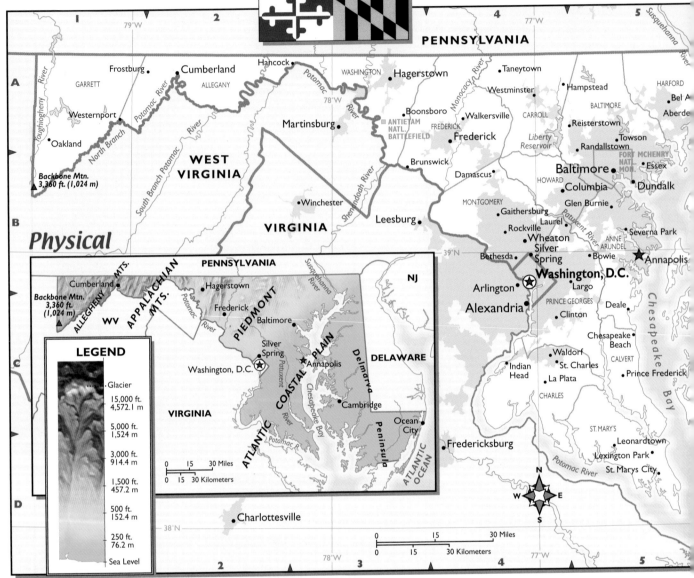

Maryland Almanac

Nicknames	Old Line State, Free State	**Lowest elevation**	sea level
State capital	Annapolis	**Land area & rank**	9,774 sq. miles (25,315 sq. km); 42nd
Date of statehood	April 28, 1788; 7th state		
State bird	Baltimore oriole	**Average January temperature**	33°F (1°C)
State flower	Black-eyed Susan		
State tree	White oak	**Average July temperature**	75°F (24°C)
State motto	*Fatti Maschii, Parole Femine* (Manly Deeds, Womanly Words)	**Average yearly precipitation**	43 inches (109 cm)
Total population & rank	5,375,156 (in 2001); 19th	**Major industries**	manufacturing, biotechnology, information technology, services, tourism
Population density	550 per sq. mile (212 per sq. km)		
Population distribution	86% urban, 14% rural		
Largest cities	Baltimore, Columbia, Silver Spring, Dundalk, Wheaton-Glenmont	**Places to visit**	Antietam National Battlefield (Sharpsburg), Fort McHenry National Monument (Baltimore), Assateague Island National Seashore
Highest elevation	Backbone Mountain, 3,360 ft. (1,024 m)	**Web site**	www.state.md.us

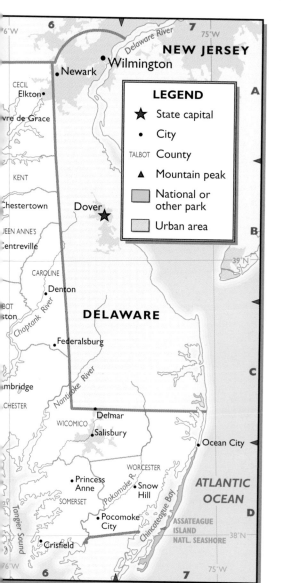

Maryland's unique shape is divided into two parts by the Chesapeake Bay. The coastal regions of the Chesapeake and Atlantic are flat and home to Maryland's commercial and recreational harbors. The western section is a mix of mountains, hills, plains, valleys, and forests. There is good farmland throughout the state, where nursery stock, fruit, grains, poultry, and tobacco are grown. In 1791, the state gave part of its land to create the new national capital, Washington, D.C. Many people who work in Washington, D.C. live in Maryland. In this densely populated state, 86% of the people live and work in urban areas such as Baltimore and Hagerstown. The border between Maryland and Pennsylvania is called the Mason-Dixon Line and is the unofficial line between the northern and southern states. Even though considered a southern state, Maryland fought with the north during the Civil War. "The Star Spangled Banner" was written by Francis Scott Key at Fort McHenry near Baltimore. There are many other historic sites as well as fabulous beaches and urban centers like the renowned Inner Harbor of Baltimore attracting visitors to Maryland.

MIDATLANTIC

MARYLAND

Did You Know?

Not many states have an official sport, and Marylands is an ancient one:

Jousting

Economy – Chief Products

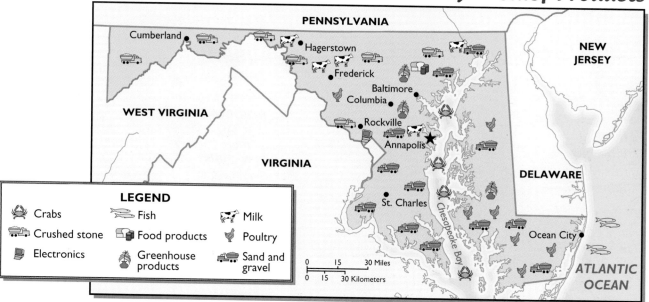

LEGEND

Crabs   Fish   Milk

Crushed stone   Food products   Poultry

Electronics   Greenhouse products   Sand and gravel

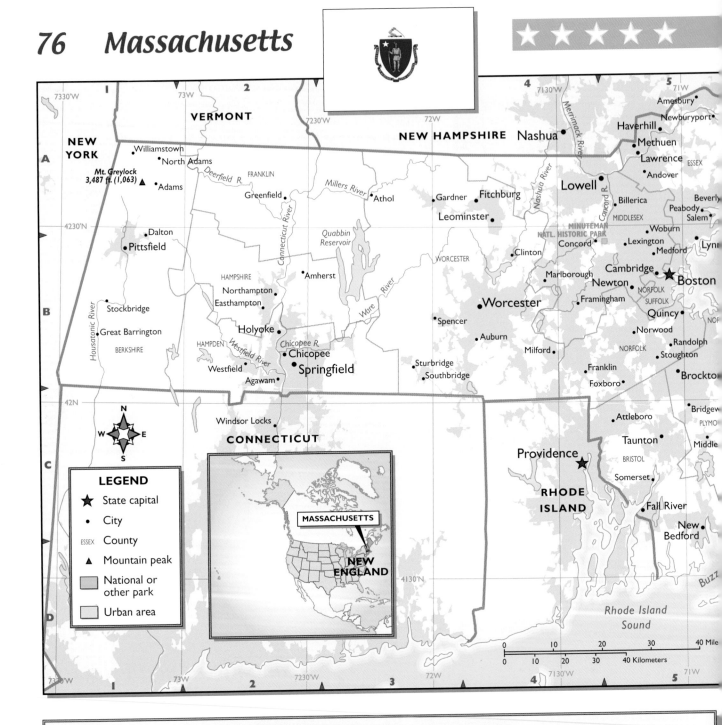

Massachusetts Almanac

Nicknames	Bay State, Old Colony	**Highest elevation**	Mt. Greylock, 3,487 ft. (1,063 m)
State capital	Boston	**Lowest elevation**	sea level
Date of statehood	Feb. 6, 1788; 6th state	**Land area & rank**	7,840 sq. miles (20,306 sq. km); 45th
State bird	Chickadee	**Average January temperature**	25°F (–4°C)
State flower	Mayflower		
State tree	American elm	**Average July temperature**	70°F (21°C)
State motto	*Ense Petit Placidam Sub Libertate Quietem* (By the Sword We Seek Peace, but Peace Only Under Liberty)	**Average yearly precipitation**	45 inches (114 cm)
		Major industries	services, trade, manufacturing
Total population & rank	6,379,304 (in 2001); 13th	**Places to visit**	Minute Man National Historical Park, Freedom Trail (Boston), Old Sturbridge Village, Plymouth: Plymouth Rock, Plimoth Plantation,
Population density	814 per sq. mile (314 per sq. km)		
Population distribution	91% urban, 9% rural		
Largest cities	Boston, Worcester, Springfield, Lowell, Cambridge	**Web site**	www.mass.gov

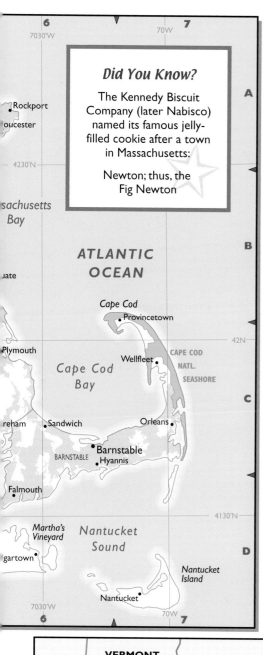

Did You Know?

The Kennedy Biscuit Company (later Nabisco) named its famous jelly-filled cookie after a town in Massachusetts:

Newton; thus, the Fig Newton

The shape of Massachusetts is defined by the curl of Cape Cod on the Atlantic coast. Massachusetts is a key state in U.S. history. It is the home of Plymouth Rock, the landing point of the Pilgrims in 1620, as well as many U.S. firsts: Harvard (the first college in the United States), the first newspaper, printing press, library, and post office. There are also many famous Revolutionary War sites. Its ports and fine harbors contributed to the success of the fishing and shipping industries. Technology came early to Massachusetts with the first power loom and continues to this day with many people working for high-tech businesses. Although Massachusetts is a very industrialized state, both its coastal lowlands and its western river valleys support agriculture. Nursery stock and cranberries are the state's leading products. The world-class museums, cultural events, historic sites, lovely New England coastal resorts, and ski areas and the natural beauty of the western forests have fostered a strong tourist business.

Physical

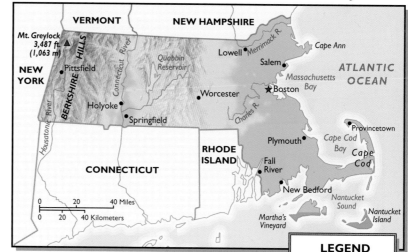

LEGEND

- Glacier
- 15,000 ft. 4,572.1 m
- 5,000 ft. 1,524 m
- 3,000 ft. 914.4 m
- 1,500 ft. 457.2 m
- 500 ft. 152.4 m
- 250 ft. 76.2 m
- Sea Level

Economy—Chief Products

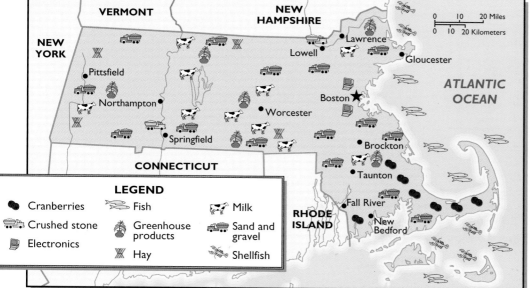

LEGEND

- Cranberries
- Crushed stone
- Electronics
- Fish
- Greenhouse products
- Hay
- Milk
- Sand and gravel
- Shellfish

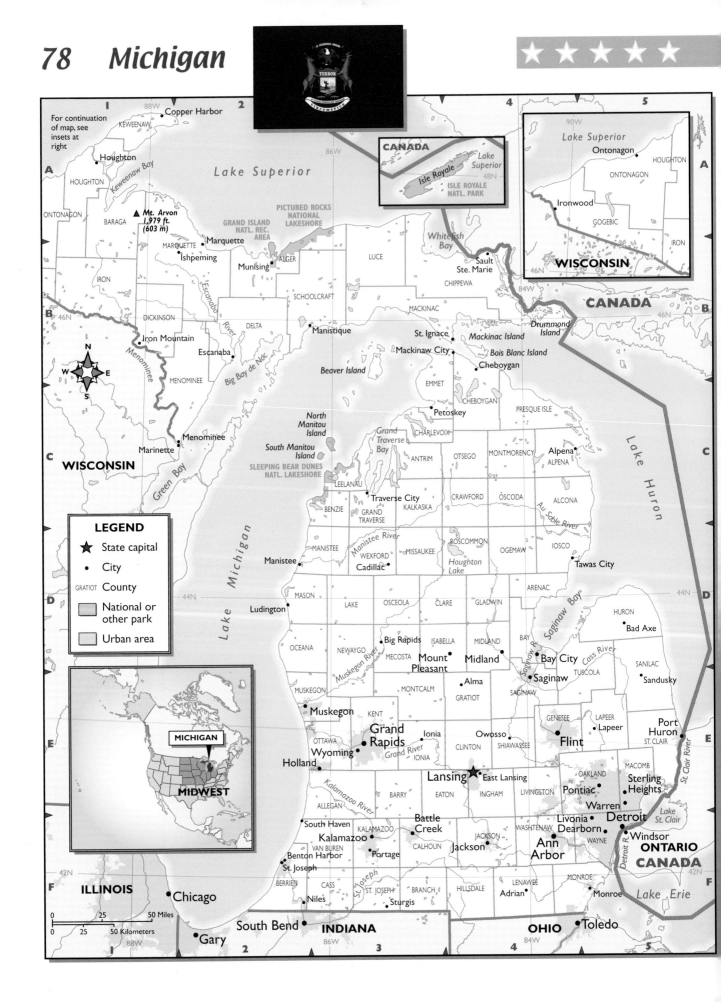

For continuation of map, see insets at right

Lake Superior

Copper Harbor
KEWEENAW
Houghton
HOUGHTON
ONTONAGON
BARAGA
▲ Mt. Arvon 1,979 ft. (603 m)
Marquette
MARQUETTE
Ishpeming
IRON
Iron Mountain
DICKINSON
Escanaba
Menominee
MENOMINEE
Marinette
Menominee River
Big Bay de Noc
Green Bay

WISCONSIN

PICTURED ROCKS NATIONAL LAKESHORE
GRAND ISLAND NATL. REC. AREA
Munising
ALGER
DELTA
SCHOOLCRAFT
LUCE
Manistique
MACKINAC

Whitefish Bay
Sault Ste. Marie
CHIPPEWA
CANADA

St. Ignace
Mackinaw City
Mackinac Island
Bois Blanc Island
Drummond Island
Cheboygan
EMMET
CHEBOYGAN
PRESQUE ISLE

Beaver Island
North Manitou Island
South Manitou Island
SLEEPING BEAR DUNES NATL. LAKESHORE
LEELANAU
BENZIE
Grand Traverse Bay
Traverse City
GRAND TRAVERSE
CHARLEVOIX
Petoskey
ANTRIM
OTSEGO
MONTMORENCY
Alpena
ALPENA
KALKASKA
CRAWFORD
OSCODA
ALCONA
Au Sable River

Lake Michigan

Manistee
Manistee River
MANISTEE
WEXFORD
Cadillac
MISSAUKEE
ROSCOMMON
Houghton Lake
OGEMAW
IOSCO
Tawas City

Ludington
MASON
LAKE
OSCEOLA
CLARE
GLADWIN
ARENAC
Saginaw Bay
HURON
Bad Axe

OCEANA
NEWAYGO
Muskegon River
Big Rapids
MECOSTA
ISABELLA
Mount Pleasant
MIDLAND
Midland
BAY
Bay City
Cass River
SANILAC
Sandusky

MUSKEGON
Muskegon
MONTCALM
Alma
GRATIOT
SAGINAW
Saginaw
TUSCOLA

KENT
Grand Rapids
OTTAWA
Wyoming
Ionia
IONIA
Grand River
Owosso
CLINTON
SHIAWASSEE
GENESEE
Flint
LAPEER
Lapeer
Port Huron
ST. CLAIR

Holland
Kalamazoo River
ALLEGAN
BARRY
EATON
INGHAM
Lansing ★ East Lansing
LIVINGSTON
OAKLAND
Pontiac
MACOMB
Sterling Heights
Warren
Lake St. Clair
St. Clair River

South Haven
KALAMAZOO
Kalamazoo
VAN BUREN
Portage
CALHOUN
Battle Creek
JACKSON
Jackson
WASHTENAW
Ann Arbor
WAYNE
Livonia
Dearborn
Detroit
Windsor
ONTARIO
CANADA

Benton Harbor
St. Joseph
BERRIEN
CASS
St. Joseph River
ST. JOSEPH
BRANCH
HILLSDALE
LENAWEE
Adrian
MONROE
Monroe
Lake Erie

Niles
Sturgis

ILLINOIS
Chicago

South Bend
INDIANA
Gary

OHIO
Toledo

Detroit R.

CANADA
Isle Royale
Lake Superior
ISLE ROYALE NATL. PARK
48N

WISCONSIN
Lake Superior
Ontonagon
HOUGHTON
ONTONAGON
Ironwood
GOGEBIC
IRON
46N
CANADA

LEGEND
★ State capital
• City
GRATIOT County
National or other park
Urban area

MICHIGAN
MIDWEST

0   25   50 Miles
0   25   50 Kilometers

★ ★ ★ ★ ★

ichigan is unique among the lower 48 states
y being divided into two large pieces. Lower
ichigan resembles a mitten with its thumb
rotruding to the right, while the Upper
eninsula sits above it, spreading from west
east like a crooked tree branch. Both parts
the state are nearly surrounded by waters
the Great Lakes. Michigan has the longest
eshwater coastline in the United States.
ith just a small fraction of the state's
pulation, the Upper Peninsula is largely
volved with forestry, dairy farming, and
tdoor recreation. Agriculture is important
Lower Michigan, particularly in the
uthern half. Cherries and other fruits are
mmon along the Lake Michigan shore
here the trees are protected from frost
mage. Michigan has long been known for
anufacturing, and the automobile industry
d food processing lead the way. Industrial
mand for workers has attracted many
migrants, including a large number from the
uthern United States.

Economy – Chief Products

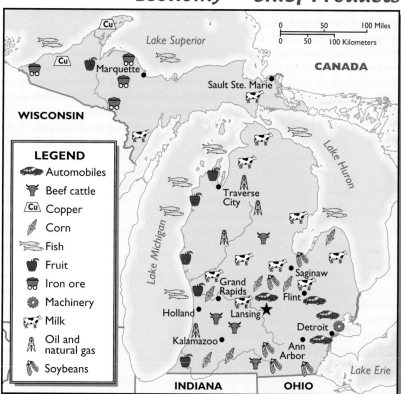

Did You Know?

Native Americans were mining copper
here long before the arrival of Europeans:
Upper Peninsula

Physical

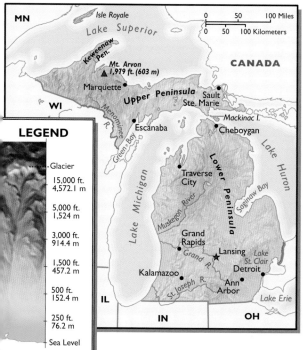

Michigan Almanac

Nicknames	Great Lakes State, Wolverine State
State capital	Lansing
Date of statehood	Jan. 26, 1837; 26th state
State bird	Robin
State flower	Apple blossom
State tree	White pine
State motto	*Si Quaeris Peninsulam Amoenam, Circumspice* (If You Seek a Pleasant Peninsula, Look About You)
Total population & rank	9,990,871 (in 2001); 8th
Population density	176 per sq. mile (70 per sq. km)
Population distribution	75% urban, 25% rural
Largest cities	Detroit, Grand Rapids, Warren, Flint, Sterling Heights
Highest elevation	Mt. Arvon, 1,979 ft. (603 m)
Lowest elevation	Lake Erie, 571 ft. (174 m)
Land area & rank	56,804 sq. miles (147,122 sq. km); 22nd
Average January temperature	20°F (–7°C)
Average July temperature	69°F (21°C)
Average yearly precipitation	32 inches (81 cm)
Major industries	manufacturing, services, tourism, agriculture, forestry/lumber
Places to visit	Greenfield Village (Dearborn), Motown Historical Museum (Detroit), Mackinac Island
Web site	www.michigan.gov

MINNESOTA

MANITOBA

CANADA

ONTARIO

MINNESOTA

MIDWEST

KITTSON
ROSEAU
• Roseau

LAKE OF THE WOODS

Lake of the Woods

Rainy River

Rainy Lake

International Falls

Kabetogama Lake

VOYAGEURS NATL. PARK

Basswood R.

Pigeon River

MARSHALL

Mud Lake

Upper Red Lake

KOOCHICHING

Vermilion Lake

Eagle Mtn. 2,301 ft. (701 m) ▲ COOK

Grand Portage

Thief River Falls •

PENNINGTON

Red Lake River

Ely •

LAKE

East Grand Forks

Grand Forks

Crookston •

RED LAKE

POLK

Lower Red Lake

BELTRAMI

Lake Winnibigoshish

Big Fork River

ITASCA

Chisholm •

Virginia •

Hibbing •

SAINT LOUIS

Lake Superior

NORTH DAKOTA

NORMAN

MAHNOMEN

CLEARWATER

Bemidji •

Cass Lake

HUBBARD

Leech Lake

CASS

Grand Rapids •

St. Louis River

West Fargo

Fargo

Moorhead

CLAY

BECKER

Detroit Lakes •

Two Harbors •

Hermantown •

Duluth

MICHIGAN

Cloquet •

Superior •

WADENA

CROW

CARLTON

Otter Tail G.

OTTER TAIL

Fergus Falls •

Leech Lake

River

Mille Lacs Lake

AITKIN

PINE

WILKIN

Bois de Sioux River

GRANT

DOUGLAS

TODD

MORRISON

Little Falls •

MILLE LACS

KANABEC

Brainerd •

Alexandria •

TRAVERSE

Chippewa River

POPE

STEVENS

Morris •

BENTON

St. Croix River

N
W E
S

LEGEND

★ State capital
• City
PINE County
▲ Mountain peak
National or other park
Swamp
Urban area

BIG STONE

SWIFT

STEARNS

Sartell •

Sauk Rapids •

St. Cloud

SHERBURNE

ISANTI

CHISAGO

ANOKA

KANDIYOHI

CHIPPEWA

MEEKER

Buffalo •

WRIGHT

Elk River •

Coon Rapids •

WASHINGTON

LAC QUI PARLE

Montevideo •

Willmar •

HENNEPIN

RAMSEY

Minneapolis

★ St. Paul

Eau Claire •

SOUTH DAKOTA

YELLOW MEDICINE

MCLEOD

CARVER

Bloomington •

Shakopee •

SCOTT

DAKOTA

Mississippi River

WISCONSIN

RENVILLE

Minnesota River

SIBLEY

NICOLLET

Northfield •

RICE

Red Wing •

GOODHUE

WABASHA

Marshall •

Redwood River

REDWOOD

LINCOLN

LYON

New Ulm •

LE SUEUR

Faribault •

Winona •

BROWN

Mankato •

BLUE EARTH

WASECA

Owatonna •

DODGE

Rochester •

OLMSTED

WINONA

PIPESTONE

MURRAY

COTTONWOOD

WATONWAN

STEELE

La Crosse •

Sioux Falls

ROCK

NOBLES

JACKSON

MARTIN

FARIBAULT

FREEBORN

MOWER

FILLMORE

HOUSTON

Worthington •

Fairmont •

Albert Lea •

Austin •

Des Moines River

0   25   50   75   100 Miles

0   25   50   75   100 Kilometers

IOWA

Taller than it is wide and capped with a small wedge of land thrusting up into Canada, Minnesota is associated with fresh water. Lake Superior washes against the remote northeastern shoreline, thousands of small lakes speckle the woodlands, and a modest lake is the source of the mighty Mississippi River. Scandinavian immigrants saw a landscape that looked familiar, and many stayed to make their home. The north, like Canada, has miles and miles of forests and a celebrated history of lumberjacks and trappers. Iron ore from its mountain ranges was crucial to the U.S. steel industry. The south, like Iowa, is fertile farmland, producing corn and soybeans. Although many U.S. cities lie close to each other, the expression "Twin Cities" means just one thing—Minneapolis and St. Paul. Each has its distinctive character, but together they blend into an attractive and comfortable metropolitan area.

Did You Know?

A commonly expressed statement says that Minnesota is the land of 10,000 lakes, but it has many more:

15,000

Minnesota Almanac

Nicknames	North Star State, Gopher State
State capital	St. Paul
Date of statehood	May 11, 1858; 32nd state
State bird	Common loon
State flower	Pink and white lady's-slipper
State tree	Norway (red) pine
State motto	*L'Etoile du Nord* (The Star of the North)
Total population & rank	4,972,294 (in 2001); 21st
Population density	62 per sq. mile (24 per sq. km)
Population distribution	71% urban, 29% rural
Largest cities	Minneapolis, St. Paul, Duluth, Rochester, Bloomington
Highest elevation	Eagle Mountain, 2,301 ft. (701 m)
Lowest elevation	Lake Superior, 602 ft. (183 m)
Land area & rank	79,610 sq. miles (206,190 sq. km); 14th
Average January temperature	9°F (–13°C)
Average July temperature	70°F (21°C)
Average yearly precipitation	26 inches (66 cm)
Major industries	agribusiness, forest products, mining, manufacturing, tourism
Places to visit	Voyageurs National Park, Walker Art Center (Minneapolis), Ironworld (Chisholm), St. Paul: Minnesota State Fair, Fort Snelling
Web site	www.state.mn.us

Economy – Chief Products

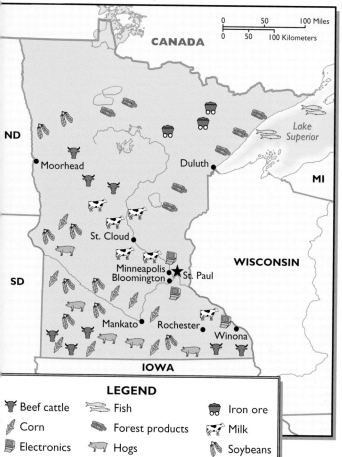

LEGEND

- 🐂 Beef cattle
- 🌽 Corn
- 💻 Electronics
- 🐟 Fish
- 🪵 Forest products
- 🐖 Hogs
- ⛏ Iron ore
- 🐄 Milk
- 🌱 Soybeans

Physical

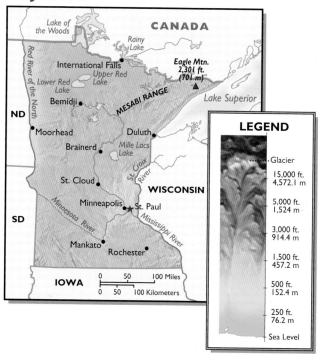

LEGEND

- Glacier
- 15,000 ft. / 4,572.1 m
- 5,000 ft. / 1,524 m
- 3,000 ft. / 914.4 m
- 1,500 ft. / 457.2 m
- 500 ft. / 152.4 m
- 250 ft. / 76.2 m
- Sea Level

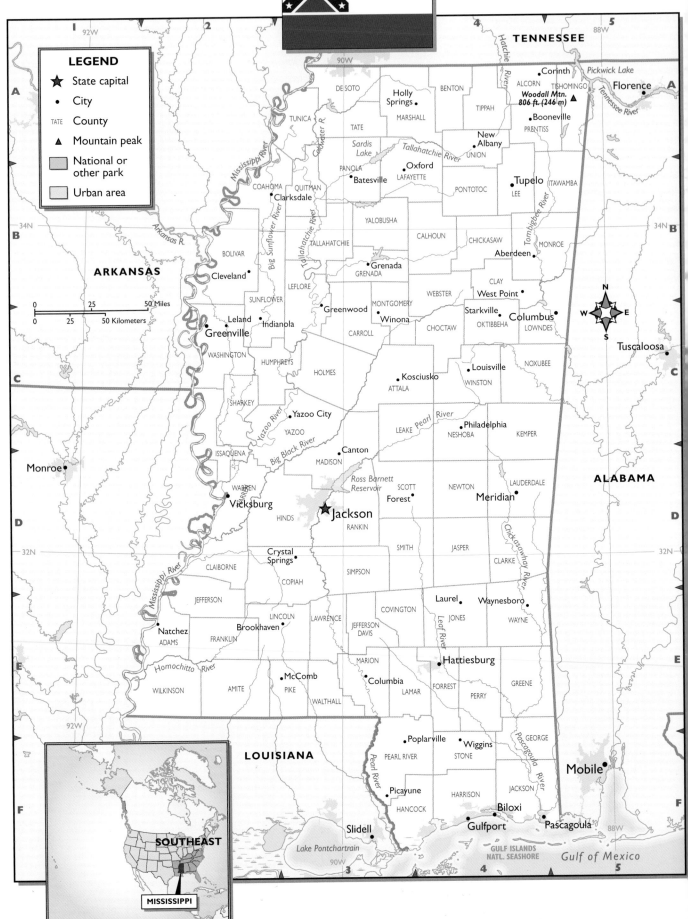

LEGEND

★ State capital
• City
TATE County
▲ Mountain peak
National or other park
Urban area

TENNESSEE

ARKANSAS

ALABAMA

LOUISIANA

Gulf of Mexico

SOUTHEAST

MISSISSIPPI

he state of Mississippi takes its name from the celebrated aterway that forms its irregular, western-facing border— e Mississippi River. By its geography, culture, and history, ississippi is one of the states belonging to the Deep South. Vithin the state, the Delta region, an oval-shaped cluster of ounties next to the Mississippi River, best matches the opular image of the Deep South. The Delta has tropical eat, unbroken flat fields growing cotton and soybeans, and e highest concentration of African Americans (60% of the elta's population) in the United States. The rest of the state lls from the northeastern hills to the Gulf Coast and oduces a mix of crops, livestock, and forest products. As all the South today, there is much in Mississippi that is ew—manufacturing, catfish farming, plus visitors who flock the Delta to hear the blues, enjoy themselves at the aches and bays, or spend time at casino facilities.

Economy – Chief Products

LEGEND

🐂	Beef cattle	🪵	Forest products	🐓	Poultry
🌾	Cotton	🐄	Milk	🦐	Shrimp
🥫	Food products	⛽	Oil and natural gas	🌱	Soybeans

Physical

LEGEND

·······	Glacier
	15,000 ft. 4,572.1 m
	5,000 ft. 1,524 m
	3,000 ft. 914.4 m
	1,500 ft. 457.2 m
	500 ft. 152.4 m
	250 ft. 76.2 m
	Sea Level

Did You Know?

Because a river's course shifts over time, some land belonging to Mississippi lies in an unexpected location: West of the Mississippi River

Mississippi Almanac

Nickname	Magnolia State	**Land area & rank**	46,907 sq. miles (121,489 sq. km); 31st
State capital	Jackson	**Average January temperature**	45°F (7°C)
Date of statehood	Dec. 10, 1817; 20th state	**Average July temperature**	81°F (27°C)
State bird	Mockingbird		
State flower	Magnolia	**Average yearly precipitation**	56 inches (142 cm)
State tree	Magnolia		
State motto	*Virtute et Armis* (By Valor and Arms)	**Major industries**	warehousing and distribution, services, manufacturing, government, wholesale and retail trade
Total population & rank	2,858,029 (in 2001); 31st		
Population density	61 per sq. mile (24 per sq. km)		
Population distribution	49% urban, 51% rural	**Places to visit**	Vicksburg National Military Park, Natchez Trace Parkway (from Natchez to Nashville, TN), Old Spanish Fort and Museum (Pascagoula)
Largest cities	Jackson, Gulfport, Biloxi		
Highest elevation	Woodall Mountain, 806 ft. (246 m)		
Lowest elevation	sea level	**Web site**	www.ms.gov

LEGEND

★ State capital
• City
OSAGE County
▲ Mountain peak
National or other park
Urban area

0   25   50 Miles
0   25   50 Kilometers

IOWA

NE

NODAWAY   WORTH   HARRISON   MERCER   PUTNAM   SCHUYLER   SCOTLAND   CLARK
ATCHISON   Maryville   GENTRY   SULLIVAN   ADAIR   KNOX   LEWIS
HOLT   ANDREW   DE KALB   DAVIESS   GRUNDY   Trenton   LINN   MACON   SHELBY   MARION   Quincy
St. Joseph   Cameron   Chillicothe   LIVINGSTON   Macon   MONROE   Hannibal
BUCHANAN   CLINTON   CALDWELL   CHARITON   RANDOLPH   Salt River   RALLS
PLATTE   CLAY   RAY   CARROLL   Moberly   PIKE   ILLINOIS
Liberty   SALINE   HOWARD   BOONE   AUDRAIN   Mexico   LINCOLN
Kansas City   Kansas City   Marshall   Columbia   MONTGOMERY
Topeka   Independence   LAFAYETTE   Boonville   CALLAWAY   WARREN   St. Charles   Florissant
Lees Summit   JACKSON   COOPER   Missouri River   ST. CHARLES   St. Louis
Belton   Warrensburg   Sedalia   MONITEAU   FRANKLIN   Washington   ST. LOUIS   East St. Louis
CASS   JOHNSON   PETTIS   COLE   OSAGE   GASCONADE   Arnold
KANSAS   Jefferson City   MORGAN   MARIES   JEFFERSON   Festus
BATES   HENRY   Clinton   BENTON   Osage River   GASCONADE   De Soto
Harry S. Truman Reservoir   Lake of the Ozarks   MILLER   River   STE. GENEVIEVE   Kaskaskia
ST. CLAIR   CAMDEN   Rolla   CRAWFORD   WASHINGTON   Park Hills   PERRY
VERNON   HICKORY   PHELPS   ST. FRANCOIS   Farmington   Perryville
Nevada   CEDAR   DALLAS   Lebanon   PULASKI   DENT   IRON   MADISON   CAPE GIRARDEAU
Stockton Lake   POLK   LACLEDE   Taum Sauk Mtn.   Jackson
BARTON   Bolivar   WEBSTER   WRIGHT   1,772 ft. (540 m)   BOLLINGER
DADE   GREENE   TEXAS   REYNOLDS   Cape Girardeau
JASPER   Carthage   LAWRENCE   Springfield   Wappapello Lake   SCOTT
Webb City   Ozark   Current River   CARTER   Black River   St. Francis River   Sikeston
Joplin   NEWTON   Monett   CHRISTIAN   DOUGLAS   HOWELL   SHANNON   MISSISSIPPI
Neosho   BARRY   STONE   TANEY   OZARK   West Plains   OREGON   RIPLEY   Poplar Bluff   Dexter
Grand Lake O' the Cherokees   MCDONALD   Table Rock Lake   Branson   White   River   BUTLER   NEW MADRID   Ohio R.
OKLAHOMA   Bull Shoals Lake   Caruthersville   PEMISCOT   Kennett   DUNKLIN
Fayetteville   KY   TENNESSEE

ARKANSAS

Ozark Natl. Scenic Riverways

N   W   E   S

MIDWEST

MISSOURI

Positioned near the center of the lower 48 states, Missouri can be recognized by the small projection dangling from the southeast corner like a toe being dipped into a swimming pool. Missouri is a state with neighbors—eight states surround it—and with two celebrated rivers. The Mississippi River forms the entire eastern boundary, and the Missouri River crosses the center of the state. The southern half, particularly the portion known as the Ozarks, is a hilly region of lakes and forests. Fertile soil provided by the rivers supports extensive farming. Like its neighbors to the north and east, the state produces plenty of corn, soybeans, and livestock. Branson, a small town in the Ozarks, attracts millions of people to its music theaters and nearby lakes. An imaginary point in Missouri is called the U.S. center of population. That means an equal number of people live north, south, east, and west of the point.

Physical

LEGEND

⋯⋯⋯	Glacier
	15,000 ft. / 4,572.1 m
	5,000 ft. / 1,524 m
	3,000 ft. / 914.4 m
	1,500 ft. / 457.2 m
	500 ft. / 152.4 m
	250 ft. / 76.2 m
	Sea Level

Missouri Almanac

Nickname	Show Me State
State capital	Jefferson City
Date of statehood	Aug. 10, 1821; 24th state
State bird	Bluebird
State flower	Hawthorn
State tree	Dogwood
State motto	*Salus Populi Suprema Lex Esto* (The Welfare of the People Shall Be the Supreme Law)
Total population & rank	5,629,707 (in 2001); 17th
Population density	82 per sq. mile (32 per sq. km)
Population distribution	69% urban, 31% rural
Largest cities	Kansas City, St. Louis, Springfield, Independence
Highest elevation	Taum Sauk Mountain, 1,772 ft. (540 m)
Lowest elevation	St Francis River in Dunklin Co., 230 ft. (70 m)
Land area & rank	68,886 sq. miles (178,415 sq. km); 18th
Average January temperature	31°F (–1°C)
Average July temperature	78°F (26°C)
Average yearly precipitation	41 inches (104 cm)
Major industries	agriculture, manufacturing, aerospace, tourism
Places to visit	Gateway Arch (St. Louis), Mark Twain Area (Hannibal), Pony Express Museum (St. Joseph)
Web site	www.state.mo.us

Economy – Chief Products

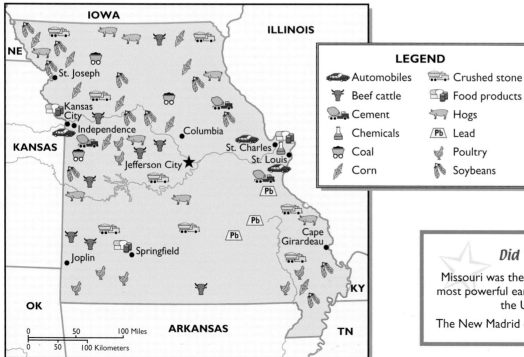

LEGEND

Automobiles	Crushed stone
Beef cattle	Food products
Cement	Hogs
Chemicals	Lead
Coal	Poultry
Corn	Soybeans

Did You Know?

Missouri was the epicenter of some of the most powerful earthquakes ever to occur in the United States:

The New Madrid earthquakes of 1811–1812

MONTANA

BRITISH COLUMBIA

ALBERTA

CANADA

SASKATCHEWAN

Milk

Plentywood
SHERIDAN
DANIELS
Lake Kocanusa
GLACIER NATL. PARK
GLACIER
Cut Bank
TOOLE
LIBERTY
Fresno Res.
Chinook
HILL
BLAINE
VALLEY
Poplar River
ROOSEVELT
Koonai R.
LINCOLN
Whitefish
Libby
FLATHEAD
Browning
Shelby
Lake Elwell
Havre
Malta
Milk R.
Glasgow
Wolf Point
Missouri
RICHLAND
Sidney
ND
Kalispell
Flathead Lake
PONDERA
Conrad
PHILLIPS
Fort Peck Lake
MCCONE
Thompson Falls
Polson
TETON
Teton
Choteau
Sun River
Missouri
UPPER MISSOURI RIVER BREAKS NATL. MON.
Fort Benton
GARFIELD
Big Dry Cr.
DAWSON
Clark Fork
SANDERS
LAKE
CHOUTEAU
River
Judith R.
MINERAL
RATTLESNAKE NATL. REC. AREA
LEWIS AND CLARK
CASCADE
Great Falls
FERGUS
PETROLEUM
Glendive
PRAIRIE
WIBAUX
Bitterroot River
MISSOULA
Lolo
Missoula
GRANITE
POWELL
Helena
Canyon Ferry Lake
BROADWATER
MEAGHER
JUDITH BASIN
Lewistown
MUSSELSHELL
Roundup
Forsyth
Miles City
CUSTER
Baker
FALLON
Deer Lodge
JEFFERSON
Boulder
Townsend
WHEATLAND
GOLDEN VALLEY
Musselshell River
ROSEBUD
Tongue River
Hamilton
Anaconda
Butte
DEER LODGE
SILVER BOW
Jefferson R.
GALLATIN
Belgrade
SWEET GRASS
YELLOWSTONE
Billings
TREASURE
Colstrip
POWDER RIVER
CARTER
RAVALLI
Big Hole R.
Bozeman
Livingston
Big Timber
STILLWATER
Laurel
Hardin
LITTLE BIGHORN BATTLEFIELD NATL. MON.
Powder River
Little Powder R.
Little Missouri R.
Dillon
MADISON
Madison River
Gallatin R.
PARK
CARBON
Red Lodge
BIGHORN CANYON NATL. REC. AREA
BIG HORN
SD
BEAVERHEAD
Granite Pk. 12,799 ft. (3,901 m)
IDAHO
YELLOWSTONE NATL. PARK
Yellowstone Lake
WYOMING
GRAND TETON NATL. PARK
Idaho Falls

0   50   100 Miles
0   50   100 Kilometers

N W E S

LEGEND

★ State capital
• City
POWELL County
▲ Mountain peak

National or other park
Urban area

MONTANA
WEST

Physical

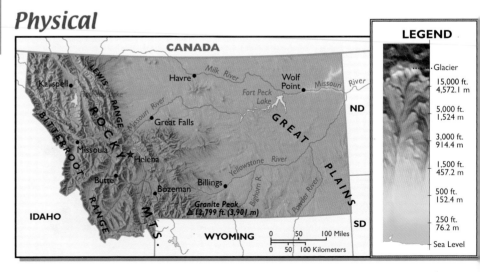

CANADA

Kalispell
Havre
Milk River
Wolf Point
Missouri
River
ND
LEWIS RANGE
ROCKY
Fort Peck Lake
Missouri River
Great Falls
GREAT
Missoula
Helena
BITTERROOT RANGE
Butte
Bozeman
Billings
Yellowstone River
PLAINS
Bighorn R.
Powder River
SD
IDAHO
MTS.
Granite Peak 12,799 ft. (3,901 m)
WYOMING

0   50   100 Miles
0   50   100 Kilometers

LEGEND

Glacier
15,000 ft. 4,572.1 m
5,000 ft. 1,524 m
3,000 ft. 914.4 m
1,500 ft. 457.2 m
500 ft. 152.4 m
250 ft. 76.2 m
Sea Level

Montana earns its "Big Sky Country" reputation from the seemingly endless horizon above the vast prairies covering the eastern two-thirds of the state. Rugged, glaciated mountains occupy the western third. Lewis and Clark explored along the Missouri River here in 1805–1806, bringing back the first descriptions of grizzly bears and other amazing plants and animals. Native Americans fought to keep their share of the land as well. General George Armstrong Custer made an ill-advised attack against a large Sioux encampment at the Battle of Little Bighorn in 1876, losing the lives of his entire company. Things have settled down since then, but Montana is still cowboy country. Rodeos, recreated cattle drives, and other ranching-related celebrations recall the heritage of this state. While many people still earn a living as real cowboys, many more work in industries such as mining, agriculture, oil, or the service sector.

Did You Know?

Montana is the only state whose rivers drain into three oceans:

Pacific, Atlantic, and Arctic Oceans

Montana Almanac

Nickname	Treasure State
State capital	Helena
Date of statehood	Nov. 8, 1889; 41st state
State bird	Western meadowlark
State flower	Bitterroot
State tree	Ponderosa pine
State motto	*Oro y Plata* (Gold and Silver)
Total population & rank	904,433 (in 2001); 44th
Population density	6 per sq. mile (2.3 per sq. km)
Population distribution	54% urban, 46% rural
Largest cities	Billings, Missoula, Great Falls, Butte
Highest elevation	Granite Peak, 12,799 ft. (3,901 m)
Lowest elevation	Kootenai River in Lincoln Co., 1,800 ft. (549 m)
Land area & rank	145,552 sq. miles (376,980 sq. km); 4th
Average January temperature	17°F (–8°C)
Average July temperature	70°F (21°C)
Average yearly precipitation	15 inches (38 cm)
Major industries	agriculture, timber, mining, tourism, oil and gas
Places to visit	Glacier National Park, Little Bighorn Battlefield National Monument, Museum of the Rockies (Bozeman), Museum of the Plains Indian (Browning)
Web site	www.state.mt.us

Economy – Chief Products

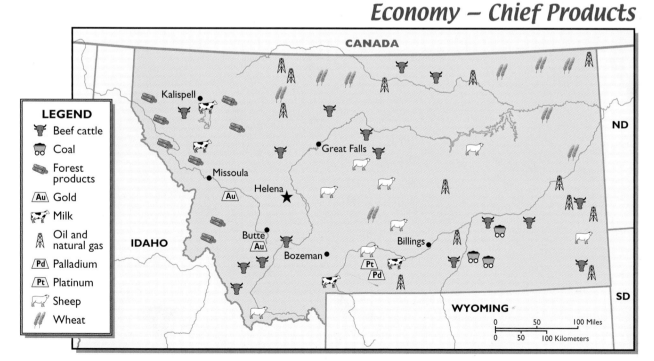

LEGEND

- Beef cattle
- Coal
- Forest products
- Au Gold
- Milk
- Oil and natural gas
- Pd Palladium
- Pt Platinum
- Sheep
- Wheat

Nebraska lies in the middle of the five states that are stacked on top of Texas and has a wide western extension called the Panhandle. The Missouri River is its eastern boundary, but another important river is the Platte. The gentle valley of the Platte River provided an easy way to travel west and was used by the Oregon Trail, Mormon pioneers, and the first transcontinental railroad. Originally covered by mile after mile of tall prairie grasses, the eastern half of Nebraska is now devoted to farming and contains most of the state's residents. The primary crops are corn and other grains. The dry and hilly western half is ranching country, particularly in the Sand Hills. The Sand Hills are permanent, grass-covered sand dunes that are ideal for raising cattle. Not surprisingly, one of the most important industries is meat packing, and many other businesses in the state are involved with food processing.

Did You Know?

Unlike those in other states, the national forests of Nebraska were created by an unusual method:

Hand-planted tree seedlings

Nebraska Almanac

Nickname	Cornhusker State	**Land area & rank**	76,872 sq. miles (199,098 sq. km); 15th
State capital	Lincoln	**Average January temperature**	23°F (–5°C)
Date of statehood	March 1, 1867; 37th state		
State bird	Western meadowlark	**Average July temperature**	76°F (24°C)
State flower	Goldenrod		
State tree	Cottonwood	**Average yearly precipitation**	22 inches (56 cm)
State motto	Equality Before the Law		
Total population & rank	1,713,235 (in 2001); 38th	**Major industries**	agriculture, manufacturing
Population density	22 per sq. mile (8 per sq. km)	**Places to visit**	Scotts Bluff National Monument, Stuhr Museum of the Prairie Pioneer (Grand Island), Agate Fossil Beds National Monument
Population distribution	70% urban, 30% rural		
Largest cities	Omaha, Lincoln		
Highest elevation	Johnson Township, 5,424 ft. (1,653 m)		
Lowest elevation	Missouri River in Richardson Co., 840 ft. (256 m)	**Web site**	www.state.ne.us

Physical

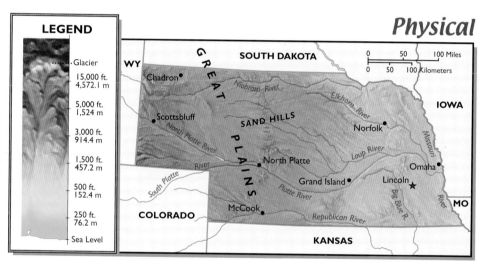

Economy – Chief Products

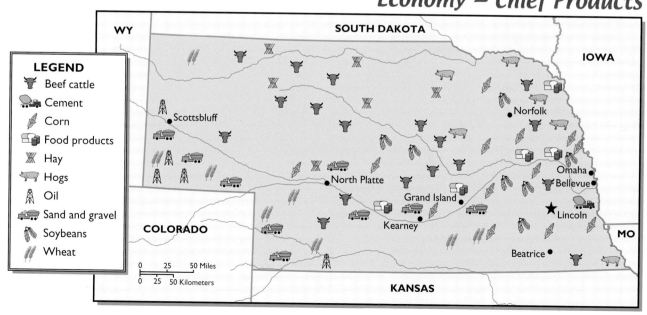

★ ★ ★ ★ ★

OREGON
IDAHO

McDermitt
Owyhee
Jackpot

A

Quinn River
HUMBOLDT
ELKO
Marys R.

Wells

Winnemucca
River
Humboldt R.
Elko
West Wendover

WASHOE
Battle
Mountain
Carlin

B

Empire
PERSHING
Humboldt River

Pyramid
Lake
Lovelock
LANDER
40°N

Stillwater
Marsh
EUREKA

Sparks
Fernley
WHITE PINE
McGill

STOREY
CHURCHILL
Austin
Eureka

Reno
Fallon
Reese River
Ruth
Ely

Virginia City
Carson R.

Carson City
Walker
GREAT BASIN
NATL. PARK

C

Lake
Tahoe
DOUGLAS
LYON
Gabbs

Gardnerville
Yerington

Walker Lake

Hawthorne
MINERAL

NYE

LEGEND

★ State capital
Tonopah
Pioche

Meadow Valley Wash

• City
Boundary Pk.
13,143 ft. (4,006 m)
Panaca

CLARK County
Goldfield
Caliente

▲ Mountain peak
CALIFORNIA
ESMERALDA
White River
LINCOLN

National or
other park

Urban area

St. George

D

Amargosa R.
Beatty
Mesquite
Virgin River

DEATH VALLEY
NATL. PARK
SPRING MOUNTAINS
NATL. REC. AREA

E

CLARK

Pahrump
North
Las Vegas

Las Vegas
Colorado River

Paradise
Henderson

Boulder City
LAKE MEAD
NATL. REC. AREA

NEVADA
ARIZONA

WEST

Cal Nev Ari

Laughlin

Bullhead City
35°N

0 25 50 75 100 Miles
0 25 50 75 100 Kilometers

The long and angled border that Nevada shares with California gives the state an outline that looks like a triangle attached to the bottom of a rectangle. Nevada lies within the U.S. geographical region called the Great Basin, the very driest part of the country. Despite this limitation, since 1990 Nevada has been the fastest growing state, climbing to the rank of 35th most populous. The distinctive terrain is called basin and range. Small mountain ranges are separated by wide, flat valleys, making a physical map of the state resemble corduroy fabric. Long known for its deposits of precious metals, Nevada leads the United States in the production of gold. Although irrigation makes farming possible and ranching occupies most of the rural land, the state's biggest business is tourism. Skiers swoosh in the mountains around Lake Tahoe, and millions of people arrive year-round to enjoy the hotels and casinos, the golf courses, and the shows and spectacles of Las Vegas.

Did You Know?

While working for a Virginia City newspaper, Samuel Clemens took the pen name for which he would be famous: Mark Twain

Nevada Almanac

Nicknames	Sagebrush State, Battle Born State, Silver State
State capital	Carson City
Date of statehood	Oct. 31, 1864; 36th state
State bird	Mountain bluebird
State flower	Sagebrush
State trees	Single-leaf piñon, bristlecone pine
State motto	All for Our Country
Total population & rank	2,106,074 (in 2001); 35th
Population density	19 per sq. mile (7.3 per sq. km)
Population distribution	92% urban, 8% rural
Largest cities	Las Vegas, Paradise, Reno, Henderson
Highest elevation	Boundary Peak, 13,143 ft. (4,006 m)
Lowest elevation	Colorado River in Clark Co., 479 ft. (146 m)
Land area & rank	109,826 sq. miles (284,449 sq. km); 7th
Average January temperature	32°F (0°C)
Average July temperature	75°F (24°C)
Average yearly precipitation	9 inches (23 cm)
Major industries	gaming, tourism, mining, manufacturing, government
Places to visit	Great Basin National Park, Hoover Dam (Boulder City), Lake Tahoe, Las Vegas
Web site	www.silver.state.nv.us

Economy – Chief Products

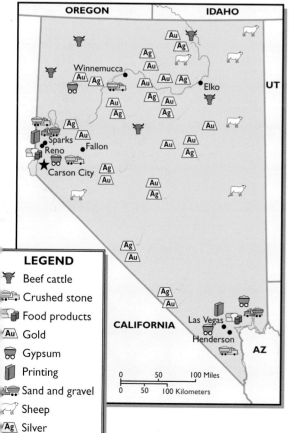

LEGEND

- 🐂 Beef cattle
- Crushed stone
- 🥫 Food products
- Au\ Gold
- Gypsum
- Printing
- Sand and gravel
- 🐑 Sheep
- Ag\ Silver

Physical

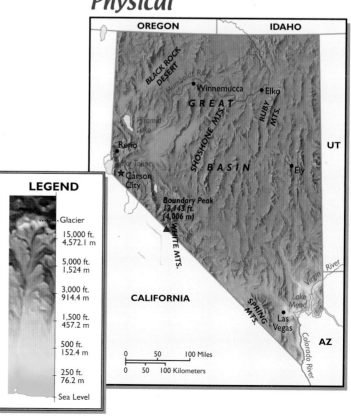

LEGEND

- Glacier
- 15,000 ft. 4,572.1 m
- 5,000 ft. 1,524 m
- 3,000 ft. 914.4 m
- 1,500 ft. 457.2 m
- 500 ft. 152.4 m
- 250 ft. 76.2 m
- Sea Level

LEGEND

⭐ State capital
• City
coos County
▲ Mountain peak

National or other park
National forest
Urban area

⭐ Montpelier

CANADA

QUÉBEC

Connecticut River

• Colebrook

COOS

Did You Know?

The highest non-tornadic gust of wind was 231 mph (372 km/h), and it was recorded in this state:

Mount Washington

• Groveton

WHITE MOUNTAIN NATL. FOREST

• Lancaster

Berlin

• Whitefield

• Gorham

MAINE

• Littleton

▲ Mt. Washington 6,288 ft. (1,917 m)

Ammonoosuc River

• Lisbon

FRANCONIA NOTCH STATE PARK

• Woodsville

North Conway

VERMONT

WHITE MOUNTAIN NATL. FOREST

• Lewiston

• Lincoln

Pemigewasset River

• Conway

0 — 15 — 30 Miles
0 — 15 — 30 Kilometers

GRAFTON

CARROLL

Baker River

• Plymouth

Lake Winnipesaukee

Saco River

• Hanover

Newfound Lake

• Portland

• Lebanon

• Bristol

• Wolfeboro

• Laconia

Winnisquam Lake

BELKNAP

• Franklin

• Claremont

Lake Sunapee

• Farmington

• Newport

SULLIVAN

MERRIMACK

Shaker Village (Canterbury)

Rochester

Salmon Falls River

STRAFFORD

• Somersworth

Dover

Contoocook R.

Merrimack River

⭐ Concord

• Durham

Piscataqua River

• Hillsborough

Great Bay

• Portsmouth

• Keene

HILLSBOROUGH

• Manchester

• Exeter

ATLANTIC OCEAN

CHESHIRE

ROCKINGHAM

• Hampton

• Peterborough

• Derry

• Milford

• Jaffrey

• Salem

• Haverhill

Nashua

• Lawrence

MASSACHUSETTS

Lowell

NEW HAMPSHIRE

NEW ENGLAND

45°N

44°N

43°N

73°W 72°W 71°W

New Hampshire, the New England state shaped like a wedge between Maine and Vermont, is a state of great natural beauty. Its mountains, forests, and lakes, home to countless species of fish and wildlife, attract outdoor enthusiasts year-round. People of New Hampshire have been known for their rugged individualism even before becoming the first of the original 13 colonies to separate from Great Britain. Since 1952, New Hampshire has had the first presidential primary, which gives it a big impact on presidential politics. It has more members in its house of representatives than any other state. Most of New Hampshire's residents live in cities in the southeastern part of the state. Cities like Portsmouth, New Hampshire's port city, and Manchester are industrial centers that produce computers and electronic equipment and metal goods. Because of the abundance of tourists to the state, the biggest part of the workforce works in the service industry, staffing hotels, restaurants, museums, stores, ski resorts, and historic sites.

Physical

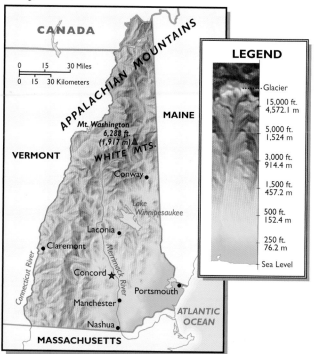

Economy – Chief Products

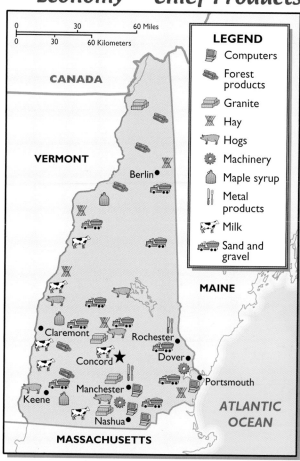

New Hampshire Almanac

Nickname	Granite State	Land area & rank	8,968 sq. miles (23,227 sq. km); 44th
State capital	Concord	Average January temperature	17°F (–8°C)
Date of statehood	June 21, 1788; 9th state		
State bird	Purple finch		
State flower	Purple lilac	Average July temperature	67°F (19°C)
State tree	White birch		
State motto	Live Free or Die	Average yearly precipitation	42 inches (107 cm)
Total population & rank	1,259,181 (in 2001); 41st	Major industries	tourism, manufacturing, agriculture, trade, mining
Population density	140 per sq. mile (54 per sq. km)		
Population distribution	59% urban, 41% rural	Places to visit	White Mountain National Forest, Mt. Washington, Canterbury Shaker Village, Franconia Notch State Park
Largest cities	Manchester, Nashua, Concord		
Highest elevation	Mt. Washington, 6,288 ft. (1,917 m)		
		Web site	www.state.nh.us
Lowest elevation	sea level		

LEGEND

★ State capital
• City
SALEM County
▲ Mountain peak
National or other park
Urban area

Did You Know?

New Jersey is one of the most densely populated states in the nation, but its truck farms, orchards, and flower gardens gave the state its nickname:

The Garden State

76°W
1
75°W
2
74°W
4
5

Scranton
Danbury

High Point
1,803 ft. (550 m)
NEW YORK
CT

DELAWARE WATER GAP
NATL. REC. AREA
SUSSEX
Ringwood
Norwalk
Stamford

41°N
Newton • Sparta
PASSAIC
Ramsey
41°N
Hopatcong
Paramus
Yonkers
Paterson
BERGEN
New Rochelle
Hackensack
Hackettstown
Dover
Clifton
WARREN
MORRIS
Passaic

PENNSYLVANIA
Washington
Morristown
EDISON NATL.
HISTORIC SITE
Newark
Jersey City
New York City
Easton • Phillipsburg
Elizabeth
Bayonne
Bethlehem
UNION
Plainfield
Allentown
SOMERSET
Staten
Island
GATEWAY
NATL.
REC.
AREA
HUNTERDON
Somerville
Raritan R.
Edison
New Brunswick
Perth Amboy
Sandy Hook
Sayreville
MIDDLESEX
Princeton
Red Bank
Long Branch
MERCER
Freehold
Trenton
MONMOUTH
Asbury Park

Burlington
Lakewood
Point Pleasant
40°N
Mount Holly
40°N
Rancocas River
Browns Mills
Toms River
Philadelphia
Camden
Cherry Hill
BURLINGTON
OCEAN
Delaware River
Woodbury
ATLANTIC
Lindenwold
OCEAN
Wilmington
GLOUCESTER
CAMDEN
Newark
Penns Grove
Glassboro
Hammonton
0   15   30 Miles
SALEM
0   15   30 Kilometers
Salem
Great Egg Harbor
ATLANTIC
Little Egg Inlet
Vineland
Bridgeton
Pleasantville
Brigantine
Millville
Atlantic City
CUMBERLAND
Great Egg Inlet
DELAWARE
Ocean
City
MD
CAPE MAY
Sea Isle City
Dover
Avalon
Delaware
Bay
39°N
Hereford Inlet
39°N
Wildwood
75°W
Cape May
74°W
1
2
3
4
5

Mullica R.

N
W   E
S

Barnegat Bay
Barnegat Inlet

NEW JERSEY
MIDATLANTIC

Passaic R.
HUDSON
ESSEX
Wallkill River
Delaware River

New Jersey's shape is delineated by the Delaware and Hudson Rivers as well as the Atlantic coast. Its location between two of the largest U.S. cities, Philadelphia and New York, has given New Jersey access to immense markets for its products and encouraged economic growth. New Jersey is one of the largest producers of medicines, chemicals, electronics, and also food products like Campbell's Soup from its many truck farms and orchards. This economic success has also led to New Jersey's standing as one of the most densely populated state, with 94% of the people living in cities. Some of the world's most famous inventors like Thomas Edison, Samuel Morse, and Albert Einstein lived in New Jersey, adding to its reputation as an innovative state. New Jersey has many colonial and Revolutionary War historic sites including Monmouth Battlefield, Trenton, and Morristown. The Atlantic coastal region is famous for its resort towns with boardwalks, casinos, and white sand beaches. Tourism has increased the number of people with jobs in the service industry.

New Jersey Almanac

Nickname	Garden State
State capital	Trenton
Date of statehood	Dec. 18, 1787; 3rd state
State bird	Eastern goldfinch
State flower	Purple violet
State tree	Red oak
State motto	Liberty and Prosperity
Total population & rank	8,484,431 (in 2001); 9th
Population density	1,144 per sq. mile (442 per sq. km)
Population distribution	94% urban, 6% rural
Largest cities	Newark, Jersey City, Paterson, Elizabeth
Highest elevation	High Point, 1,803 ft. (550 m)
Lowest elevation	sea level
Land area & rank	7,417 sq. miles (19,210 sq. km); 46th
Average January temperature	31°F (–1°C)
Average July temperature	74°F (23°C)
Average yearly precipitation	45 inches (114 cm)
Major industries	pharmaceuticals/drugs, telecommunications, biotechnology, printing and publishing
Places to visit	Edison National Historic Site (West Orange), Liberty State Park (Jersey City), Pine Barrens wilderness area, Atlantic City
Web site	www.state.nj.us

Economy – Chief Products

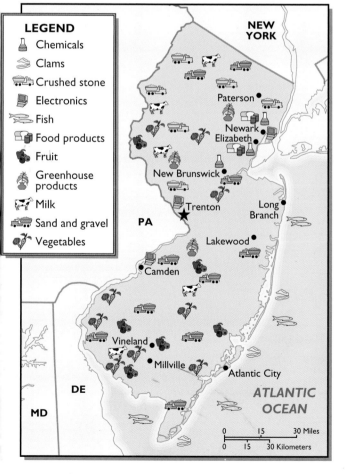

LEGEND
- 🧪 Chemicals
- 🐚 Clams
- 🚛 Crushed stone
- 💻 Electronics
- 🐟 Fish
- 🥫 Food products
- 🍓 Fruit
- 🌱 Greenhouse products
- 🐄 Milk
- 🚛 Sand and gravel
- 🥬 Vegetables

Physical

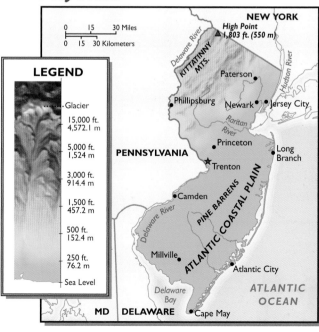

LEGEND
- Glacier
- 15,000 ft. 4,572.1 m
- 5,000 ft. 1,524 m
- 3,000 ft. 914.4 m
- 1,500 ft. 457.2 m
- 500 ft. 152.4 m
- 250 ft. 76.2 m
- Sea Level

UT

COLORADO 106°W

OK

A

Shiprock Aztec Chama Raton Cimarron River
Farmington Bloomfield Questa COLFAX UNION Clayton
SAN JUAN Navajo Reservoir TAOS Wheeler Pk. 13,161 ft (4,011 m) Taos HARDING
RIO ARRIBA RIO CHAMA Mora River
Chaco River Abiquiu Res. Espanola Chimayo MORA
CHACO CULTURE NATL. HISTORIC PARK Los Alamos LOS ALAMOS Mora River
36°N 36°N

B

MCKINLEY BANDELIER NATL. MON. ★ Santa Fe Las Vegas Conchas Lake
Gallup SANDOVAL SANTA FE SAN MIGUEL HARDING
Puerco River Bernalillo Rio Grande Pecos River Tucumcari
Zuni Pueblo Grants Rio Rancho QUAY
EL MALPAIS NATL. MON. AND CONS. AREA CIBOLA Albuquerque BERNALILLO
Los Lunas Santa Rosa CURRY
VALENCIA Belen GUADALUPE Clovis
TORRANCE Portales

C

34°N Socorro DE BACA ROOSEVELT 34°N
CATRON SOCORRO LINCOLN

D

Elephant Butte Reservoir Ruidoso Roswell CHAVES
Truth or Consequences Tularosa Lovington
Caballo Reservoir SIERRA Alamogordo Artesia Pecos River
Silver City Bayard WHITE SANDS NATL. MON. Hobbs
GRANT OTERO EDDY LEA
Gila River DONA ANA Eunice
Lordsburg Deming Carlsbad

E

LUNA Las Cruces CARLSBAD CAVERNS NATL. PARK Jal
32°N Anthony Red Bluff Reservoir 32°N
HIDALGO TEXAS
Sunland Park El Paso
Ciudad Juárez 106°W 104°W

F

N W E S MEXICO

0 25 50 75 100 Miles
0 25 50 75 100 Kilometers

108°W

LEGEND

★ State capital   National or other park
• City   Urban area
SIERRA County
▲ Mountain peak

NEW MEXICO

SOUTHWEST

New Jersey's shape is delineated by the Delaware and Hudson Rivers as well as the Atlantic coast. Its location between two of the largest U.S. cities, Philadelphia and New York, has given New Jersey access to immense markets for its products and encouraged economic growth. New Jersey is one of the largest producers of medicines, chemicals, electronics, and also food products like Campbell's Soup from its many truck farms and orchards. This economic success has also led to New Jersey's standing as one of the most densely populated state, with 94% of the people living in cities. Some of the world's most famous inventors like Thomas Edison, Samuel Morse, and Albert Einstein lived in New Jersey, adding to its reputation as an innovative state. New Jersey has many colonial and Revolutionary War historic sites including Monmouth Battlefield, Trenton, and Morristown. The Atlantic coastal region is famous for its resort towns with boardwalks, casinos, and white sand beaches. Tourism has increased the number of people with jobs in the service industry.

New Jersey Almanac

Nickname	Garden State
State capital	Trenton
Date of statehood	Dec. 18, 1787; 3rd state
State bird	Eastern goldfinch
State flower	Purple violet
State tree	Red oak
State motto	Liberty and Prosperity
Total population & rank	8,484,431 (in 2001); 9th
Population density	1,144 per sq. mile (442 per sq. km)
Population distribution	94% urban, 6% rural
Largest cities	Newark, Jersey City, Paterson, Elizabeth
Highest elevation	High Point, 1,803 ft. (550 m)
Lowest elevation	sea level
Land area & rank	7,417 sq. miles (19,210 sq. km); 46th
Average January temperature	31°F (–1°C)
Average July temperature	74°F (23°C)
Average yearly precipitation	45 inches (114 cm)
Major industries	pharmaceuticals/drugs, telecommunications, biotechnology, printing and publishing
Places to visit	Edison National Historic Site (West Orange), Liberty State Park (Jersey City), Pine Barrens wilderness area, Atlantic City
Web site	www.state.nj.us

Economy – Chief Products

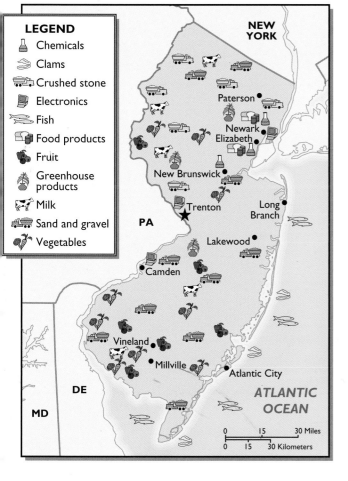

LEGEND
- Chemicals
- Clams
- Crushed stone
- Electronics
- Fish
- Food products
- Fruit
- Greenhouse products
- Milk
- Sand and gravel
- Vegetables

Physical

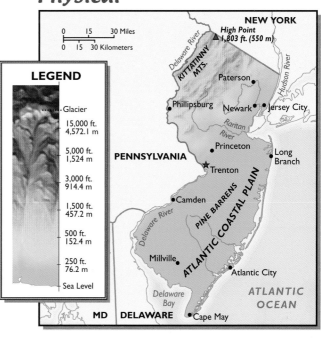

UT

OK

AZ

COLORADO

TEXAS

MEXICO

108°W
106°W
104°W

36°N
34°N
32°N

Shiprock
Aztec
Farmington
Bloomfield

SAN JUAN

Navajo Reservoir

Chama

Questa

Raton

Cimarron River

COLFAX

UNION

Clayton

RIO ARRIBA

Rio Chama

Abiquiu Res.

Wheeler Pk.
13,161 ft (4,011 m)

TAOS

Taos

MORA

Mora River

HARDING

Chaco River

CHACO CULTURE NATL. HISTORIC PARK

Espanola
Chimayo

Canadian River

MCKINLEY

Puerco River

Gallup

LOS ALAMOS

Los Alamos

BANDELIER NATL. MON.

SANDOVAL

Santa Fe

Las Vegas

SAN MIGUEL

Conchas Lake

SANTA FE

Pecos River

Zuni Pueblo

Grants

Bernalillo

Rio Rancho

Albuquerque

BERNALILLO

Tucumcari

QUAY

EL MALPAIS NATL. MON. AND CONS. AREA

CIBOLA

Rio Puerco

Rio Grande

VALENCIA

Los Lunas

Belen

TORRANCE

Santa Rosa

GUADALUPE

CURRY

Clovis

Portales

CATRON

Socorro

SOCORRO

DE BACA

ROOSEVELT

LINCOLN

Elephant Butte Reservoir

Ruidoso

Roswell

CHAVES

Pecos River

Lovington

Caballo Reservoir

Truth or Consequences

SIERRA

Tularosa

Silver City

Bayard

GRANT

Alamogordo

Artesia

Hobbs

LEA

WHITE SANDS NATL. MON.

OTERO

EDDY

Eunice

Gila River

Lordsburg

Deming

LUNA

Rio Grande

DONA ANA

Las Cruces

Carlsbad

CARLSBAD CAVERNS NATL. PARK

Jal

HIDALGO

Anthony

Red Bluff Reservoir

Sunland Park

El Paso

Ciudad Juárez

LEGEND

★ State capital

• City

SIERRA County

▲ Mountain peak

National or other park

Urban area

N
W   E
S

25   50   75   100 Miles
25 50 75 100 Kilometers

NEW MEXICO

SOUTHWEST

New York's shape has been described as a "lopsided funnel," with all of the wealth of the state flowing through the southernmost funnel of New York City. It is a state with two separate cultures: the big city, world-class culture of New York City, and the rural, small-town, natural beauty of "Upstate" New York. New York City is a world leader in trade, manufacturing, and business. The dazzling array of cultural activities, museums, theaters, art, and music in the city make it an international tourist destination as well. Because of the United Nations Headquarters, the city is often viewed as a world capital. Upstate New York is home to many amazing natural wonders including Niagara Falls, the Finger Lakes region, and Adirondack Park (the nation's largest), as well as many historic sites. The Port of New York is among the busiest anywhere. In its harbor stands the Statue of Liberty—a symbol of freedom throughout the world.

New York Almanac

Nickname	Empire State
State capital	Albany
Date of statehood	July 26, 1788; 11th state
State bird	Bluebird
State flower	Rose
State tree	Sugar maple
State motto	*Excelsior* (Ever Upward)
Total population & rank	19,011,378 (in 2001); 3rd
Population density	403 per sq. mile (156 per sq. km)
Population distribution	88% urban, 12% rural
Largest cities	New York City, Buffalo, Rochester, Yonkers, Syracuse
Highest elevation	Mt. Marcy, 5,344 ft. (1,629 m)
Lowest elevation	sea level
Land area & rank	47,214 sq. miles (122,284 sq. km); 30th
Average January temperature	21°F (–6°C)
Average July temperature	69°F (21°C)
Average yearly precipitation	40 inches (102 cm)
Major industries	manufacturing, finance, communications, tourism, transportation, services
Places to visit	National Baseball Hall of Fame (Cooperstown), Niagara Falls, New York City: Central Park, Statue of Liberty and Ellis Island, Bronx Zoo, World Trade Center Site
Web site	www.state.ny.us

Did You Know?

In 1853, a resort in this town was home to the invention of this all-time favorite snack food—the potato chip:

Saratoga Springs

Economy – Chief Products

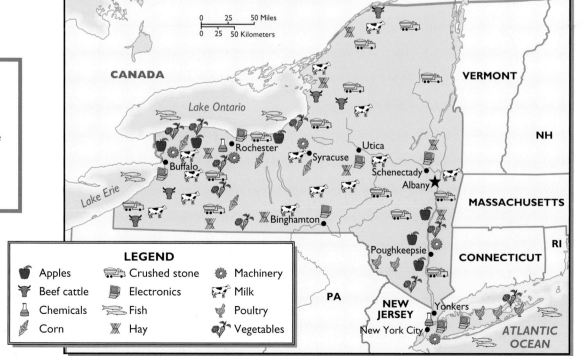

LEGEND

🍎 Apples
🐂 Beef cattle
⚗ Chemicals
🌽 Corn
🚚 Crushed stone
💻 Electronics
🐟 Fish
✕ Hay
⚙ Machinery
🐄 Milk
🐔 Poultry
🥕 Vegetables

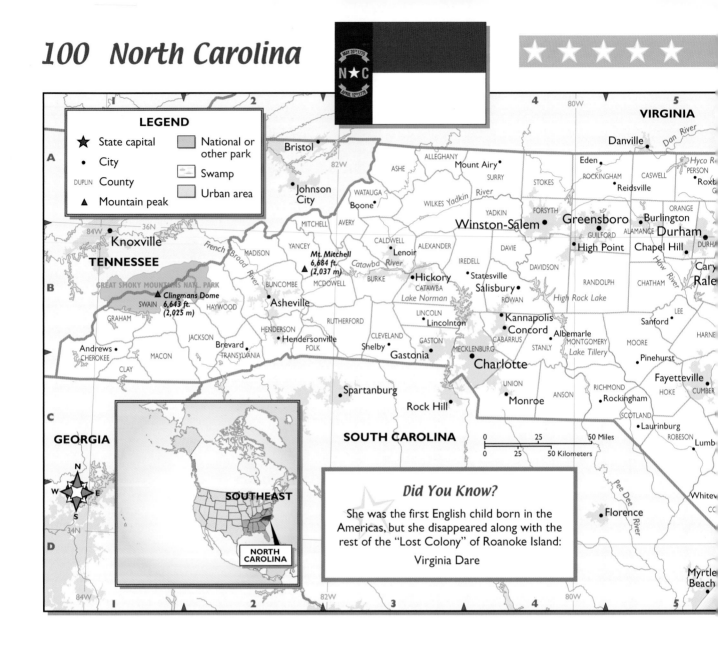

North Carolina Almanac

Nicknames	Tar Heel State, Old North State	**Lowest elevation**	sea level
State capital	Raleigh	**Land area & rank**	48,711 sq. miles (126,161 sq. km); 29th
Date of statehood	Nov. 21, 1789; 12th state		
State bird	Cardinal	**Average January temperature**	40°F (4°C)
State flower	Dogwood		
State tree	Pine	**Average July temperature**	77°F (25°C)
State motto	Esse Quam Videri (To Be Rather Than to Seem)	**Average yearly precipitation**	50 inches (127 cm)
Total population & rank	8,186,268 (in 2001); 11th	**Major industries**	manufacturing, agriculture, tourism
Population density	168 per sq. mile (65 per sq. km)		
Population distribution	60% urban, 40% rural	**Places to visit**	Great Smoky Mountains National Park, Cape Hatteras National Seashore, Wright Brothers National Memorial
Largest cities	Charlotte, Raleigh, Greensboro, Durham, Winston-Salem		
Highest elevation	Mt. Mitchell, 6,684 ft. (2,037 m)	**Web site**	www.ncgov.com

North Carolina is one of the widest states, stretching for 500 miles (800 km) from the wave-lapped beaches of the Atlantic Ocean to its mountainous western tip. As in all large states, the geographical variety is remarkable. Delicate barrier islands are dangerous to ships but protect the bays where pirates once roamed and fishermen still work. The cool and green mountains feature the most-visited national park, Great Smoky Mountains, and the highest point east of the Mississippi River. Its cities are concentrated in the Piedmont among gently rolling hills. For years and years, North Carolina has been associated with three products—tobacco, textiles, and furniture. Recently, the state has become known for fast-growing, high-tech businesses involved with medicine, electronics, and research. With its attractive environment and appealing cities, North Carolina has been one of the fastest growing states.

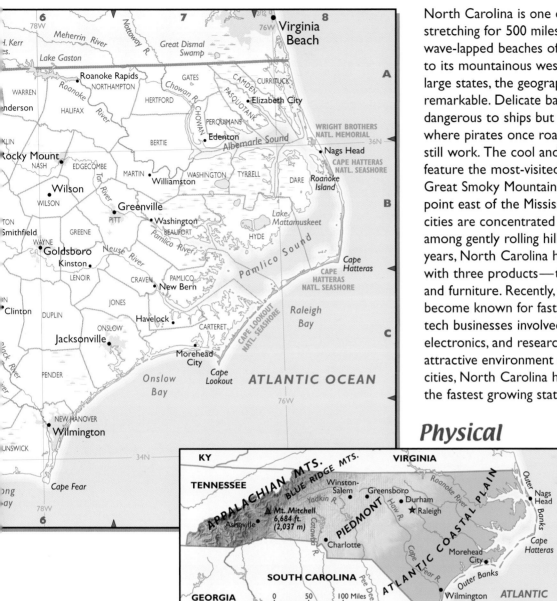

Physical

LEGEND

- Glacier
- 15,000 ft. / 4,572.1 m
- 5,000 ft. / 1,524 m
- 3,000 ft. / 914.4 m
- 1,500 ft. / 457.2 m
- 500 ft. / 152.4 m
- 250 ft. / 76.2 m
- Sea Level

Economy – Chief Products

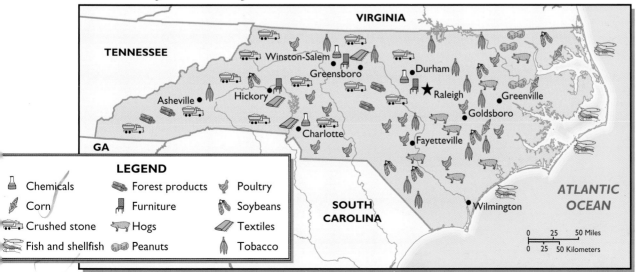

LEGEND

- Chemicals
- Corn
- Crushed stone
- Fish and shellfish
- Forest products
- Furniture
- Hogs
- Peanuts
- Poultry
- Soybeans
- Textiles
- Tobacco

LEGEND
★ State capital
• City
SIOUX County
▲ Mountain peak
National or other park
Urban area

NORTH DAKOTA

MIDWEST

North Dakota is the nearly rectangular, top and center state of the lower 48 states. Only the eastern boundary, established by the Red River, is a natural feature. Immigration to the United States was at its peak during the years that North Dakota was being settled. Many of the state's first residents came from Europe, especially Scandinavia and Germany. Their descendants still live there. In the last ten years, however, the population has grown very little, and many of the rural counties are losing people. The gently rolling land may lack spectacular scenery, but a closer look reveals details like the prairie potholes, small lakes and ponds that are important for waterfowl. North Dakota's soil, formed under a vast carpet of grass, is perfect for growing grains. Only one other state produces more wheat, and North Dakota harvests the most of the special wheat used for spaghetti and noodles. Colorful fields of sunflowers are also common.

North Dakota Almanac

Nickname	Peace Garden State	**Land area & rank**	68,976 sq. miles (178,648 sq. km); 17th
State capital	Bismarck	**Average January temperature**	7°F (−14°C)
Date of statehood	Nov. 2, 1889; 39th state		
State bird	Western meadowlark	**Average July temperature**	69°F (21°C)
State flower	Wild prairie rose		
State tree	American elm	**Average yearly precipitation**	17 inches (36 cm)
State motto	Liberty and Union, Now and Forever, One and Inseparable	**Major industries**	agriculture, mining, tourism, manufacturing, telecommunications, energy, food processing,
Total population & rank	634,448 (in 2001); 48th		
Population density	9 per sq. mile (3.5 per sq. km)	**Places to visit**	Theodore Roosevelt National Park, Bonanzaville (Fargo), North Dakota Heritage Center (Bismarck), Dakota Dinosaur Museum (Dickinson)
Population distribution	56% urban, 44% rural		
Largest cities	Fargo, Bismarck, Grand Forks, Minot		
Highest elevation	White Butte, 3,506 ft. (1,069 m)		
Lowest elevation	Red River in Pembina Co., 750 ft. (229 m)	**Web site**	www.discovernd.com

Physical

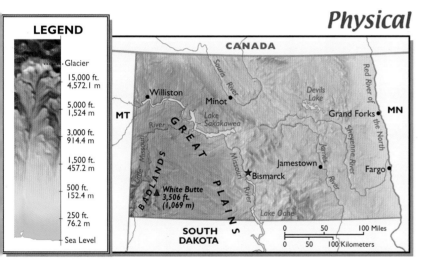

Did You Know?

Theodore Roosevelt wrote about a North Dakota phenomenon that has slowly and steadily endured for more than 80 years:

Underground fire in beds of lignite coal

Economy – Chief Products

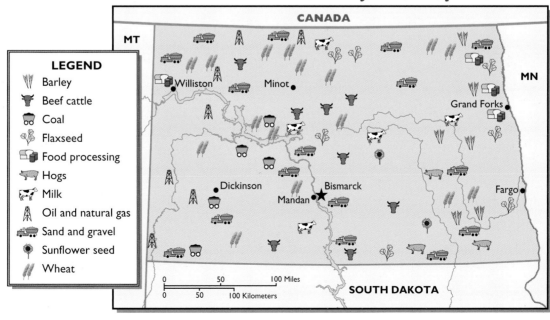

LEGEND

★ State capital
• City
SCIOTO County
▲ Mountain peak

National or other park
Urban area

MICHIGAN

INDIANA

KENTUCKY

ONTARIO

CANADA

Lake Erie

PA

WEST VIRGINIA

82W
42N
84W
40N
84W
82W

Detroit

Toledo
LUCAS
Oregon
Maumee
FULTON
WILLIAMS
OTTAWA
WOOD
Bowling Green
DEFIANCE
HENRY
Defiance
PAULDING
PUTNAM
SENECA
Findlay
HANCOCK
Fremont
SANDUSKY
Tiffin
ERIE
Sandusky
Norwalk
HURON

Fort Wayne
St. Joseph River
St. Marys River
Wabash River
Auglaize River
Maumee River
Sandusky River

Van Wert
VAN WERT
ALLEN
Lima
HARDIN
WYANDOT
CRAWFORD
Bucyrus
RICHLAND
Galion
MARION
Marion
MORROW
MERCER
Celina
Grand Lake
AUGLAIZE
SHELBY
Sidney
LOGAN
Bellefontaine
▲ Campbell Hill 1,549 ft. (472 m)
UNION
Delaware
DELAWARE
KNOX
Mount Vernon

Cleveland
Euclid
Lorain
LORAIN
Elyria
Parma
Cleveland Heights
CUYAHOGA
Painesville
LAKE
Mentor
ASHTABULA
Ashtabula
Conneaut
GEAUGA
Medina
MEDINA
Ashland
ASHLAND
WAYNE
Wooster
CUYAHOGA VALLEY NATL. PARK
SUMMIT
Cuyahoga Falls
Akron
Barberton
PORTAGE
Alliance
STARK
Canton
Massillon
TRUMBULL
Warren
Youngstown
Boardman
MAHONING
COLUMBIANA
East Liverpool
CARROLL
New Philadelphia
TUSCARAWAS
Coshocton
COSHOCTON
JEFFERSON
Steubenville
HARRISON
Wheeling

Mansfield
HOLMES
Mohican R.
Walhonding River
Tuscarawas River

DARKE
Greenville
Piqua
MIAMI
Troy
CHAMPAIGN
Springfield
CLARK
MADISON
Westerville
Gahanna
Columbus
FRANKLIN
LICKING
Newark
MUSKINGUM
GUERNSEY
Cambridge
BELMONT

Richmond
PREBLE
MONTGOMERY
Dayton
Kettering
Xenia
GREENE
FAYETTE
Washington Court House
PICKAWAY
Circleville
FAIRFIELD
Lancaster
PERRY
MORGAN
Zanesville
NOBLE
MONROE
Ohio River

Great Miami River
Little Miami River

Oxford
BUTLER
WARREN
Middletown
Hamilton
Fairfield
CLINTON
Wilmington
HIGHLAND
ROSS
Chillicothe
Scioto River
HOCKING
Hocking River
ATHENS
Athens
Marietta
WASHINGTON
Parkersburg

HAMILTON
Cincinnati
Covington
CLERMONT
BROWN
ADAMS
PIKE
SCIOTO
Portsmouth
JACKSON
VINTON
GALLIA
MEIGS
LAWRENCE
Ironton
Muskingum River

Huntington

★ Frankfort

N W E S

0   25   50 Miles
0   25   50 Kilometers

OHIO

MIDWEST

The outline of Ohio comes close to being a square, although this square is missing its lower corners. The irregular southern boundary of the state is formed by the Ohio River as it twists and turns on its way to the Mississippi River. Most of the state's rivers flow south and do not enter Lake Erie. Ohio's many urban areas are one reason the state has the seventh-largest population. However, the very largest cities, historic centers of heavy industry, have actually had shrinking populations in the last 10 years. Despite its modest size, Ohio features geographic variety. The southeastern quarter of the state is hilly and wooded. The rest of the state, once covered by unbroken forest, is now primarily farmland producing a typical Midwestern mix of corn, soybeans, and livestock. Continuing to follow their traditional way of life, more Amish live in Ohio than any other state. Their communities are now popular tourist attractions.

Did You Know?

In 1967, Cleveland elected the first African-American mayor of a major U.S. city: Carl B. Stokes

Ohio Almanac

Nickname	Buckeye State
State capital	Columbus
Date of statehood	March 1, 1803; 17th state
State bird	Cardinal
State flower	Scarlet carnation
State tree	Buckeye
State motto	With God, All Things Are Possible
Total population & rank	11,373,541 (in 2001); 7th
Population density	278 per sq. mile (107 per sq. km)
Population distribution	77% urban, 23% rural
Largest cities	Columbus, Cleveland, Cincinnati, Toledo, Akron, Dayton
Highest elevation	Campbell Hill, 1,549 ft. (472 m)
Lowest elevation	Ohio River in Hamilton Co., 455 ft. (139 m)
Land area & rank	40,948 sq. miles (106,055 sq. km); 35th
Average January temperature	27°F (−3°C)
Average July temperature	73°F (23°C)
Average yearly precipitation	38 inches (97 cm)
Major industries	manufacturing, trade, services
Places to visit	Mound City Group (Chillicothe), Pro Football Hall of Fame (Canton), Rock and Roll Hall of Fame and Museum (Cleveland), Air Force Museum (Dayton)
Web site	www.state.oh.us

Economy – Chief Products

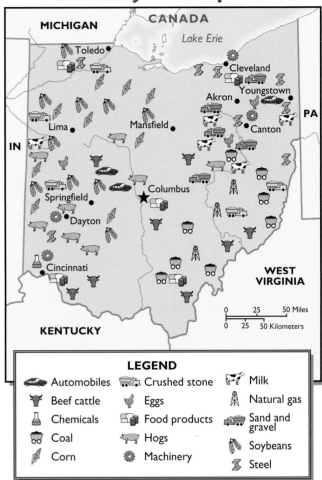

LEGEND

- Automobiles
- Beef cattle
- Chemicals
- Coal
- Corn
- Crushed stone
- Eggs
- Food products
- Hogs
- Machinery
- Milk
- Natural gas
- Sand and gravel
- Soybeans
- Steel

Physical

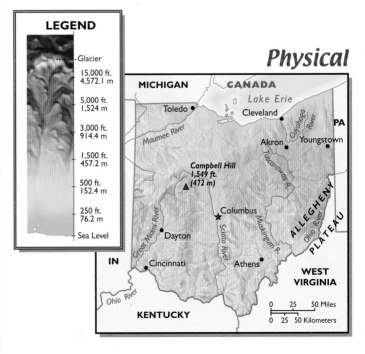

LEGEND

- Glacier
- 15,000 ft. / 4,572.1 m
- 5,000 ft. / 1,524 m
- 3,000 ft. / 914.4 m
- 1,500 ft. / 457.2 m
- 500 ft. / 152.4 m
- 250 ft. / 76.2 m
- Sea Level

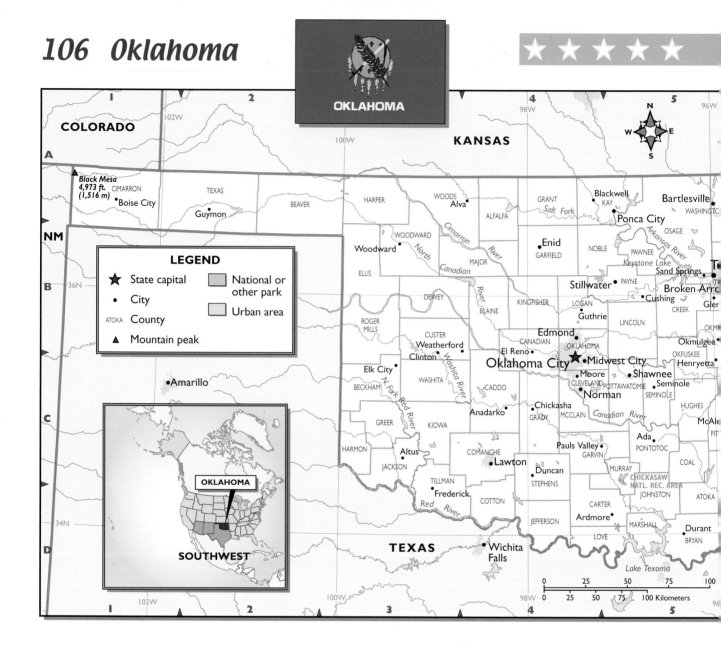

Oklahoma Almanac

Nickname	Sooner State	**Lowest elevation**	Little River in McCurtain Co., 289 ft. (88 m)
State capital	Oklahoma City		
Date of statehood	Nov. 16, 1907; 46th state	**Land area & rank**	68,667 sq. miles (177,848 sq. km); 19th
State bird	Scissor-tailed flycatcher		
State flower	Mistletoe	**Average January temperature**	37°F (3°C)
State tree	Redbud		
State motto	Labor Omnia Vincit (Labor Conquers All Things)	**Average July temperature**	82°F (28°C)
Total population & rank	3,460,097 (in 2001); 28th	**Average yearly precipitation**	34 inches (86 cm)
Population density	50 per sq. mile (19 per sq. km)	**Major industries**	manufacturing, mineral and energy exploration and production, agriculture, services
Population distribution	65% urban, 35% rural		
Largest cities	Oklahoma City, Tulsa, Norman, Lawton	**Places to visit**	Indian City U.S.A. (Anadarko), Cherokee Heritage Center (Tahlequah), National Cowboy Hall of Fame (Oklahoma City), Oklahoma City National Memorial
Highest elevation	Black Mesa, 4,973 ft. (1,516 m)		
		Web site	www.state.ok.us

Like an upside-down baseball cap, Oklahoma sits on the northern shoulder of Texas. The "bill" of the baseball cap is a narrow, western extension called the Panhandle. The Red River separates most of Texas and Oklahoma, but the Arkansas River is more important. Using it, ocean-going ships can reach port facilities near Tulsa. Many residents of Oklahoma are Native American. The percentage is nearly ten times the U.S. average. More than 60 tribal groups live in the state, but few of those lived there 200 years ago. Most were moved to Oklahoma by the U.S. government after 1830. Oklahoma grows wheat and raises cattle, and the eastern hills contain more forestland than states to its north, but Oklahoma's most valuable resources are oil and natural gas. There are even oil wells on the grounds of the state capitol. Many businesses are involved with oil and natural gas production. Tourists come to Oklahoma to visit museums and places associated with the Native American cultures and with its Old West heritage.

Physical

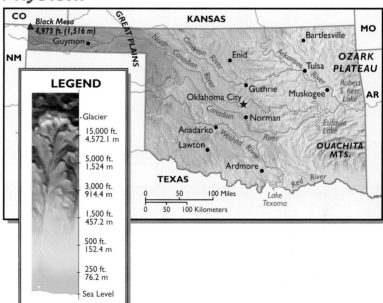

Did You Know?

In just one day, Oklahoma City grew from zero residents to more than 10,000 residents:

April 22, 1889

LEGEND

Glacier

15,000 ft.
4,572.1 m

5,000 ft.
1,524 m

3,000 ft.
914.4 m

1,500 ft.
457.2 m

500 ft.
152.4 m

250 ft.
76.2 m

Sea Level

Economy – Chief Products

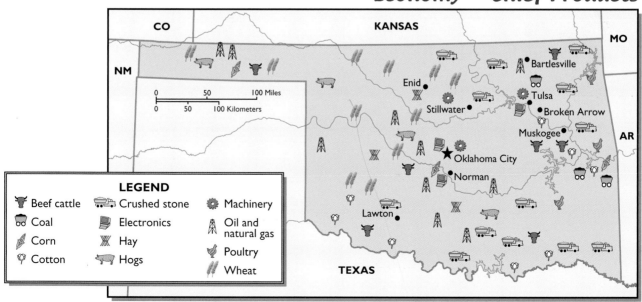

LEGEND

- Beef cattle
- Coal
- Corn
- Cotton
- Crushed stone
- Electronics
- Hay
- Hogs
- Machinery
- Oil and natural gas
- Poultry
- Wheat

STATE OF OREGON
1859

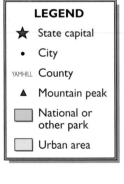

LEGEND

★ State capital

• City

YAMHILL County

▲ Mountain peak

National or other park

Urban area

OREGON

WEST

Oregon is a Pacific Coast state that treasures its 296-mi (476-km) coastline. All of the beaches are public proper and the unique sand dunes of the central coast are protected within a national scenic area. Although its population is only one-tenth that of its southern neighbo California, the state is well known for its residents' involvement in social causes. Sometimes this involves the way the government works, but often it involves environmental issues. Some people think Oregon is enti made up of misty forests, rich and fertile farmland, and solitary, snow-capped volcanic peaks — like Mt. Hood — this describes only the western third of the state. The r of Oregon is a mix of mountains, hills, and plateaus whe water is too valuable to waste, and the scattered communities depend on lumber, cattle, and sheep. The southeastern corner is a desert. Many people who live i Portland and the other cities along the banks of the Willamette River work in high-tech businesses.

Oregon Almanac

Nickname	Beaver State	Land area & rank	95,997 sq. miles (248,632 sq. km); 10th
State capital	Salem	Average January temperature	33°F (1°C)
Date of statehood	Feb. 14, 1859; 33rd state	Average July temperature	66°F (19°C)
State bird	Western meadowlark		
State flower	Oregon grape		
State tree	Douglas fir	Average yearly precipitation	27 inches (69 cm)
State motto	She Flies with Her Own Wings	Major industries	manufacturing, services, trade, finance, insurance, real estate, government, construction
Total population & rank	3,472,867 (in 2001); 27th		
Population density	36 per sq. mile (14 per sq. km)		
Population distribution	79% urban, 21% rural	Places to visit	Crater Lake National Park, Oregon Caves National Monument, Fort Clatsop National Memorial
Largest cities	Portland, Eugene, Salem		
Highest elevation	Mt. Hood, 11,239 ft. (3,426 m)		
Lowest elevation	sea level	Web site	www.oregon.gov

Physical

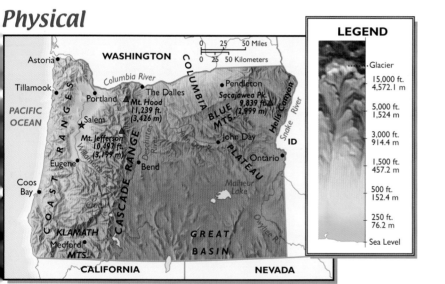

LEGEND

Glacier

15,000 ft. 4,572.1 m

5,000 ft. 1,524 m

3,000 ft. 914.4 m

1,500 ft. 457.2 m

500 ft. 152.4 m

250 ft. 76.2 m

Sea Level

Did You Know?

The deepest lake in the United States is found in the bowl-shaped depression atop an extinct Oregon volcano:

Crater Lake

Economy— Chief Products

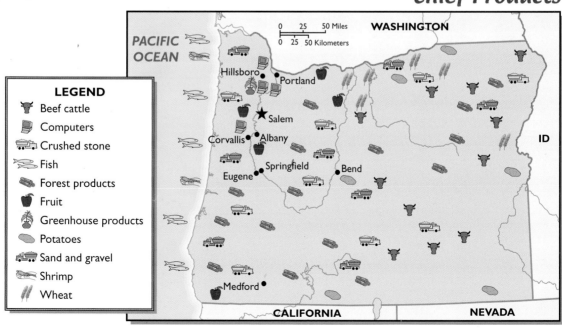

LEGEND

- 🐂 Beef cattle
- 💻 Computers
- 🚚 Crushed stone
- 🐟 Fish
- 🪵 Forest products
- 🫑 Fruit
- 🌱 Greenhouse products
- 🥔 Potatoes
- 🚛 Sand and gravel
- 🦐 Shrimp
- 🌾 Wheat

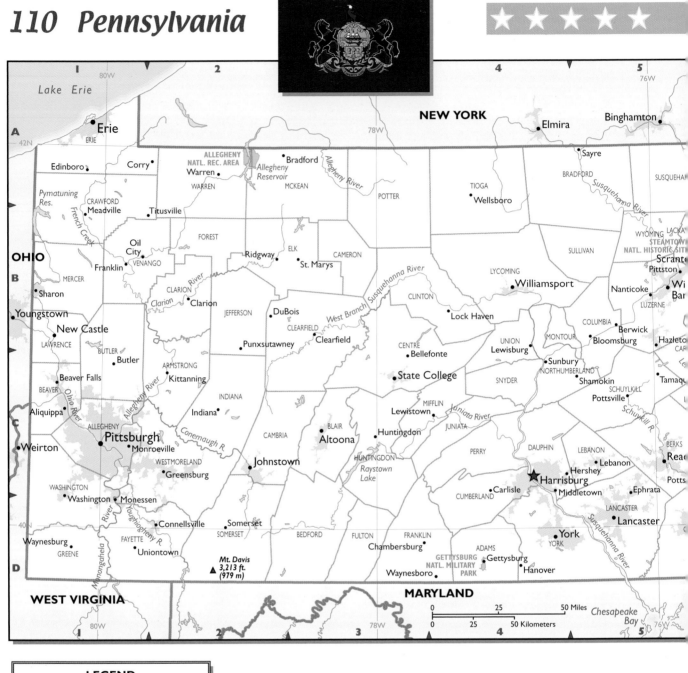

Lake Erie

NEW YORK

Erie
ERIE

Edinboro • Corry •
Warren •
Bradford •
ALLEGHENY NATL. REC. AREA
Allegheny Reservoir
WARREN
MCKEAN
POTTER
Elmira •
Sayre •
Binghamton •
78W
BRADFORD
Susquehanna River
SUSQUEHA

Pymatuning Res.
CRAWFORD
Meadville •
Titusville •
FOREST
TIOGA
Wellsboro •
SULLIVAN
WYOMING   LACKA
STEAMTOWN NATL. HISTORIC SIT
Scrant

OHIO
Oil City •
Franklin •
VENANGO
Ridgway •
ELK
St. Marys •
CAMERON
Susquehanna River
LYCOMING
Williamsport •
COLUMBIA
Nanticoke •
LUZERNE
Wi Bar
Pittston •

Sharon •
MERCER
CLARION
Clarion •
Clarion
JEFFERSON
DuBois •
CLEARFIELD
CLINTON
Lock Haven •
West Branch Susquehanna River
Berwick •
Bloomsburg •
Hazleto
CA

Youngstown •
New Castle •
LAWRENCE
BUTLER
Butler •
ARMSTRONG
Kittanning •
Punxsutawney •
Clearfield •
CENTRE
Bellefonte •
State College •
UNION
Lewisburg •
MONTOUR
NORTHUMBERLAND
Sunbury •
Shamokin •
SCHUYLKILL
Pottsville •
Tamaqu

Beaver Falls •
BEAVER
Aliquippa •
Ohio River
ALLEGHENY
INDIANA
Indiana •
CAMBRIA
BLAIR
Altoona •
Huntingdon •
MIFFLIN
Lewistown •
JUNIATA
Juniata River
SNYDER
PERRY
DAUPHIN
LEBANON
Lebanon •
Hershey •
BERKS
Rea

Weirton •
Pittsburgh
Monroeville •
WESTMORELAND
Greensburg •
Conemaugh R.
Johnstown •
HUNTINGDON
Raystown Lake
Carlisle •
CUMBERLAND
Harrisburg
Middletown •
Ephrata •
LANCASTER
Lancaster •
Potts

Washington •
WASHINGTON
Monessen •
Youghiogheny R.
Connellsville •
SOMERSET
Somerset •
BEDFORD
FULTON
FRANKLIN
Chambersburg •
ADAMS
Gettysburg •
GETTYSBURG NATL. MILITARY PARK
York •
YORK
Susquehanna River

Waynesburg •
GREENE
FAYETTE
Uniontown •
Monongahela River
Mt. Davis
3,213 ft.
(979 m)
Waynesboro •
Hanover •

WEST VIRGINIA
MARYLAND
Chesapeake Bay

0   25   50 Miles
0   25   50 Kilometers

LEGEND

★ State capital
• City
CENTRE County
▲ Mountain peak

National or other park
Urban area

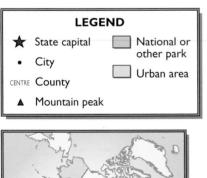

MIDATLANTIC

PENNSYLVANIA

Physical

Lake Erie
Erie •
NEW YORK

OH
Allegheny River
ALLEGHENY PLATEAU
New Castle •
Williamsport •
M O U N T A I N S
Scranton •
POCONO MTS.
Delaware River

Ohio River
APPALACHIAN
ALLEGHENY MTS.
W. Branch Susquehanna R.
Susquehanna River
Allentown •
NJ

Pittsburgh •
Johnstown •
Harrisburg •
Reading •

Monongahela River
Mt. Davis
3,213 ft.
(979 m) ▲
APPALACHIAN
York •
Philadelphia •

WV
VA
MD
DE

0   25   50 Miles
0   25   50 Kilometers

LEGEND

Glacier
15,000
4,572.
5,000
1,524
3,000
914.4
1,500
457.2
500 ft.
152.4
250 ft.
76.2 m
Sea Lev

Pennsylvania's nickname, the Keystone State, is appropriate for both its geographic location at the center of the original 13 colonies and its position as a key state in U.S. history. Both the Declaration of Independence and the U.S. Constitution were written, debated, and signed in Philadelphia. There are hundreds of museums and historic sites, including the Philadelphia Art Museum, Independence Hall, the Liberty Bell, Valley Forge, and Gettysburg. The state's abundant forests, lakes, rivers, and recreational parks are sandwiched between its two largest financial, business, and manufacturing centers: Philadelphia and Pittsburgh. Pennsylvania is also known for some of the richest farmland in the United States, and it has the largest rural population in the United States. Because Pennsylvania was founded in the Quaker tradition of tolerance and religious freedom, many plain sects such as the Mennonites and Amish settled in the state and continue to thrive here.

Pennsylvania Almanac

Nickname	Keystone State
State capital	Harrisburg
Date of statehood	Dec. 12, 1787; 2nd state
State bird	Ruffed grouse
State flower	Mountain laurel
State tree	Hemlock
State motto	Virtue, Liberty and Independence
Total population & rank	12,287,150 (in 2001); 6th
Population density	274 per sq. mile (106 per sq. km)
Population distribution	77% urban, 23% rural
Largest cities	Philadelphia, Pittsburgh, Allentown, Erie
Highest elevation	Mt. Davis, 3,213 ft. (979 m)
Lowest elevation	sea level
Land area & rank	44,817 sq. miles (116,076 sq. km); 32nd
Average January temperature	27°F (–3°C)
Average July temperature	71°F (22°C)
Average yearly precipitation	41 inches (104 cm)
Major industries	agribusiness, manufacturing, health care, tourism, biotechnology, printing and publishing, research and consulting
Places to visit	Gettysburg National Military Park, Independence Hall (Philadelphia), Pennsylvania Dutch country (Lancaster Co.), Steamtown National Historic Site, Hershey
Web site	www.pennsylvania.gov

Did You Know?

This bloody Civil War battle broke the strength of the Confederate army, which would no longer be able to mount an offensive against the North:

Gettysburg

Economy – Chief Products

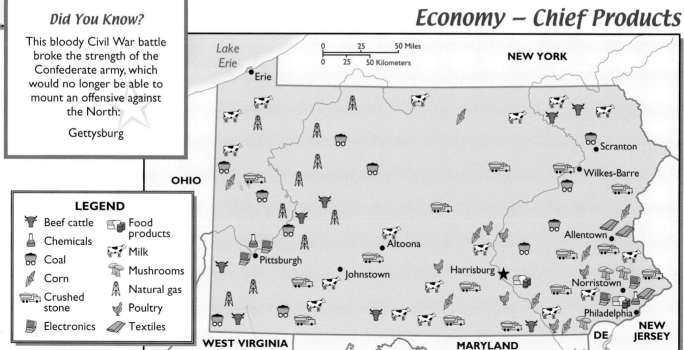

LEGEND

- Beef cattle
- Chemicals
- Coal
- Corn
- Crushed stone
- Electronics
- Food products
- Milk
- Mushrooms
- Natural gas
- Poultry
- Textiles

HOPE

LEGEND
★ State capital
• City
KENT County
▲ Mountain peak
Urban area

Blackstone

7130'W

42N

42N

Woonsocket

Pawtucket
Reservoir

Manville

Pascoag
Harrisville

River

Chepachet River

North
Providence
Central
Falls
Pawtucket

MASSACHUSETTS

Greenville

Woonasquatucket R.

Jerimoth Hill
812 ft.
(247 m)
▲

PROVIDENCE

Pongansett R.

★ Providence

East Providence

Cranston

Taunton River

CONNECTICUT

Scituate
Reservoir

Providence River

Barrington

Warren

Flat River
Res.
West
Warwick
Pawtuxet River

Warwick

BRISTOL

Mount Hope Bay

Fall
River

KENT

East Greenwich

Bristol

Wood River

Greenwich
Bay

Tiverton

Stafford
Pond

Prudence
Island

Portsmouth

Narragansett
Bay

NEWPORT

Queen River

Wickford

Rhode
Island

Sakonnet

Chipuxet R.

Middletown

4130'N

4130'N

Hope Valley

Jamestown

Newport

WASHINGTON

Kingston

Wood River

Sakonnet
Point

Ashaway

River

Worden
Pond

Wakefield

Narragansett Pier

Pawcatuck

Bradford

Watchaug
Pond

Charlestown

Point
Judith

Rhode Island Sound

Westerly

Pawcatuck

Ninigret
Pond

NEW
YORK

Block Island Sound

ATLANTIC
OCEAN

NEW
ENGLAND

RHODE ISLAND

Block Island

0   5   10 Miles
0   5   10 Kilometers

7130'W

71W

N
W   E
S

Rhode Island is the smallest state in the United States, yet it is also one of the most densely populated. In 1776, it became the first colony to declare independence from Great Britain and has contributed significantly to the history of the United States ever since. Situated on the scenic Narragansett Bay, it attracts many tourists who delight in boating, fishing, and viewing the great beauty of the state's beaches and resort islands. Narragansett Bay is also home to Rhode Island's fishing industry. Rhode Island is famous for the immense Victorian mansions in the Newport area, such as Cornelius Vanderbilt's "Breakers." Newport is known as the "sailing capital of America" and is the historic site of the America's Cup yacht race. Providence, Rhode Island's capital and home to most of Rhode Island's residents, is also a center for the arts, jewelry trade, tourism, and service industries. Metal products and scientific instruments are manufactured in Rhode Island as well.

Economy – Chief Products

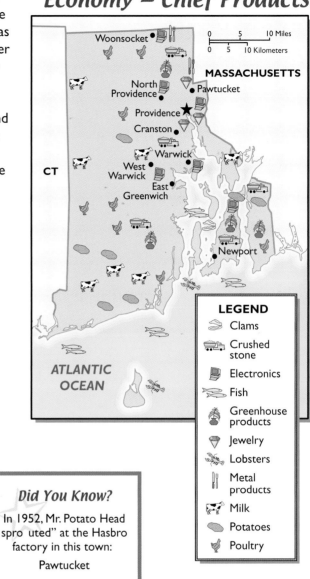

LEGEND

Clams	
Crushed stone	
Electronics	
Fish	
Greenhouse products	
Jewelry	
Lobsters	
Metal products	
Milk	
Potatoes	
Poultry	

Physical

LEGEND

- Glacier
- 15,000 ft. / 4,572.1 m
- 5,000 ft. / 1,524 m
- 3,000 ft. / 914.4 m
- 1,500 ft. / 457.2 m
- 500 ft. / 152.4 m
- 250 ft. / 76.2 m
- Sea Level

Did You Know?

In 1952, Mr. Potato Head spro uted" at the Hasbro factory in this town: Pawtucket

Rhode Island Almanac

Nicknames	Little Rhody, Ocean State	**Lowest elevation**	sea level
State capital	Providence	**Land area & rank**	1,045 sq. miles (2,707 sq. km); 50th
Date of statehood	May 29, 1790; 13th state		
State bird	Rhode Island red	**Average January temperature**	29°F (−2°C)
State flower	Violet		
State tree	Red maple	**Average July temperature**	71°F (22°C)
State motto	Hope		
Total population & rank	1,058,920 (in 2001); 43rd	**Average yearly precipitation**	45 inches (114 cm)
Population density	1,013 per sq. mile (391 per sq. km)	**Major industries**	services, manufacturing
Population distribution	91% urban, 9% rural	**Places to visit**	Newport mansions and Cliff Walk, Block Island, Touro Synagogue (Newport)
Largest cities	Providence, Warwick, Cranston, Pawtucket		
Highest elevation	Jerimoth Hill, 812 ft. (247 m)	**Web site**	www.state.ri.us

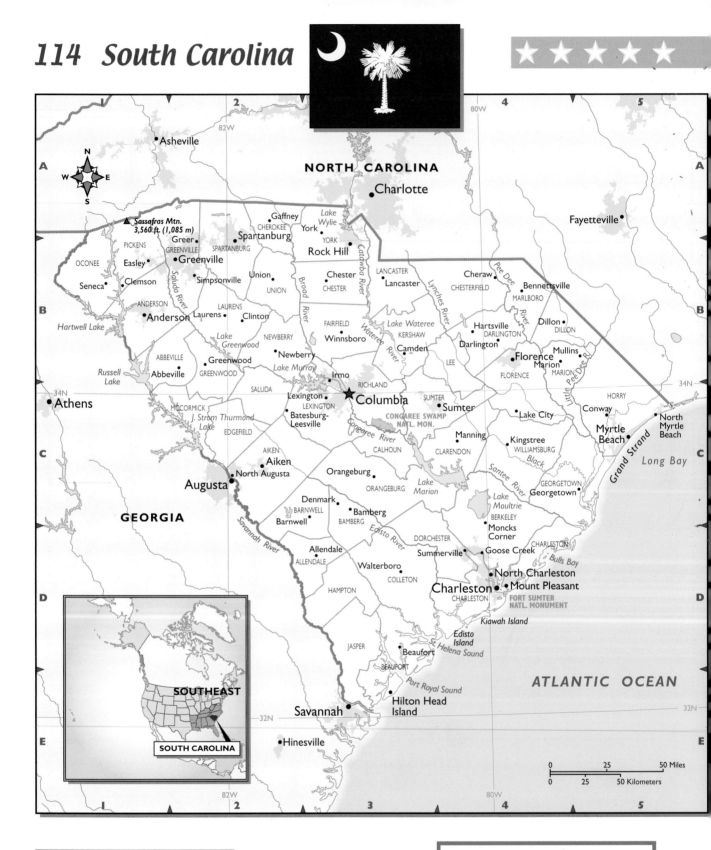

NORTH CAROLINA

Asheville

Charlotte

Fayetteville

▲ *Sassafras Mtn.*
3,560 ft. (1,085 m)

PICKENS

Gaffney
CHEROKEE
York
Lake
Wylie
YORK
Rock Hill

Spartanburg
SPARTANBURG

Greer
GREENVILLE

Easley
Greenville

Chester
CHESTER

Lancaster
LANCASTER

Cheraw
CHESTERFIELD

Pee Dee

Bennettsville
MARLBORO

OCONEE

Seneca
Clemson

Simpsonville

Union
UNION

Hartsville
DARLINGTON

Dillon
DILLON

ANDERSON

Laurens
LAURENS

Clinton

FAIRFIELD

Newberry
NEWBERRY

Winnsboro

Lake Wateree
KERSHAW

Camden

Darlington

Florence
FLORENCE

Mullins

Marion
MARION

Saluda River

Broad River

Catawba River

Lynches River

Little Pee Dee R.

Hartwell Lake

Anderson

ABBEVILLE

Greenwood
GREENWOOD

Lake Greenwood

Abbeville

Lake Murray

Newberry

Irmo

RICHLAND

Lexington
LEXINGTON

Columbia

SUMTER

Sumter

HORRY

Conway

34N

Russell Lake

Athens

MCCORMICK

J. Strom Thurmond Lake

EDGEFIELD

SALUDA

Batesburg-Leesville

Congaree River

CONGAREE SWAMP
NATL. MON.

Manning

Lake City

Wateree River

LEE

CLARENDON

Kingstree
WILLIAMSBURG

Myrtle Beach

North Myrtle Beach

Grand Strand

Long Bay

AIKEN

Aiken

North Augusta

Orangeburg
ORANGEBURG

CALHOUN

Santee River

Black River

GEORGETOWN

Georgetown

Augusta

GEORGIA

Denmark

BARNWELL

Bamberg
BAMBERG

Lake Marion

Lake Moultrie

BERKELEY

Moncks Corner

CHARLESTON

Edisto River

Barnwell

DORCHESTER

Summerville

Goose Creek

Bulls Bay

Savannah River

Allendale
ALLENDALE

Walterboro

COLLETON

North Charleston
Mount Pleasant

Charleston
CHARLESTON

FORT SUMTER
NATL. MONUMENT

HAMPTON

Edisto Island

Kiawah Island

JASPER

Beaufort
BEAUFORT

St. Helena Sound

ATLANTIC OCEAN

Hilton Head Island

Port Royal Sound

Savannah

Hinesville

32N

SOUTHEAST

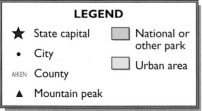

SOUTH CAROLINA

LEGEND

★ State capital

• City

AIKEN County

▲ Mountain peak

■ National or other park

■ Urban area

Did You Know?

In the Revolutionary War, two battles in South Carolina helped to turn the tide of war in the south:

Kings Mountain and Cowpens

0   25   50 Miles
0   25   50 Kilometers

It's easy to pick out the triangular shape of South Carolina with its nearly straight Atlantic Ocean edge. Look more closely to see that the coastline is actually pierced with bays and dotted with islands. With its population almost equally divided between urban and rural residents and with many small towns, South Carolina has been able to preserve a way of life that is disappearing in other southern states. A fascinating community of African Americans is the Gullah, descendants of slaves who lived in isolation for many years on the coastal islands. Mountains are limited to the northwestern corner, and a large part of the state is good for farming. A wide variety of crops are grown. The manufacture of fabrics and clothing remains an important industry, but tourism has become even more valuable. Many visitors vacation at the sandy beaches of the northern coast or at the coastal islands devoted to golf and tennis. Others come to Charleston to enjoy its gardens, architecture, and culture.

Economy – Chief Products

Physical

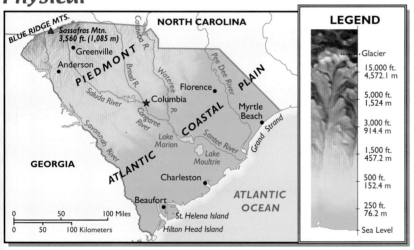

South Carolina Almanac

Nickname	Palmetto State	**Lowest elevation**	sea level
State capital	Columbia	**Land area & rank**	30,109 sq. miles (77,982 sq. km); 40th
Date of statehood	May 23, 1788; 8th state		
State bird	Carolina wren	**Average January temperature**	44°F (7°C)
State flower	Yellow jessamine		
State tree	Palmetto	**Average July temperature**	79°F (26°C)
State motto	*Dum Spiro Spero* (While I Breathe, I Hope)	**Average yearly precipitation**	48 inches (122 cm)
Total population & rank	4,063,011 (in 2001); 26th	**Major industries**	tourism, agriculture, manufacturing
Population density	135 per sq. mile (52 per sq. km)	**Places to visit**	Fort Sumter National Monument, Charleston Museum, Historic Charleston, Grand Strand and Hilton Head beaches
Population distribution	60% urban, 40% rural		
Largest cities	Columbia, Charleston, North Charleston, Greenville		
Highest elevation	Sassafras Mountain, 3,560 ft. (1,085 m)	**Web site**	www.myscgov.com

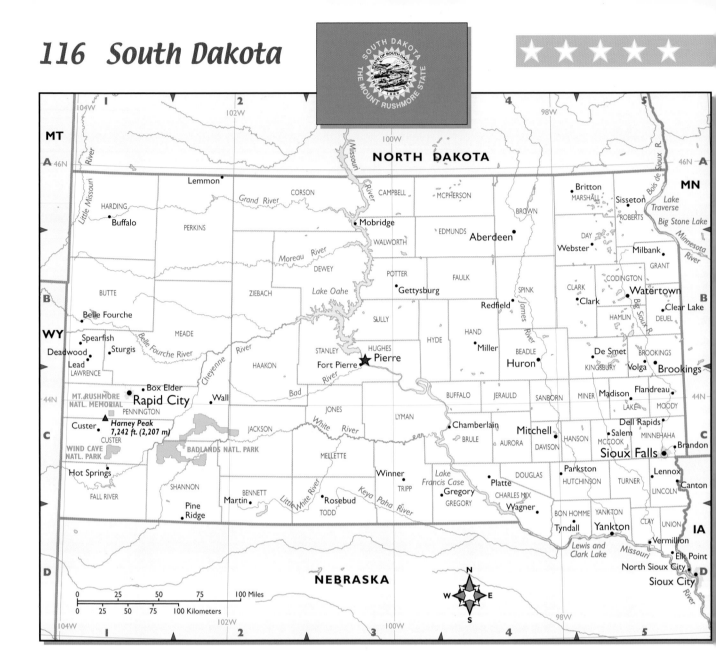

STATE OF SOUTH DAKOTA
THE MOUNT RUSHMORE STATE

MT

NORTH DAKOTA

46N A

Lemmon
CORSON
CAMPBELL
MCPHERSON
BROWN
Britton
MARSHALL
Sisseton
Lake
Traverse

MN

HARDING
Buffalo
PERKINS
Grand River
Mobridge
WALWORTH
EDMUNDS
Aberdeen
DAY
Webster
Milbank
GRANT
Big Stone Lake
ROBERTS

BUTTE
ZIEBACH
Moreau River
DEWEY
POTTER
FAULK
SPINK
Redfield
CODINGTON
CLARK
Clark
HAMLIN
Watertown
Clear Lake
DEUEL

B

Belle Fourche
MEADE
Lake Oahe
SULLY
HYDE
HAND
Miller
BEADLE
Huron
KINGSBURY
De Smet
Volga
BROOKINGS
Brookings

WY
Spearfish
Deadwood
Sturgis
Lead
LAWRENCE
Belle Fourche River
HAAKON
STANLEY
Fort Pierre
HUGHES
Pierre
James River
Big Sioux R.
44N

Box Elder
MT. RUSHMORE
NATL. MEMORIAL
Rapid City
Wall
Bad River
JONES
LYMAN
BUFFALO
JERAULD
SANBORN
MINER
Madison
LAKE
Flandreau
MOODY
44N

Custer
Harney Peak
7,242 ft. (2,207 m)
CUSTER
CUSTER
JACKSON
White River
Cheyenne River
Chamberlain
BRULE
AURORA
DAVISON
Mitchell
HANSON
MCCOOK
Salem
MINNEHAHA
Dell Rapids
Brandon

C
WIND CAVE
NATL. PARK
BADLANDS NATL. PARK
MELLETTE
Winner
Lake
Francis Case
Platte
DOUGLAS
Parkston
HUTCHINSON
TURNER
Sioux Falls
Lennox
LINCOLN
Canton

Hot Springs
FALL RIVER
SHANNON
BENNETT
Martin
Little White River
Rosebud
TODD
Keya Paha River
TRIPP
Gregory
GREGORY
CHARLES MIX
Wagner
BON HOMME
YANKTON
Tyndall
Yankton
CLAY
UNION
IA

Pine
Ridge

NEBRASKA
Lewis and
Clark Lake
Missouri River
Vermillion
Elk Point
North Sioux City
Sioux City

D

104W
102W
100W
98W

0   25   50   75   100 Miles
0   25   50   75   100 Kilometers

N
W   E
S

LEGEND
★ State capital
• City
BRULE County
▲ Mountain peak
◻ National or other park
◻ Urban area

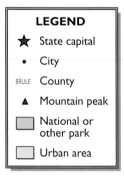

SOUTH DAKOTA

MIDWEST

South Dakota is second from the top in the column of nearly rectangular states that rises above Texas like a stack of Legos. The Missouri River wiggles up through the center of South Dakota, creating a distinct eastern half and western half. Most of the residents live in the eastern half, but many Native Americans live on reservations in the western half. The southwestern corner contains the most obvious geographical feature of the entire state, the Black Hills. Native Americans consider the Black Hills to be sacred land, and an immense sculpture of the Sioux warrior Crazy Horse is slowly being carved in the rock. Another famous mountain sculpture is nearby—the faces of four U.S. presidents carved in Mount Rushmore. Rich soils in the eastern half of the state support agriculture, but more people work in manufacturing and services. Businesses related to banking and insurance are the most important.

South Dakota Almanac

Nicknames	Mount Rushmore State, Coyote State	**Land area & rank**	75,885 sq. miles (196,542 sq. km); 16th
State capital	Pierre	**Average January temperature**	16°F (–9°C)
Date of statehood	Nov. 2, 1889; 40th state		
State bird	Chinese ring-necked pheasant	**Average July temperature**	73°F (23°C)
State flower	Pasqueflower		
State tree	Black Hills spruce	**Average yearly precipitation**	19 inches (48 cm)
State motto	Under God the People Rule		
Total population & rank	756,600 (in 2001); 46th	**Major industries**	agriculture, services, manufacturing
Population density	10 per sq. mile (3.9 per sq. km)	**Places to visit**	Mount Rushmore National Memorial, Badlands National Park, Wind Cave National Park, Deadwood
Population distribution	52% urban, 48% rural		
Largest cities	Sioux Falls, Rapid City		
Highest elevation	Harney Peak, 7,242 ft. (2,207 m)	**Web site**	www.state.sd.us
Lowest elevation	Big Stone Lake in Roberts Co., 966 ft. (294 m)		

Physical

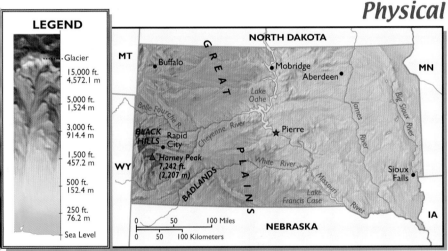

LEGEND

- Glacier
- 15,000 ft. / 4,572.1 m
- 5,000 ft. / 1,524 m
- 3,000 ft. / 914.4 m
- 1,500 ft. / 457.2 m
- 500 ft. / 152.4 m
- 250 ft. / 76.2 m
- Sea Level

Did You Know?

The outside of an exhibition building in Mitchell is decorated every year with murals made of multicolored corn, barley, and other grains:

The Corn Palace

Economy – Chief Products

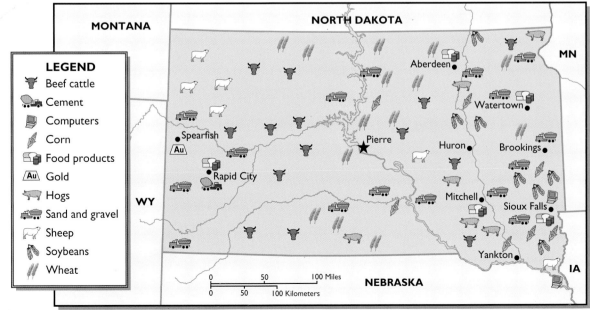

LEGEND

- Beef cattle
- Cement
- Computers
- Corn
- Food products
- Au Gold
- Hogs
- Sand and gravel
- Sheep
- Soybeans
- Wheat

Looking a bit like a sharpened pencil lying on its side, Tennessee has the flattest shape of all the states. Spanning hundreds of miles from the crest of the Appalachian Mountains to the Mississippi River, Tennessee boasts three distinct geographical regions. The Tennessee River generally forms their boundaries as it flows south from the mountains, makes a detour through Alabama, and turns north to cross the western part of the state. Tennessee was one of the first areas across the Appalachians to be settled, and it is one of the oldest non-colonial states. The first settlements were made in the mountains, and examples of traditional ways of life have been preserved in Great Smoky Mountains National Park. Western Tennessee, flat and fertile, is the most important farming area. Many tourists visit Memphis and Nashville to appreciate music. Memphis is famous for the blues, while Nashville is the capital of country and western.

Nickname	Volunteer State
State capital	Nashville
Date of statehood	June 1, 1796; 16th state
State bird	Mockingbird
State flower	Iris
State tree	Tulip poplar
State motto	Agriculture and Comme
Total population & rank	5,740,021 (in 2001); 16t

Physical

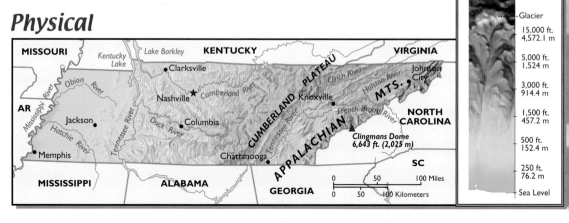

Clingmans Dome 6,643 ft. (2,025 m)

LEGEND

Glacier
15,000 ft. 4,572.1 m
5,000 ft. 1,524 m
3,000 ft. 914.4 m
1,500 ft. 457.2 m
500 ft. 152.4 m
250 ft. 76.2 m
Sea Level

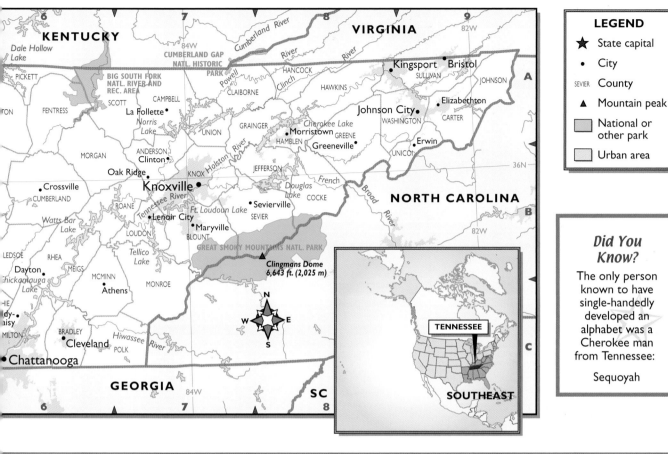

TENNESSEE

SOUTHEAST

LEGEND

★ State capital
• City
SEVIER County
▲ Mountain peak
National or other park
Urban area

Did You Know?

The only person known to have single-handedly developed an alphabet was a Cherokee man from Tennessee:

Sequoyah

Tennessee Almanac

Population density	139 per sq. mile (54 per sq. km)	Average January temperature	37°F (3°C)
Population distribution	64% urban, 36% rural	Average July temperature	77°F (25°C)
Largest cities	Memphis, Nashville, Knoxville, Chattanooga, Clarksville	Average yearly precipitation	52 inches (132 cm)
		Major industries	manufacturing, trade, services, tourism, finance, insurance, real estate
Highest elevation	Clingmans Dome, 6,643 ft. (2,025 m)	Places to visit	Great Smoky Mountains National Park, Cumberland Gap National Historic Park, Grand Old Opry (Nashville), Graceland (Memphis),
Lowest elevation	Mississippi River in Shelby Co., 178 ft. (54 m)		
Land area & rank	41,217 sq. miles (106,752 sq. km); 34th	Web site	www.state.tn.us

Economy – Chief Products

LEGEND

🚗 Automobiles
🐄 Beef cattle
⚗ Chemicals
Coal
🌸 Cotton
🚚 Crushed stone
🐄 Milk
🐓 Poultry
🌾 Soybeans
🌿 Tobacco
Zn Zinc

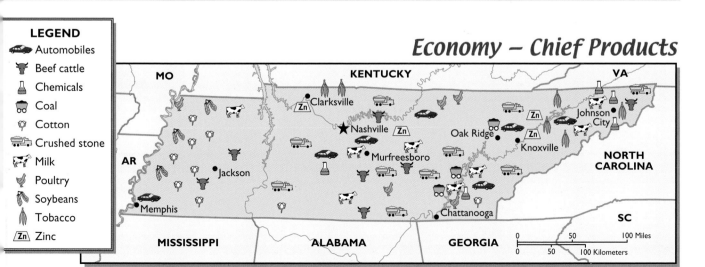

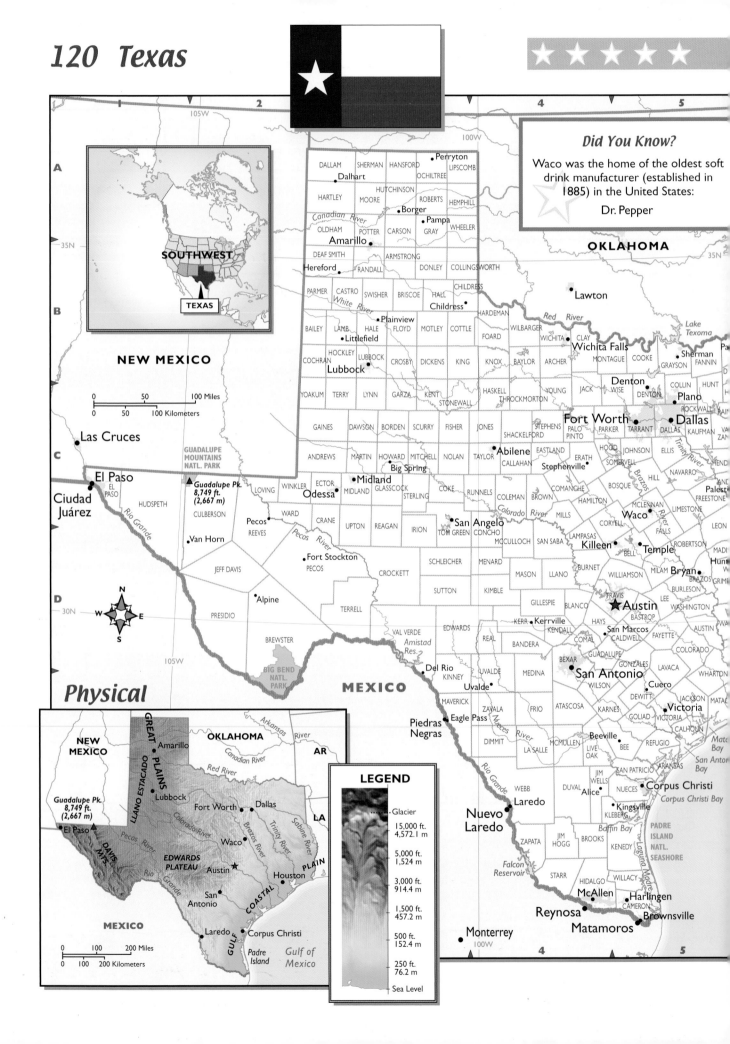

Did You Know?

Waco was the home of the oldest soft drink manufacturer (established in 1885) in the United States:

Dr. Pepper

SOUTHWEST

TEXAS

NEW MEXICO

OKLAHOMA

0 50 100 Miles
0 50 100 Kilometers

DALLAM SHERMAN HANSFORD •Perryton LIPSCOMB
•Dalhart OCHILTREE
HARTLEY HUTCHINSON ROBERTS HEMPHILL
MOORE
Canadian River •Borger
OLDHAM POTTER CARSON •Pampa WHEELER
Amarillo• GRAY
DEAF SMITH ARMSTRONG
Hereford• RANDALL DONLEY COLLINGSWORTH
CHILDRESS
PARMER CASTRO SWISHER BRISCOE HALL
White River •Childress HARDEMAN
•Plainview WILBARGER Red River
BAILEY LAMB HALE FLOYD MOTLEY COTTLE FOARD WICHITA CLAY
•Littlefield Wichita Falls• MONTAGUE COOKE
COCHRAN HOCKLEY LUBBOCK CROSBY DICKENS KING KNOX BAYLOR ARCHER
Lubbock• Denton• COLLIN HUNT
YOAKUM TERRY LYNN GARZA KENT STONEWALL HASKELL THROCKMORTON YOUNG JACK WISE DENTON •Plano ROCKWALL
Fort Worth• •Dallas
GAINES DAWSON BORDEN SCURRY FISHER JONES SHACKELFORD STEPHENS PALO PARKER TARRANT DALLAS KAUFMAN
PINTO HOOD JOHNSON ELLIS
ANDREWS MARTIN HOWARD MITCHELL NOLAN TAYLOR •Abilene EASTLAND ERATH SOMERVELL NAVARRO
•Big Spring CALLAHAN •Stephenville HILL Palest•
LOVING WINKLER ECTOR •Midland COKE RUNNELS COLEMAN BROWN COMANCHE BOSQUE LIMESTONE FREESTONE
Odessa• MIDLAND GLASSCOCK STERLING HAMILTON •Waco LEON
WARD CRANE UPTON REAGAN IRION TOM GREEN CONCHO MCCULLOCH SAN SABA CORYELL FALLS ROBERTSON MADI
Pecos• •San Angelo Killeen• •Temple Hun•
REEVES Pecos River LAMPASAS BELL MILAM •Bryan GRIM
•Fort Stockton SCHLEICHER MENARD MASON LLANO BURNET WILLIAMSON BRAZOS BURLESON
PECOS CROCKETT TRAVIS LEE WASHINGTON
SUTTON KIMBLE GILLESPIE BLANCO ★Austin
•Alpine TERRELL BASTROP
PRESIDIO EDWARDS KERR •Kerrville HAYS San Marcos• AUSTIN
KENDALL CALDWELL FAYETTE
Amistad REAL COMAL COLORADO
Res. BANDERA BEXAR GONZALES LAVACA WHARTON
•Del Rio UVALDE MEDINA San Antonio• •Cuero JACKSON MATA
KINNEY Uvalde• WILSON DEWITT Victoria• CALHOUN
MAVERICK FRIO ATASCOSA KARNES GOLIAD VICTORIA
Piedras Eagle Pass• ZAVALA Nueces REFUGIO
Negras DIMMIT LA SALLE MCMULLEN BEE •Beeville ARANSAS
LIVE Corpus Christi•
Nuevo WEBB OAK JIM SAN PATRICIO
Laredo Rio Grande WELLS DUVAL Alice• NUECES
Laredo• •Kingsville Corpus Christi Bay
ZAPATA JIM KLEBERG PADRE
Falcon HOGG BROOKS Baffin Bay ISLAND
Reservoir STARR KENEDY NATL.
HIDALGO WILLACY SEASHORE
McAllen• •Harlingen
•Monterrey Reynosa• CAMERON •Brownsville
Matamoros

NEW MEXICO

Las Cruces•

El Paso•
EL PASO
Ciudad Juárez

Rio Grande

HUDSPETH

GUADALUPE MOUNTAINS NATL. PARK

▲ Guadalupe Pk. 8,749 ft. (2,667 m)
CULBERSON

•Van Horn

JEFF DAVIS

N
W   E
S

30N

105W

BREWSTER

BIG BEND NATL. PARK

MEXICO

100W

Physical

NEW MEXICO

GREAT PLAINS

LLANO ESTACADO

Guadalupe Pk. 8,749 ft. (2,667 m)

•El Paso

DAVIS MTS.

Pecos River

Rio Grande

OKLAHOMA

Arkansas River

•Amarillo

Canadian River

Red River

•Lubbock

Colorado River

Fort Worth• •Dallas

•Waco

Brazos River

Trinity River

Sabine River

AR

LA

EDWARDS PLATEAU

Austin★

San Antonio•

•Houston

COASTAL PLAIN

•Laredo

GULF

Padre Island

•Corpus Christi

Gulf of Mexico

MEXICO

0 100 200 Miles
0 100 200 Kilometers

LEGEND

Glacier

15,000 ft. 4,572.1 m

5,000 ft. 1,524 m

3,000 ft. 914.4 m

1,500 ft. 457.2 m

500 ft. 152.4 m

250 ft. 76.2 m

Sea Level

Just like the biggest and strongest cheerleader holding up his partners in formation, Texas, at the bottom center of the United States, looks like it is supporting a stack of states upon its arms and shoulders. In many ways, Texas is a state that is big. Its borders enclose a tremendous geographical variety, from the damp and thick forests of the east across the mixed prairies and woodlands of the midlands to the dry and barren mesas of the west. Texas is the second most populated state, and its people are as varied as its landscape. Texas claims more than half of the entire U.S. border with Mexico, a border formed by the curving Rio Grande, and Mexican immigration has influenced the food, music, and language of Texas. The state is famous for its struggle for independence from Mexico, for cities that have grown rapidly in the last 25 years, and for a 100-year-old oil and natural gas industry. Sometimes forgotten is the contribution of agriculture. Texas is a leading producer of cattle and cotton, as well as fruits and vegetables.

Economy – Chief Products

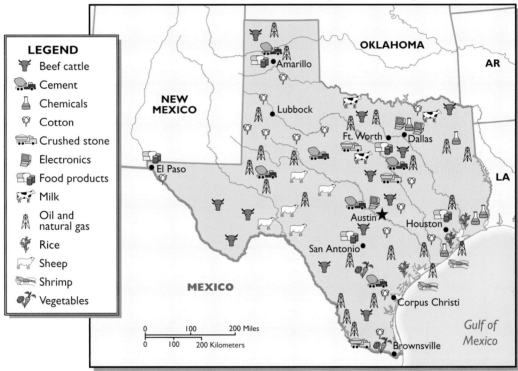

LEGEND
- Beef cattle
- Cement
- Chemicals
- Cotton
- Crushed stone
- Electronics
- Food products
- Milk
- Oil and natural gas
- Rice
- Sheep
- Shrimp
- Vegetables

Texas Almanac

Nickname	Lone Star State		**Lowest elevation**	sea level
State capital	Austin		**Land area & rank**	261,797 sq. miles (678,054 sq. km); 2nd
Date of statehood	Dec. 29, 1845; 28th state		**Average January temperature**	48°F (9°C)
State bird	Mockingbird			
State flower	Bluebonnet		**Average July temperature**	83°F (28°C)
State tree	Pecan			
State motto	Friendship		**Average yearly precipitation**	28 inches (71 cm)
Total population & rank	21,325,018 (in 2001); 2nd			
Population density	81 per sq. mile (31 per sq. km)		**Major industries**	manufacturing, trade, oil and gas extraction, services
Population distribution	82% urban, 18% rural		**Places to visit**	The Alamo (San Antonio), Big Bend National Park, Guadalupe Mountains National Park, Lyndon B. Johnson Space Center (Houston), Padre Island National Seashore
Largest cities	Houston, Dallas, San Antonio, Austin, El Paso, Fort Worth			
Highest elevation	Guadalupe Peak, 8,749 ft. (2,667 m)		**Web site**	www.state.tx.us

UTAH
16 47
1896

★ ★ ★ ★ ★

IDAHO

WYOMING

0   25   50   75   100 Miles
0   25   50   75   100 Kilometers

LEGEND

★ State capital
• City
JUAB County
▲ Mountain peak
National or other park
Urban area

WEST

UTAH

Smithfield

Logan

Tremonton

CACHE

Bear Lake

RICH

BOX ELDER

Brigham City

WEBER

Roy Ogden

Layton

MORGAN

Farmington

DAVIS

Antelope I.

Great Salt Lake

Bountiful

Salt Lake City

SALT LAKE

Wendover

West Valley City

Sandy

Tooele

TOOELE

Lehi

Orem

Provo

Utah Lake

Spanish Fork

Payson

UTAH

40N

▲ Ibapah Pk. 12,087 ft. (3,684 m)

NV

JUAB

Nephi

Park City

Heber City

WASATCH

Jordan R.

Salt Lake

Weber River

Bear River

River

SUMMIT

FLAMING GORGE NATL. REC. AREA

DAGGETT

▲ Kings Pk. 13,528 ft. (4,123 m)

DUCHESNE

Roosevelt

Duchesne River

Strawberry River

UINTAH

DINOSAUR NATL. MON.

Green River

Yampa River

Vernal

White River

COLORADO

N
W   E
S

40N

Delta

MILLARD

Sevier Lake (dry lake)

Beaver River

Sevier River

Fillmore

Salina

Richfield

SEVIER

SANPETE

Ephraim

Manti

Castle Dale

San Rafael River

EMERY

Helper

Price

CARBON

Price River

Green River

GRAND

Colorado River

River

Grand Junction

D

ARCHES NATL. PARK

CANYONLANDS NATL. PARK (HORSESHOE CANYON UNIT)

Moab

Mt. Peale ▲ 12,721 ft. (3,877 m)

Dolores River

Milford

BEAVER

Beaver

PIUTE

Delano Pk. 12,169 ft. ▲ (3,709 m)

Loa

Muddy Creek

Fremont R.

Dirty Devil River

CANYONLANDS NATL. PARK

WAYNE

CAPITOL REEF NATL. PARK

38N

Mt. Pennell ▲ 11,371 ft. (3,466 m)

38N

IRON

Parowan

Panguitch

GARFIELD

CEDAR BREAKS NATL. MON.

Cedar City

Enterprise

BRYCE CANYON NATL. PARK

Sevier River

Escalante

Escalante River

Colorado River

Monticello

SAN JUAN

Blanding

NATURAL BRIDGES NATL. MON.

GLEN CANYON NATL. REC. AREA

GRAND STAIRCASE-ESCALANTE NATL. MON.

WASHINGTON

ZION NATL. PARK

St. George

Washington

Virgin River

Kanab

KANE

Paria River

Lake Powell

San Juan River

Bluff

Page

ARIZONA

NM

Utah burst onto the international scene during the 2002 Winter Olympics, when visitors from around the world saw a Utah that was both natural and sophisticated. High, snow-capped mountains lend a magnificent backdrop to the towns and cities. In the more arid southern half of the state, mountains give way to a rugged landscape full of awe-inspiring national parks like Zion and Arches, broken by the long, meandering man-made Lake Powell. The Great Salt Lake is the largest saltwater lake in the Western Hemisphere. The Mormons settled the Utah Territory in 1847, and the state remains heavily influenced by their beliefs. World War I and World War II saw a large influx of outsiders as the wartime economy boomed, resulting in a more diverse mix of people. The economy now relies strongly on the services industry, joined by tourism, mining, and ranching. The state boasts that its powder snow is the best on earth, and many skiers visit the mountain resorts to test that statement personally.

Economy – Chief Products

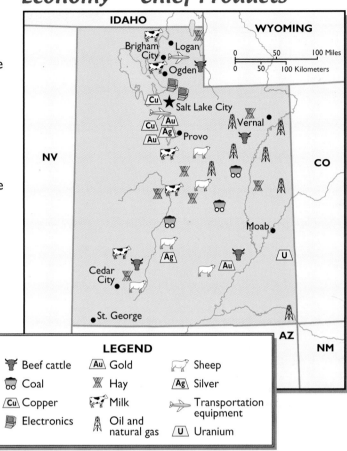

LEGEND

- 🐂 Beef cattle
- Coal
- Cu Copper
- 💻 Electronics
- Au Gold
- Hay
- 🐄 Milk
- Oil and natural gas
- 🐑 Sheep
- Ag Silver
- ✈ Transportation equipment
- U Uranium

Did You Know?

Salt Lake City has the highest per captita consumption, and it's the official state snack food:

Jell-O™

Utah Almanac

Nickname	Beehive State
State capital	Salt Lake City
Date of statehood	Jan. 4, 1896; 45th state
State bird	Seagull
State flower	Sego lily
State tree	Blue spruce
State motto	Industry
Total population & rank	2,269,789 (in 2001); 34th
Population density	28 per sq. mile (11 per sq. km)
Population distribution	88% urban, 12% rural
Largest cities	Salt Lake City, West Valley City, Provo
Highest elevation	Kings Peak, 13,528 ft. (4,123 m)
Lowest elevation	Beaver Dam Wash, 2,000 ft. (610 m)
Land area & rank	82,144 sq. miles (212,753 sq. km); 12th
Average January temperature	26°F (−3°C)
Average July temperature	73°F (23°C)
Average yearly precipitation	12 inches (30 cm)
Major industries	services, trade, manufacturing, government, transportation, utilities
Places to visit	Bryce Canyon National Park, Zion National Park, Arches National Park, Great Salt Lake, Temple Square (Salt Lake City)
Web site	www.utah.gov

Physical

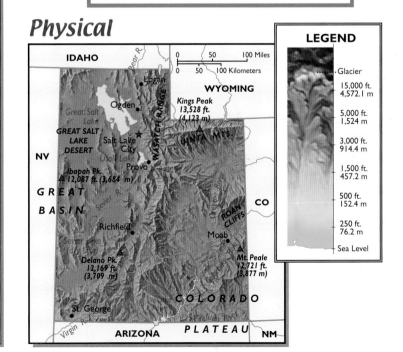

LEGEND

- Glacier
- 15,000 ft. 4,572.1 m
- 5,000 ft. 1,524 m
- 3,000 ft. 914.4 m
- 1,500 ft. 457.2 m
- 500 ft. 152.4 m
- 250 ft. 76.2 m
- Sea Level

CANADA

QUÉBEC

45N

A

Swanton

Richford

Lake
Memphremagog

Newport

Missisquoi River

FRANKLIN

St. Albans

ORLEANS

Island Pond

Black River

ESSEX

*Lake
Champlain*

Barton

GRAND
ISLE

Plattsburgh

LAMOILLE

Lamoille River

Milton

Mt. Mansfield
4,393 ft.
(1,339 m)

Morrisville

Lyndonville

B

Winooski

Essex Junction

Stowe

Passumpsic River

CALEDONIA
St. Johnsbury

Burlington

South Burlington

CHITTENDEN

Winooski River

Waterbury
Reservoir

Moore
Reservoir

Shelburne

Waterbury

WASHINGTON

N

W   E

S

Montpelier

Plainfield

**NEW
HAMPSHIRE**

Vergennes

Barre

Bristol

Northfield

Wells River

C

ADDISON

Middlebury

ORANGE

44N

NEW YORK

Lemon Fair River

GREEN MOUNTAIN
NATL. FOREST

Randolph

LEGEND

Otter Creek

Bethel

★ State capital

Lake
Winnipesaukee

Brandon

White River

• City

ESSEX County

Connecticut River

▲ Mountain peak

D

Lake
Bomoseen

Proctor

Rutland

White River Junction

National forest

Fair Haven

RUTLAND

Ottauquechee River

WINDSOR

Lebanon

Urban area

Lake
George

Wallingford

Windsor

Black River

Claremont

Mettawee River

Glens Falls

Hudson River

E

Springfield

Chester

43N

Manchester

Batten Kill River

Bellows Falls

VERMONT

Arlington

West River

**NEW
ENGLAND**

GREEN MOUNTAIN NATL. FOREST

BENNINGTON

Saratoga
Springs

Putney

Keene

F

North
Bennington

WINDHAM

Bennington

Brattleboro

0   10   20   30   40 Miles

Pownal

*Harriman
Reservoir*

0   10   20   30   40 Kilometers

Albany

MASSACHUSETTS

Nashua

73W

73W

72W

72W

Vermont's most spectacular geographic feature is the Green Mountains area that runs like a spine down the center of the state. Forests cover much of the state. While Vermont is the only New England state without an Atlantic coastline, it is bounded by water on two sides. On the east is the Connecticut River, and on the west is Lake Champlain. Vermont has a small population, the smallest east of the Mississippi River, and the lowest percentage of urban residents in the United States. Most of the people live in picturesque New England towns that become ski resorts during Vermont's long, snowy winters. This happy coexistence of mountains, trees, lakes, rivers, wilderness trails, and charming small towns makes Vermont an exceptionally scenic state and one of the most popular tourist destinations in the nation. Vermont's delicious maple syrup is famous. The lumber industry and paper products, along with marble and granite, are also important in Vermont's economy.

Economy – Chief Products

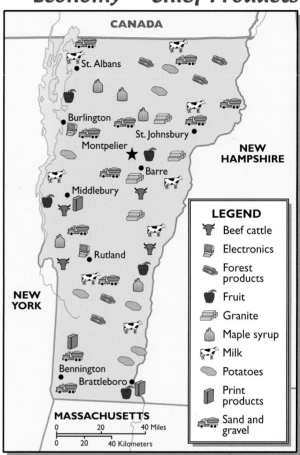

LEGEND

- 🐂 Beef cattle
- Electronics
- Forest products
- 🫑 Fruit
- Granite
- Maple syrup
- 🐄 Milk
- Potatoes
- Print products
- Sand and gravel

Physical

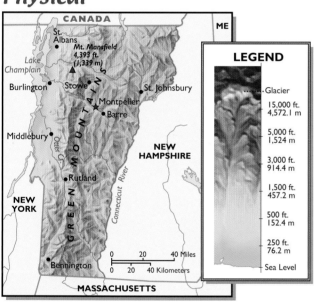

LEGEND

- Glacier
- 15,000 ft. 4,572.1 m
- 5,000 ft. 1,524 m
- 3,000 ft. 914.4 m
- 1,500 ft. 457.2 m
- 500 ft. 152.4 m
- 250 ft. 76.2 m
- Sea Level

Did You Know?

In 1978, Ben and Jerry started making ice cream in a renovated garage in this northern town:

Burlington

Vermont Almanac

Nickname	Green Mountain State	**Land area & rank**	9,250 sq. miles (23,958 sq. km); 43rd
State capital	Montpelier	**Average January temperature**	17°F (–8°C)
Date of statehood	March 4, 1791; 14th state		
State bird	Hermit thrush	**Average July temperature**	68°F (20°C)
State flower	Red clover		
State tree	Sugar maple	**Average yearly precipitation**	40 inches (102 cm)
State motto	Freedom and Unity		
Total population & rank	613,090 (in 2001); 49th	**Major industries**	manufacturing, tourism, agriculture, trade, finance, insurance, real estate, government
Population density	66 per sq. mile (25 per sq. km)		
Population distribution	38% urban, 62% rural		
Largest cities	Burlington, Essex	**Places to visit**	Green Mountain National Forest, Vermont Marble Exhibit (Proctor), Maple Grove Maple Museum (St. Johnsbury)
Highest elevation	Mt. Mansfield, 4,393 ft. (1,339 m)		
Lowest elevation	Lake Champlain, 95 ft. (29 m)	**Web site**	www.state.vt.us

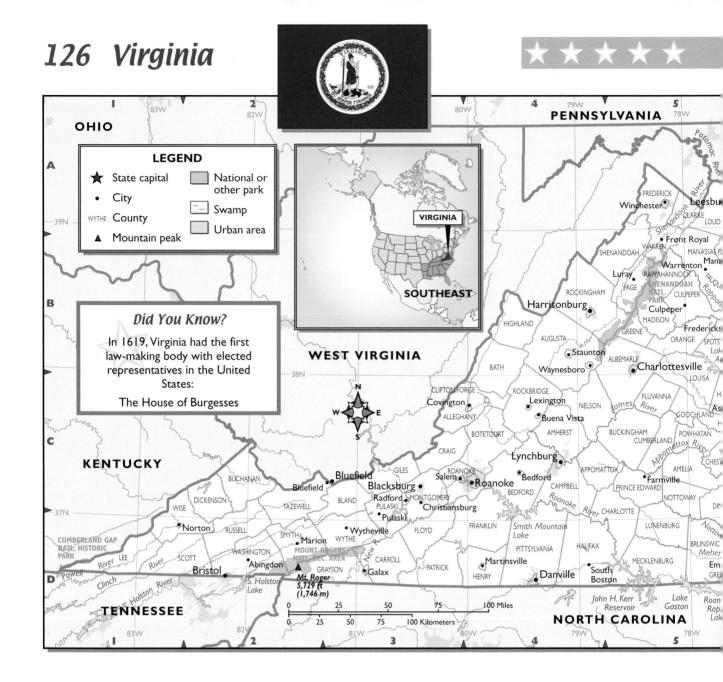

Virginia Almanac

Nickname	Old Dominion	**Lowest elevation**	sea level
State capital	Richmond	**Land area & rank**	39,594 sq. miles (102,548 sq. km); 37th
Date of statehood	June 25, 1788; 10th state		
State bird	Cardinal	**Average January temperature**	35°F (3°C)
State flower	Dogwood		
State tree	Dogwood	**Average July temperature**	75°F (24°C)
State motto	Sic Semper Tyrannis (Thus Always to Tyrants)	**Average yearly precipitation**	43 inches (109 cm)
Total population & rank	7,187,734 (in 2001); 12th	**Major industries**	services, trade, government, manufacturing, tourism, agriculture
Population density	182 per sq. mile (70 per sq. km)		
Population distribution	73% urban, 27% rural	**Places to visit**	Shenandoah National Park, Colonial Williamsburg, Arlington National Cemetery, George Washington's Home (Mount Vernon), Thomas Jefferson's Home—Monticello (Charlottesville),
Largest cities	Virginia Beach, Norfolk, Chesapeake, Richmond, Newport News		
Highest elevation	Mt. Rogers, 5,729 ft. (1,746 m)	**Web site**	www.myvirginia.org

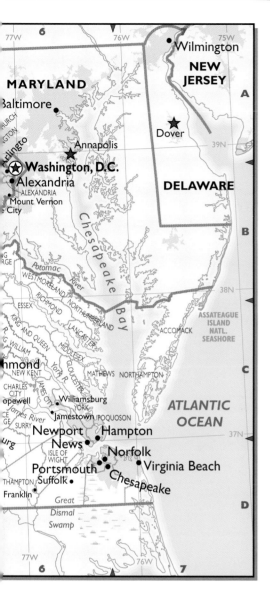

Virginia is the site of Jamestown, the first permanent English settlement in North America. From colonial sites like Williamsburg to Revolutionary and Civil War battlefields, historic plantations like Thomas Jeffersons Mo nticello and George Washington's Mount Vernon to Arlington National Cemetery—the burial place of President John F. Kennedy and honored U.S. soldiers—Virginia's historic sites span the history of the United States. It is the birthplace of eight presidents—more than any other state. Virginia is also a place of great natural beauty. The Blue Ridge Mountains, the Shenandoah Valley, Luray Caverns and Virginia's beaches are all major tourist attractions. The economy of Virginia started strong with the establishment of tobacco farming in colonial times. Virginia is thriving today because many diverse industries like shipbuilding, tobacco processing, tourism, government, and financial businesses make their home here. All of these industries create good jobs for Virginia's residents, so population growth is consistently higher here than in the rest of the United States. Most of the people live in the urban areas along Chesapeake Bay and the Atlantic coast.

Physical

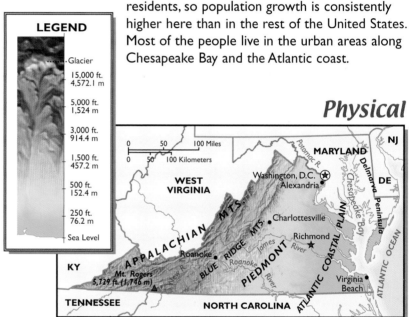

Economy – Chief Products

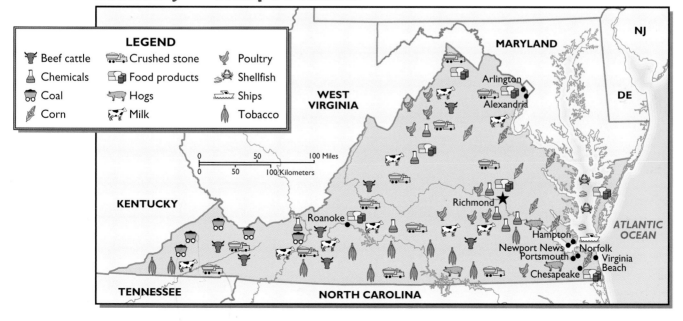

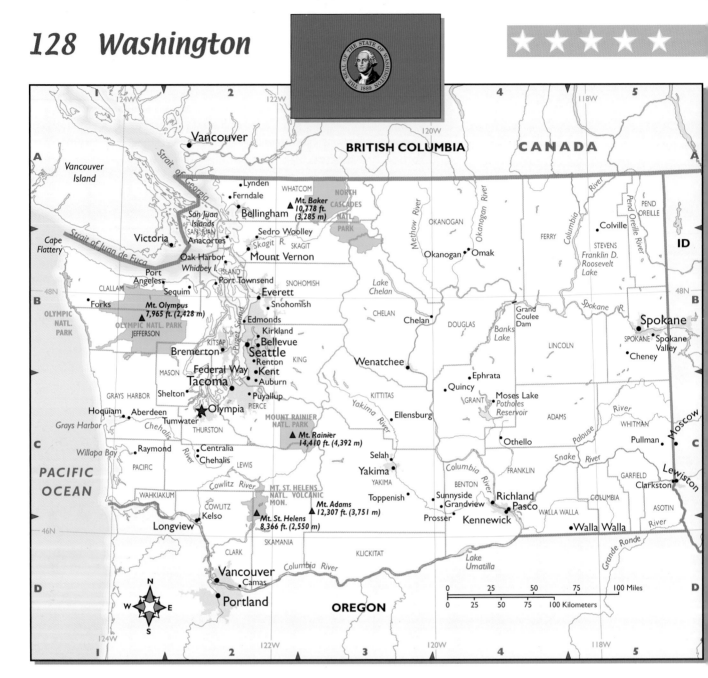

PACIFIC OCEAN

LEGEND
★ State capital
• City
SKAGIT County
▲ Mountain peak
⬜ National or other park
⬜ Urban area

WASHINGTON

WEST

Located in the upper-left corner of the lower 48 states, Washington has many important connections to Alaska, Canada, and countries across the Pacific Ocean. A number of people who live in Washington and many who visit as tourists come from Asia. Most of the state's residents live next to or very close to Puget Sound. Seattle is often selected as one of the most comfortable and appealing cities in the United States. The mountains of western Washington are famous for receiving much rain and snow and for having forests filled with tall trees. Mount Rainier a 14,410-foot (4,392-m) active volcano and site of a popular national park in the Cascade Range. The eastern half of the state is quite dry. Fortunately, the Columbia River makes large S-curve through central Washington and provides water for cities and farms. This geographical variety allows the state to produce many different agricultural products especially wheat, apples, and grapes. The most important industrial products are airplanes and computer software.

Washington Almanac

Nickname	Evergreen State	**Land area & rank**	66,544 sq. miles (172,349 sq. km); 20th
State capital	Olympia	**Average January temperature**	32°F (0°C)
Date of statehood	Nov. 11, 1889; 42nd state	**Average July temperature**	65°F (18°C)
State bird	Willow goldfinch	**Average yearly precipitation**	38 inches (97 cm)
State flower	Western rhododendron	**Major industries**	advanced technology, aerospace, biotechnology, international trade, forestry, tourism, recycling, agriculture
State tree	Western hemlock		
State motto	Alki (By and By)		
Total population & rank	5,987,973 (in 2001); 15th	**Places to visit**	Mount Rainier National Park, Olympic National Park, Mount St. Helens National Volcanic Monument, Grand Coulee Dam, Seattle Center
Population density	90 per sq. mile (35 per sq. km)		
Population distribution	82% urban, 18% rural		
Largest cities	Seattle, Spokane, Tacoma, Vancouver		
Highest elevation	Mount Rainier, 14,410 ft. (4,392 m)	**Web site**	www.access.wa.gov
Lowest elevation	sea level		

Physical

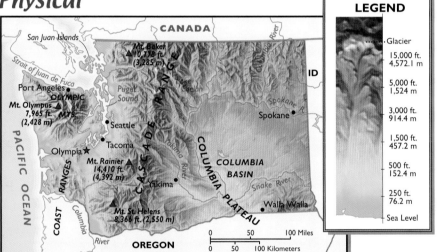

Did You Know?

On May 18, 1980, a powerful and violent eruption lowered a volcano's elevation by more than 1,000 feet (305 m) and killed 57 people:

Mount St. Helens

Economy – Chief Products

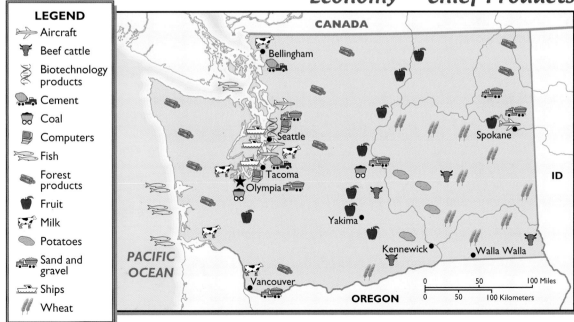

Mansfield
Canton
Altoona
Johnstown
Weirton
Pittsburgh

OHIO
PENNSYLVANIA

Newark
Wheeling
Moundsville

New Martinsville
Paden City

MARYLAND
Cumberland
Berkeley Springs
Morgantown
Martinsville
Hagerstown

Marietta
Fairmont
Keyser
Vienna
Clarksburg
Grafton
Parkersburg
Bridgeport
Charles Town
Harrisville
Philippi
Winchester
Weston
Moorefield
Ravenswood
Buckhannon
Petersburg
Ripley
Elkins
Spencer
Point Pleasant
Sutton
Spruce Knob 4,861 ft. (1,482 m)
Franklin

Harrisonburg

VIRGINIA

Huntington
St. Albans
Charleston
Summersville

Madison
Fayetteville
Oak Hill
White Sulphur Springs
Logan
Lewisburg
Williamson
Beckley
Hinton
KENTUCKY

Welch
Princeton
Bluefield
Roanoke
Bluefield
Blacksburg

25   50 Miles
25   50 Kilometers

WEST VIRGINIA

SOUTHEAST

LEGEND

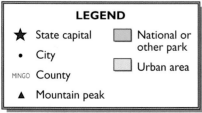

★ State capital
• City
MINGO County
▲ Mountain peak

National or other park
Urban area

Did You Know?

Long frequented by Native Americans, and later surveyed by George Washington, this site became the first public spa in the United States:

Berkeley Springs

West Virginia is called the mountain state for good reason—there is hardly any flat land in the entire state. Made up of the Appalachian Mountains, rolling hills, and steep river valleys, West Virginia is the highest state east of the Mississippi River. Valuable hardwood forests cover four-fifths of the state. Because of the rugged terrain, large-scale farming is difficult. As a result, the wild character of the land has been maintained, attracting many visitors to the wilderness areas and whitewater rivers. West Virginia's mountains also contain another of its most important natural resources—coal and other mineral deposits. Before the Civil War, the state was part of Virginia. However, since West Virginia was not part of the slave plantation economy in the rest of Virginia, it sided with the Northern states in the war and became a state in 1863. This independent spirit is reflected in West Virginia's people, who are justly proud of their lovely state with its Appalachian music and dance as well as traditional crafts like pottery, quilting, and glassmaking.

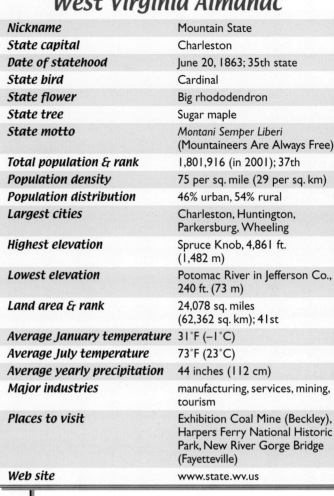

West Virginia Almanac

Nickname	Mountain State
State capital	Charleston
Date of statehood	June 20, 1863; 35th state
State bird	Cardinal
State flower	Big rhododendron
State tree	Sugar maple
State motto	*Montani Semper Liberi* (Mountaineers Are Always Free)
Total population & rank	1,801,916 (in 2001); 37th
Population density	75 per sq. mile (29 per sq. km)
Population distribution	46% urban, 54% rural
Largest cities	Charleston, Huntington, Parkersburg, Wheeling
Highest elevation	Spruce Knob, 4,861 ft. (1,482 m)
Lowest elevation	Potomac River in Jefferson Co., 240 ft. (73 m)
Land area & rank	24,078 sq. miles (62,362 sq. km); 41st
Average January temperature	31°F (−1°C)
Average July temperature	73°F (23°C)
Average yearly precipitation	44 inches (112 cm)
Major industries	manufacturing, services, mining, tourism
Places to visit	Exhibition Coal Mine (Beckley), Harpers Ferry National Historic Park, New River Gorge Bridge (Fayetteville)
Web site	www.state.wv.us

Economy— Chief Products

LEGEND
- Beef cattle
- Chemicals
- Coal
- Forest products
- Fruit
- Glass
- Hay
- Oil and natural gas
- Poultry
- Steel
- Tobacco

Physical

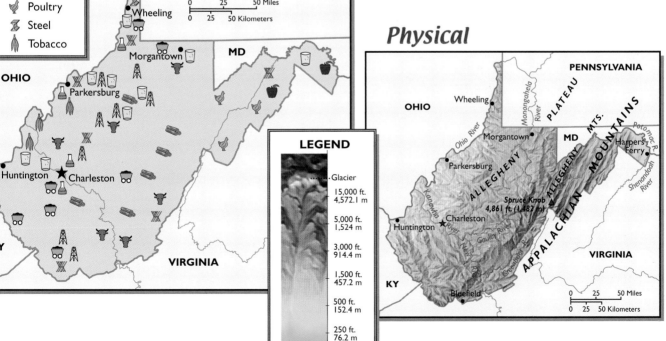

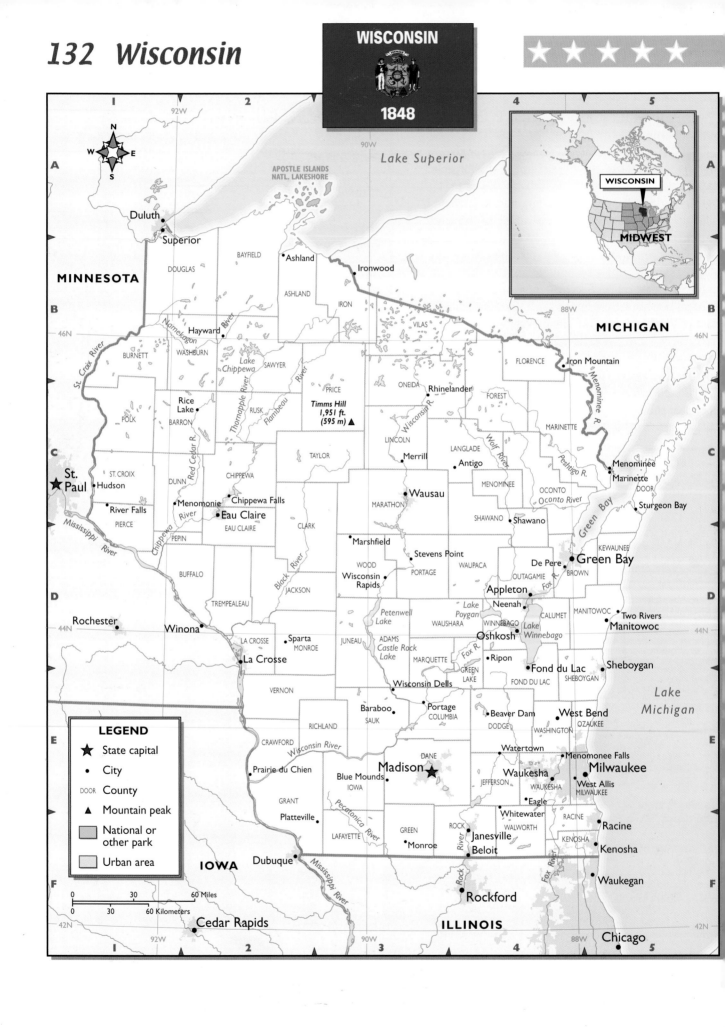

WISCONSIN

1848

MIDWEST

LEGEND

★ State capital

• City

DOOR County

▲ Mountain peak

National or other park

Urban area

Lake Superior

APOSTLE ISLANDS
NATL. LAKESHORE

Duluth

Superior

MINNESOTA

Ashland

Ironwood

BAYFIELD

DOUGLAS

ASHLAND

IRON

MICHIGAN

Hayward

BURNETT

WASHBURN

VILAS

FLORENCE

Iron Mountain

Rice
Lake

Lake
Chippewa

SAWYER

PRICE

ONEIDA

Rhinelander

FOREST

MARINETTE

POLK

BARRON

RUSK

Timms Hill
1,951 ft.
(595 m) ▲

LINCOLN

Merrill

Antigo

LANGLADE

Menominee

Marinette

DOOR

St.
Paul

Hudson

ST. CROIX

DUNN

CHIPPEWA

TAYLOR

CLARK

Wausau

MARATHON

MENOMINEE

SHAWANO

Shawano

OCONTO

Oconto River

Sturgeon Bay

River Falls

PIERCE

Menomonie

Chippewa Falls

Eau Claire

EAU CLAIRE

Marshfield

WOOD

Stevens Point

PORTAGE

WAUPACA

De Pere

Green Bay

BROWN

GREEN BAY

KEWAUNEE

PEPIN

BUFFALO

JACKSON

Wisconsin
Rapids

OUTAGAMIE

Appleton

Neenah

Fox

MANITOWOC

Two Rivers

Manitowoc

Rochester

TREMPEALEAU

Petenwell
Lake

Lake
Poygan

CALUMET

Winona

Sparta

MONROE

WAUSHARA

WINNEBAGO

Lake
Winnebago

Oshkosh

La Crosse

LA CROSSE

JUNEAU

ADAMS

Castle Rock
Lake

MARQUETTE

Ripon

Fond du Lac

Sheboygan

GREEN
LAKE

FOND DU LAC

SHEBOYGAN

VERNON

Wisconsin Dells

Baraboo

SAUK

Portage

COLUMBIA

Beaver Dam

DODGE

West Bend

OZAUKEE

WASHINGTON

Lake
Michigan

RICHLAND

CRAWFORD

Wisconsin River

Watertown

Menomonee Falls

Prairie du Chien

Madison

DANE

Waukesha

Milwaukee

Blue Mounds

IOWA

JEFFERSON

WAUKESHA

West Allis

MILWAUKEE

GRANT

Eagle

Platteville

Pecatonica River

Whitewater

RACINE

Racine

GREEN

ROCK

WALWORTH

Monroe

Dubuque

LAFAYETTE

Janesville

Beloit

Rock
River

KENOSHA

Kenosha

IOWA

Mississippi River

Rockford

Fox
River

Waukegan

Cedar Rapids

ILLINOIS

Chicago

St. Croix River

Namekagon River

Thornapple River

Flambeau River

Red Cedar R.

Chippewa River

Black River

Wisconsin R.

Wolf River

Peshtigo R.

Green Bay

Menominee R.

Fox R.

92W

90W

88W

46N

44N

42N

Wisconsin is a land of rolling hills and fertile farmlands. The extreme southwestern corner was somehow spared the effects of continental glaciation, and here many of the state's prettiest valleys and ridges can be found. About half of the state is farmland, and dairying is the most prevalent agricultural activity. Situated in the upper Midwest, Wisconsin has warm summers and winters that can be both long and severe. The presence of Lakes Superior and Michigan helps moderate the temperatures near the shore, but they can also provide more moisture for snow. These two lakes and the many smaller interior ones provide recreational activities for residents and tourists alike. Wisconsin's early settlers were immigrants from Germany, Poland, and Ireland. In the early 1900s, Wisconsin instituted many social, educational, political, and economic policies for the betterment of the people, and for decades Milwaukee, in the heavily populated southeast, elected socialists to political office. Today, Wisconsin remains one of the most socially conscious states.

Economy – Chief Products

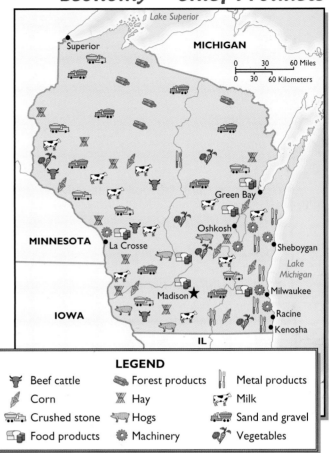

LEGEND

Beef cattle	Forest products	Metal products
Corn	Hay	Milk
Crushed stone	Hogs	Sand and gravel
Food products	Machinery	Vegetables

Did You Know?

This town on the shore of Lake Michigan claims to have invented the ice cream sundae in 1881:

Two Rivers

Wisconsin Almanac

Nickname	Badger State
State capital	Madison
Date of statehood	May 29, 1848; 30th state
State bird	Robin
State flower	Wood violet
State tree	Sugar maple
State motto	Forward
Total population & rank	5,401,906 (in 2001); 18th
Population density	99 per sq. mile (39 per sq. km)
Population distribution	68% urban, 32% rural
Largest cities	Milwaukee, Madison, Green Bay, Kenosha, Racine
Highest elevation	Timms Hill, 1,951 ft. (595 m)
Lowest elevation	Lake Michigan, 579 ft. (176 m)
Land area & rank	54,310 sq. miles (140,663 sq. km); 25th
Average January temperature	15°F (–9°C)
Average July temperature	70°F (21°C)
Average yearly precipitation	31 inches (79 cm)
Major industries	services, manufacturing, trade, government, agriculture, tourism
Places to visit	Circus World Museum (Baraboo), Old World Wisconsin (Eagle), Cave of the Mounds (Blue Mounds), Wisconsin Dells
Web site	www.wisconsin.gov

Physical

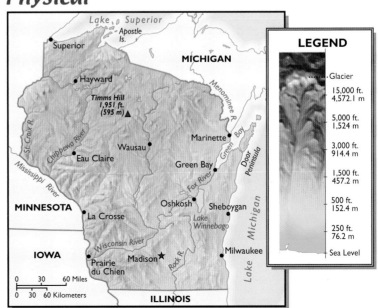

LEGEND

Glacier

15,000 ft. 4,572.1 m

5,000 ft. 1,524 m

3,000 ft. 914.4 m

1,500 ft. 457.2 m

500 ft. 152.4 m

250 ft. 76.2 m

Sea Level

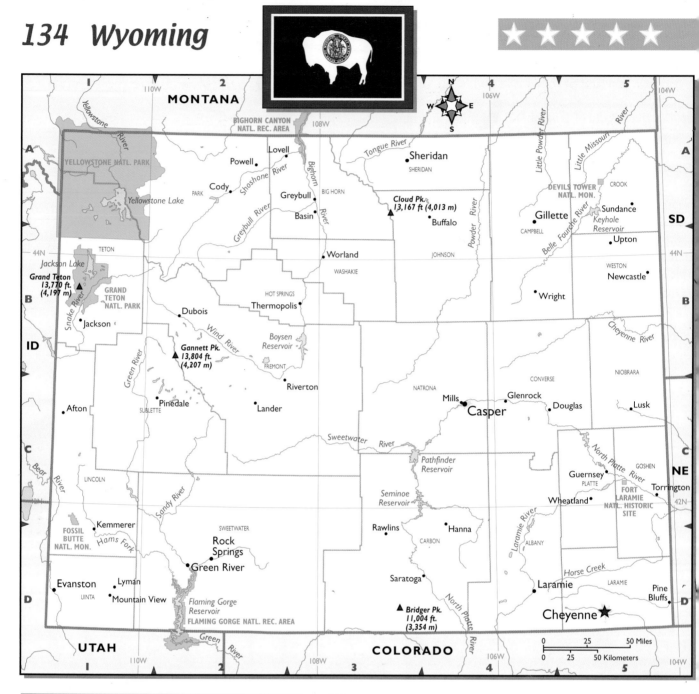

LEGEND

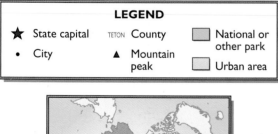

⭐ State capital   TETON County   🟩 National or other park

● City   ▲ Mountain peak   ⬜ Urban area

WEST

Wyoming is the ninth largest state in size but has the smallest population of any state, with less than half a million people. Like Colorado, its neighbor to the south, Wyoming has a rectangular shape. Within its boundaries are wide arid plains, high snow-capped mountains, refreshing evergreen forests, and spectacular parklands. Yellowstone National Park with its Old Faithful geyser and hot springs, Grand Teton National Park, and Devil's Tower National Monument are all located here. Known as the Equality State, Wyoming Territory was the first to grant women the right to vote in 1869. The population is concentrated in a number of small cities, leaving vast expanses of open land used for cattle and sheep ranching and recreation. This shared environment draws the people of Wyoming together. It results in a friendly and open attitude toward each other and toward visitors. This is important, since tourism is slowly replacing the traditional economic foundations of coal and trona (soda ash) mining and ranching.

Wyoming Almanac

Nicknames	Equality State, Cowboy State	**Land area & rank**	97,100 sq. miles (251,489 sq. km); 9th
State capital	Cheyenne	**Average January temperature**	19°F (−7°C)
Date of statehood	July 10, 1890; 44th state	**Average July temperature**	67°F (19°C)
State bird	Western meadowlark	**Average yearly precipitation**	13 inches (33 cm)
State flower	Indian paintbrush	**Major industries**	mineral extraction, oil, natural gas, tourism and recreation, agriculture
State tree	Plains cottonwood		
State motto	Equal Rights	**Places to visit**	Yellowstone National Park, Grand Teton National Park, Fort Laramie National Historic Site
Total population & rank	494,423 (in 2001); 50th		
Population density	5 per sq. mile (2 per sq. km)		
Population distribution	65% urban, 35% rural	**Web site**	www.state.wy.us
Largest cities	Cheyenne, Casper, Laramie		
Highest elevation	Gannett Peak, 13,804 ft. (4,207 m)		
Lowest elevation	Belle Fourche River in Crook Co., 3,099 ft. (945 m)		

Physical

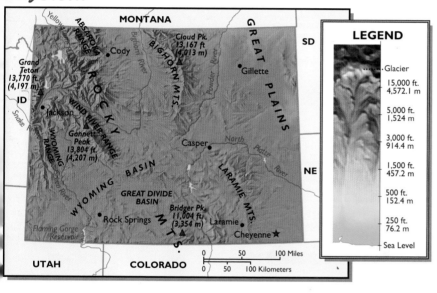

Did You Know?

The fastest animal in the Western Hemisphere is a Wyoming native:

Pronghorn antelope

Economy–
Chief Products

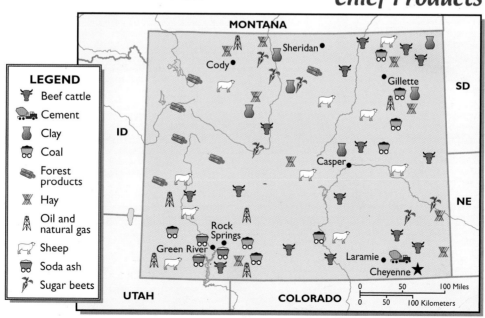

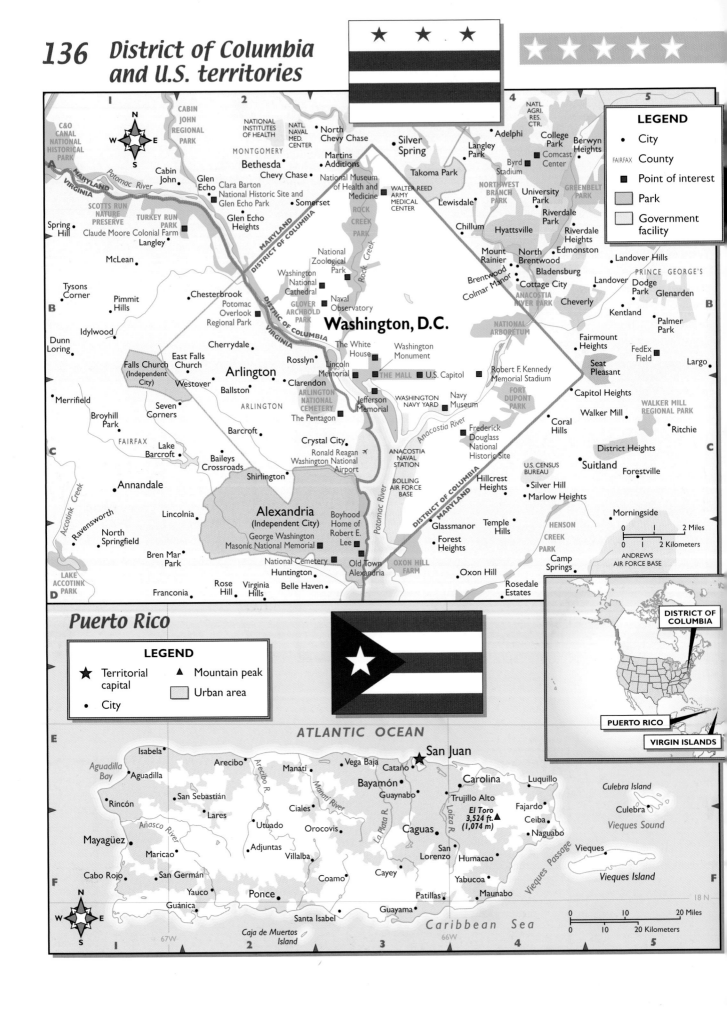

LEGEND
- City
- FAIRFAX County
- Point of interest
- Park
- Government facility

Washington, D.C.

C&O CANAL NATIONAL HISTORICAL PARK
CABIN JOHN REGIONAL PARK
MARYLAND
VIRGINIA
NATIONAL INSTITUTES OF HEALTH
NATL. NAVAL MED. CENTER
MONTGOMERY
NATL. AGRI. RES. CTR.
North Chevy Chase
Adelphi
College Park
Berwyn Heights
Silver Spring
Langley Park
Byrd Stadium
Comcast Center
Bethesda
Martins Additions
Chevy Chase
Takoma Park
NORTHWEST BRANCH PARK
University Park
GREENBELT PARK
Cabin John
Glen Echo
Clara Barton National Historic Site and Glen Echo Park
Somerset
National Museum of Health and Medicine
WALTER REED ARMY MEDICAL CENTER
Lewisdale
Riverdale Park
Riverdale Heights
Spring Hill
SCOTTS RUN NATURE PRESERVE
TURKEY RUN PARK
Glen Echo Heights
Claude Moore Colonial Farm
Langley
ROCK CREEK PARK
Chillum
Hyattsville
Mount Rainier
North Brentwood
Edmonston
Landover Hills
McLean
National Zoological Park
Washington National Cathedral
Rock Creek
Brentwood
Colmar Manor
Cottage City
Bladensburg
Landover
PRINCE GEORGE'S
Tysons Corner
Chesterbrook
Naval Observatory
GLOVER ARCHBOLD PARK
ANACOSTIA RIVER PARK
Dodge Park
Glenarden
Pimmit Hills
Potomac Overlook Regional Park
NATIONAL ARBORETUM
Cheverly
Kentland
Palmer Park
Idylwood
Cherrydale
The White House
Washington Monument
Fairmount Heights
FedEx Field
Largo
Dunn Loring
East Falls Church
Rosslyn
Lincoln Memorial
THE MALL
U.S. Capitol
Robert F. Kennedy Memorial Stadium
Seat Pleasant
Falls Church (Independent City)
Arlington
Ballston
Clarendon
ARLINGTON NATIONAL CEMETERY
Jefferson Memorial
WASHINGTON NAVY YARD
Navy Museum
FORT DUPONT PARK
Capitol Heights
WALKER MILL REGIONAL PARK
Merrifield
Westover
ARLINGTON
The Pentagon
Coral Hills
Walker Mill
Ritchie
Broyhill Park
Seven Corners
Barcroft
Crystal City
Frederick Douglass National Historic Site
District Heights
FAIRFAX
Lake Barcroft
Baileys Crossroads
Ronald Reagan Washington National Airport
ANACOSTIA NAVAL STATION
Hillcrest Heights
U.S. CENSUS BUREAU
Suitland
Forestville
Annandale
Shirlington
BOLLING AIR FORCE BASE
Silver Hill
Marlow Heights
Morningside
Lincolnia
Potomac River
Glassmanor
Temple Hills
HENSON CREEK PARK
North Springfield
Alexandria (Independent City)
George Washington Masonic National Memorial
Boyhood Home of Robert E. Lee
Forest Heights
Bren Mar Park
National Cemetery
Old Town Alexandria
OXON HILL FARM
Oxon Hill
Camp Springs
LAKE ACCOTINK PARK
Franconia
Rose Hill
Virginia Hills
Huntington
Belle Haven
Rosedale Estates
ANDREWS AIR FORCE BASE
Accotink Creek
Ravensworth

DISTRICT OF COLUMBIA
MARYLAND
VIRGINIA

0 1 2 Miles
0 1 2 Kilometers

Puerto Rico

LEGEND
- ★ Territorial capital
- ▲ Mountain peak
- • City
- Urban area

DISTRICT OF COLUMBIA
PUERTO RICO
VIRGIN ISLANDS

ATLANTIC OCEAN

Isabela
Aguadilla Bay
Aguadilla
Arecibo
Manatí
Vega Baja
Cataño
San Juan
Rincón
San Sebastián
Arecibo R.
Ciales
Bayamón
Carolina
Luquillo
Lares
Manatí River
Guaynabo
Trujillo Alto
Fajardo
Culebra Island
Mayagüez
Utuado
Orocovis
La Plata R.
El Toro 3,524 ft. ▲ (1,074 m)
Ceiba
Naguabo
Culebra
Vieques Sound
Maricao
Adjuntas
Villalba
Caguas
Loíza R.
Añasco River
San Lorenzo
Humacao
Vieques Passage
Vieques
Cabo Rojo
San Germán
Coamo
Cayey
Yabucoa
Vieques Island
Yauco
Ponce
Patillas
Maunabo
Guánica
Guayama
18 N
Santa Isabel
Caja de Muertos Island
Caribbean Sea
67W
66W

0 10 20 Miles
0 10 20 Kilometers

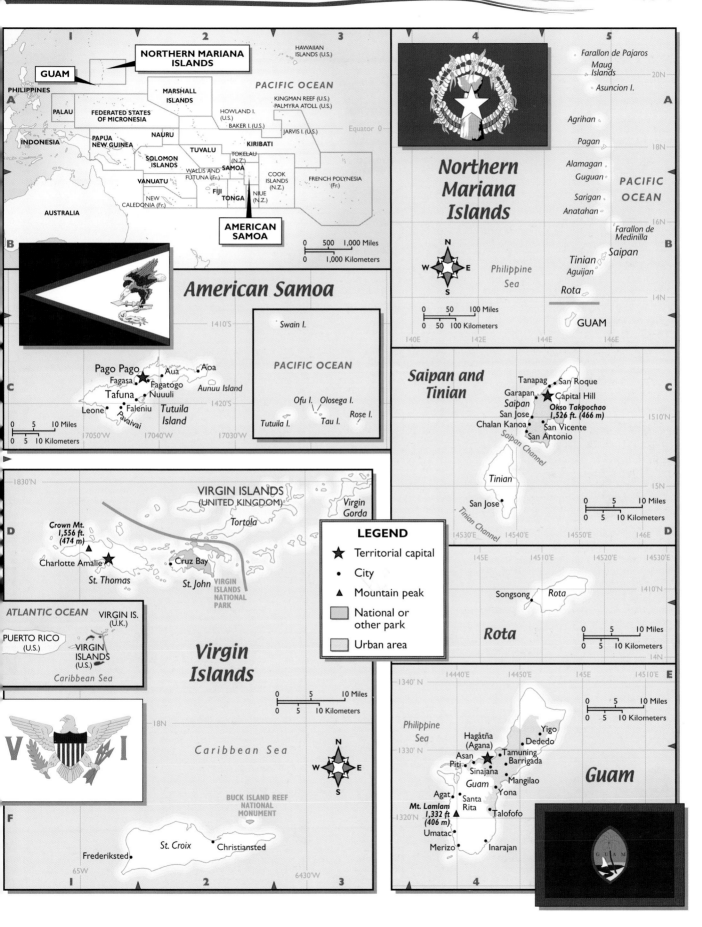

NORTHERN MARIANA ISLANDS

GUAM

PHILIPPINES

PACIFIC OCEAN

HAWAIIAN
ISLANDS (U.S.)

MARSHALL
ISLANDS

KINGMAN REEF (U.S.)
PALMYRA ATOLL (U.S.)

PALAU

FEDERATED STATES
OF MICRONESIA

HOWLAND I.
(U.S.)

BAKER I. (U.S.)

JARVIS I. (U.S.)

Equator 0

INDONESIA

NAURU

PAPUA
NEW GUINEA

TUVALU

KIRIBATI

SOLOMON
ISLANDS

WALLIS AND
FUTUNA (Fr.)

SAMOA

TOKELAU
(N.Z.)

COOK
ISLANDS
(N.Z.)

FRENCH POLYNESIA
(Fr.)

VANUATU

FIJI

TONGA

NIUE
(N.Z.)

NEW
CALEDONIA (Fr.)

AUSTRALIA

AMERICAN
SAMOA

0   500   1,000 Miles

0   1,000 Kilometers

American Samoa

1410'S

Swain I.

PACIFIC OCEAN

Pago Pago
Fagasa ★
Aua
Aoa

Tafuna
Nuuuli

Aunuu Island

Leone
Faleniu
Pavaivai

Tutuila
Island

1420'S

Ofu I.   Olosega I.

Tutuila I.   Tau I.   Rose I.

0   5   10 Miles

0   5   10 Kilometers

17050'W   17040'W   17030'W

Northern Mariana Islands

Farallon de Pajaros

Maug
Islands

20N

Asuncion I.

Agrihan

18N

Pagan

Alamagan

Guguan

PACIFIC
OCEAN

Sarigan

Anatahan

16N

Farallon de
Medinilla

Tinian   Saipan

Philippine
Sea

Aguijan

14N

Rota

GUAM

140E   142E   144E   146E

0   50   100 Miles

0   50   100 Kilometers

Saipan and Tinian

Tanapag   San Roque

Garapan   ★ Capital Hill

Saipan

Okso Takpochao
1,526 ft. (466 m)

San Jose

Chalan Kanoa

San Vicente

San Antonio

Saipan Channel

Tinian

1510'N

San Jose

15N

Tinian Channel

0   5   10 Miles

0   5   10 Kilometers

14530'E   14540'E   14550'E   146E

145E   14510'E   14520'E   14530'E

Songsong   Rota

1410'N

Rota

14N

0   5   10 Miles

0   5   10 Kilometers

LEGEND

★ Territorial capital

• City

▲ Mountain peak

National or
other park

Urban area

1830'N

VIRGIN ISLANDS
(UNITED KINGDOM)

Virgin
Gorda

Tortola

Crown Mt.
1,556 ft.
(474 m)

Charlotte Amalie ★

Cruz Bay

St. Thomas

St. John

VIRGIN
ISLANDS
NATIONAL
PARK

ATLANTIC OCEAN

VIRGIN IS.
(U.K.)

PUERTO RICO
(U.S.)

VIRGIN
ISLANDS
(U.S.)

Caribbean Sea

Virgin Islands

18N

Caribbean Sea

BUCK ISLAND REEF
NATIONAL
MONUMENT

0   5   10 Miles

0   5   10 Kilometers

Frederiksted

St. Croix

Christiansted

65W   6430'W

1   2   3

1340' N

Philippine
Sea

Yigo

Hagåtña
(Agana)

Dededo

Asan
Piti

Tamuning
Barrigada

1330'N

Sinajana

Guam

Mangilao

Agat

Santa
Rita

Yona

Mt. Lamlam
1,332 ft
(406 m)

Talofofo

Umatac

1320'N

Merizo

Inarajan

Guam

14440'E   14450'E   145E   14510'E

0   5   10 Miles

0   5   10 Kilometers

Figures after entries indicate population, page number, and grid reference.

A

Abbeville LA, *11887* **70** D2
Abbeville SC, *5840* **114** B2
Aberdeen MD, *13842* **74** A5
Aberdeen MS, *6415* **82** B4
Aberdeen SD, *24658* **116** B4
Aberdeen WA, *16461* **128** C1
Abilene KS, *6543* **66** B4
Abilene TX, *115930* **120** C4
Abingdon VA, *7780* **126** D2
Ada OK, *15691* **106** C5
Adams MA, *5784* **76** A1
Adel GA, *5307* **54** E3
Adelphi MD, *14998* **136** A4
Adirondack Mts., *mountains* **7** B9
Adjuntas PR, *4980* **136** F2
Adrian MI, *21574* **78** F4
Afton WY, *1818* **134** C1
Agat GU, *3988* **137** F4
Agawam MA, *28144* **76** B2
Aguadilla PR, *16776* **136** E1
Aiken SC, *25337* **114** C2
Ajo AZ, *3705* **40** E2
Akron OH, *217074* **104** C4
Alabama R., *river* **7** E8
Alamogordo NM, *35582* **96** D3
Alamosa CO, *7960* **46** D3
Alaska Range, *mountains* **6** F1
Albany GA, *76939* **54** E2
Albany NY, *95658* **99** D6
Albany OR, *40852* **108** B1
Albemarle NC, *15680* **100** B4
Albert Lea MN, *18356* **80** F3
Albuquerque NM, *448607* **96** C3
Aleutian Is., *islands* **6** F1
Alexander City AL, *15008* **36** C4
Alexandria LA, *46342* **70** C2
Alexandria MN, *8820* **80** D2
Alexandria VA, *128283* **127** B6
Algona IA, *5741* **64** A2
Alice TX, *19010* **120** E4
Aliquippa PA, *11734* **110** C1
Allegheny Mts., *mountains* **7** C8
Allegheny Plat., *plateau* **7** B9
Allegheny R., *river* **7** C9
Allendale SC, *4052* **114** D3
Allentown PA, *106632* **111** C6
Alliance NE, *8959* **88** B1
Alliance OH, *23253* **104** C5
Alma MI, *9275* **78** E4
Alpena MI, *11304* **78** C4
Alpine TX, *5786* **120** D2
Altamaha R., *river* **7** E9
Alton IL, *30496* **60** D2
Altoona PA, *49523* **110** C3
Alturas CA, *2892* **44** A2
Altus OK, *21447* **106** C3
Alva OK, *5288* **106** A4
Amana IA, *700* **64** C4
Amarillo TX, *173627* **120** B3
American Falls ID, *4111* **58** F4
Americus GA, *17013* **54** D2
Ames IA, *50731* **64** B3
Amesbury MA, *12327* **76** A5
Amherst MA, *17050* **76** B2
Amsterdam NY, *18355* **99** C6
Anaconda MT, *9417* **86** C2
Anacortes WA, *14557* **128** B2
Anadarko OK, *6645* **106** C4
Anaheim CA, *328014* **44** F4
Anamosa IA, *5494* **64** B5
Anchorage AK, *260283* **38** C3
Andalusia AL, *8794* **36** E3
Anderson CA, *9022* **44** B2
Anderson IN, *59734* **62** C4
Anderson SC, *25514* **114** B1
Andover MA, *7900* **76** A5
Andrews NC, *1602* **100** B1
Angola IN, *7344* **62** A5
Ankeny IA, *27117* **64** C3
Annandale VA, *54994* **136** C1
Annapolis MD, *35838* **74** B5
Ann Arbor MI, *114024* **78** F4
Anniston AL, *24276* **36** B4
Ansonia CT, *18554* **48** C2
Anthony NM, *7904* **96** E3
Antigo WI, *8560* **132** C4
Aoa AS, *507* **137** C2
Apalachicola R., *river* **7** E8
Appalachian Mts., *mountains* **7** C9
Appleton WI, *70087* **132** D4
Arcata CA, *16651* **44** A1
Arco ID, *1026* **58** E3
Ardmore OK, *23711* **106** D5
Arecibo PR, *49318* **136** E2
Arkadelphia AR, *10912* **42** D2
Arkansas City KS, *11963* **66** D4
Arkansas R., *river* **6** C5
Arkansas R., *river* **7** D7
Arlington VT, *1199* **124** E2
Arlington VA, *189453* **127** B6
Arnold MO, *19965* **84** C4
Artesia NM, *10692* **96** D4
Arvada CO, *102153* **46** B3
Asan GU, *1002* **137** F4
Asbury Park NJ, *16930* **94** C4
Ashaway RI, *1537* **112** E1
Ashdown AR, *4781* **42** E1
Asheville NC, *68889* **100** B2
Ashland KY, *21981* **69** B7
Ashland OH, *21249* **104** C3
Ashland OR, *19522* **108** D2
Ashland VA, *6619* **126** C5
Ashland WI, *8620* **132** B2
Ashtabula OH, *20962* **104** A5
Aspen CO, *5914* **46** B2
Astoria OR, *9813* **108** A1
Atascadero CA, *26411* **44** E2
Atchison KS, *10232* **66** B5
Athens AL, *18967* **36** A3
Athens GA, *101489* **54** B3
Athens OH, *21342* **104** E4
Athens TN, *13220* **119** C6
Athol MA, *8370* **76** A3
Atlanta GA, *416474* **54** B2
Atlantic IA, *7257* **64** C2
Atlantic City NJ, *40517* **94** E3
Atlantic Coastal Plain, *plain* **7** D9
Atmore AL, *7676* **36** E2
Attleboro MA, *42068* **76** C5
Aua AS, *2193* **137** C2
Auburn AL, *42987* **36** D4
Auburn CA, *12462* **44** C2
Auburn IN, *12074* **62** A5
Auburn ME, *23203* **72** E2
Auburn MA, *15901* **76** B4
Auburn NE, *3350* **88** C5
Auburn NY, *28574* **98** C4
Auburn WA, *40314* **128** C2
Augusta GA, *199775* **54** C4
Augusta KS, *8423* **66** C4
Augusta ME, *18560* **72** E2
Aurora CO, *276393* **46** B3
Aurora IL, *142990* **60** B4
Aurora NE, *4225* **88** C4
Austin MN, *23314* **80** F3
Austin NV, *600* **90** C3
Austin TX, *656562* **120** D5
Avalon NJ, *2143* **94** F3
Avenal CA, *14674* **44** D3
Aztec NM, *6378* **96** A2

B

Bad Axe MI, *3462* **78** D5
Baileys Crossroads VA, *23166* **136** C2
Bainbridge GA, *11722* **54** E2
Baker MT, *1695* **86** C5
Baker City OR, *9860* **108** B4
Bakersfield CA, *247057* **44** E3
Ballston VA, **136** C2
Baltimore MD, *651154* **74** B5
Bamberg SC, *3733* **114** C3
Bangor ME, *31473* **72** D3
Baraboo WI, *10711* **132** E3
Barberton OH, *27899* **104** C4
Barcroft VA, **136** C2
Bardstown KY, *10374* **68** C4
Bar Harbor ME, *2680* **72** E4
Barnstable MA, *47821* **77** C6
Barnwell SC, *5035* **114** C3
Barre VT, *9291* **124** C3
Barrigada GU, *4417* **137** F4
Barrington RI, *16819* **112** C4
Barrow AK, *4581* **38** A3
Barrow, Pt., *cape* **6** E1
Barstow CA, *21119* **44** E4
Bartlesville OK, *34748* **106** A5
Bartlett TN, *40543* **118** C1
Barton VT, *742* **124** A4
Basin WY, *1238* **134** A3
Bastrop LA, *12988* **70** A3
Batavia NY, *16256* **98** C2
Batesburg-Leesville SC, *5517* **114** C2
Batesville AR, *9445* **42** C3
Batesville MS, *7113* **82** B3
Bath ME, *9266* **72** E2
Bath NY, *5641* **98** D3
Baton Rouge LA, *227818* **70** D3
Battle Creek MI, *53364* **78** F3
Battle Mountain NV, *2871* **90** B3
Bayamón PR, *1699* **136** E3
Bayard NM, *2534* **96** E1
Bay City MI, *36817* **78** D4
Bay Minette AL, *7820* **36** F2
Bayonne NJ, *61842* **94** B4
Beach ND, *1116* **102** C1
Beatrice NE, *12496* **88** D5
Beatty NV, *1154* **90** E3
Beaufort SC, *12950* **114** D3
Beaumont TX, *113866* **121** D6
Beaver UT, *2454* **122** E2
Beaver Dam WI, *15169* **132** E4
Beaver Falls PA, *9920* **110** C1
Beaverton OR, *76129* **108** A2
Beckley WV, *17254* **130** D2
Bedford IN, *13768* **62** E3
Bedford VA, *6299* **126** C4
Beeville TX, *13129* **120** E5
Bel Air MD, *10080* **74** A5
Belcourt ND, *2440* **102** A3
Belen NM, *6901* **96** C3
Belfast ME, *6381* **72** E3
Belgrade MT, *5728* **86** C3
Bellefontaine OH, *13069* **104** C2
Bellefonte PA, *6395* **110** C3
Belle Fourche SD, *4565* **116** B1
Belle Glade FL, *14906* **52** D5
Belle Haven VA, *480* **136** D3
Belleville IL, *41410* **60** E3
Bellevue NE, *44382* **88** C5
Bellevue WA, *109569* **128** B2
Bellingham WA, *67171* **128** A2
Bellows Falls VT, *3165* **124** E3
Beloit KS, *4019* **66** B3
Beloit WI, *35775* **132** F4
Belton MO, *21730* **84** C1
Bemidji MN, *11917* **80** C2
Bend OR, *52029* **108** B3
Bennettsville SC, *9425* **114** B4
Bennington VT, *9168* **124** F2
Benton IL, *6880* **60** E3
Benton Harbor MI, *11182* **78** F2
Bentonville AR, *19730* **42** B1
Berea KY, *9851* **68** C5
Berkeley CA, *102743* **44** C2
Berkeley Springs WV, *663* **130** B5
Berlin NH, *10331* **92** C4
Bernalillo NM, *6611* **96** B3
Berwick PA, *10774* **110** B5
Berwyn Heights MD, *2942* **136** A4
Bessemer AL, *29672* **36** C3
Bethany Beach DE, *903* **50** F4
Bethel AK, *5471* **38** C2
Bethel VT, *800* **124** D3
Bethesda MD, *55277* **74** B4
Bethlehem PA, *71329* **111** C6
Bettendorf IA, *31275* **64** C5
Beulah ND, *3152* **102** C2
Beverly MA, *39862* **76** A5
Biddeford ME, *20942* **72** F2
Bighorn R., *river* **6** B4
Big Rapids MI, *10849* **78** D3
Big Spring TX, *25233* **120** C3
Big Timber MT, *1650* **86** C3
Billerica MA, *38981* **76** A5
Billings MT, *89847* **86** C4
Biloxi MS, *50644* **82** F4
Binghamton NY, *47380* **98** D4
Birmingham AL, *242820* **36** C3
Bisbee AZ, *6090* **40** F5
Bishop CA, *3575* **44** D3
Bismarck ND, *55532* **102** C3
Bitterroot Range, *mountains* **6** A3
Blackfoot ID, *10419* **58** E4
Black Hills, *mountains* **6** B5
Blacksburg VA, *39573* **126** C3
Blackwell OK, *7668* **106** A4
Bladensburg MD, *7661* **136** B4
Blair NE, *7512* **88** B5
Blakely GA, *5696* **54** E1
Blanding UT, *3162* **122** F5
Bloomfield NM, *6417* **96** A2
Bloomington IL, *64808* **60** C3
Bloomington IN, *69291* **62** E3
Bloomington MN, *85172* **80** E3
Bloomsburg PA, *12375* **110** B5
Bluefield VA, *5078* **126** C3
Bluefield WV, *11451* **130** E2
Blue Mounds WI, *708* **132** E3
Blue Ridge, *mountains* **7** D9
Bluff UT, *320* **122** F5
Bluffton IN, *9536* **62** B4
Blythe CA, *12155* **44** F5
Blytheville AR, *18272* **42** B5
Boardman OH, *37215* **104** C5
Boca Raton FL, *74764* **52** E5
Bogalusa LA, *13365* **70** C4
Boise ID, *185787* **58** E2
Boise City OK, *1483* **106** A1
Bolivar MO, *9143* **84** D2
Bolivar TN, *5802* **118** C2
Bonners Ferry ID, *2515* **58** A2
Boone IA, *12803* **64** B3
Boone NC, *13472* **100** A3
Booneville MS, *8625* **82** A4
Boonsboro MD, *2803* **74** A3
Boonville MO, *8202* **84** B3
Boothbay ME, *550* **72** E3
Borger TX, *14302* **120** A3
Bossier City LA, *56461* **70** A1
Boston MA, *589141* **76** B5
Boston Mts., *mountains* **7** D6
Bottineau ND, *2336* **102** A3
Boulder CO, *94673* **46** B3
Boulder MT, *1300* **86** C2
Boulder City NV, *14966* **90** F4
Bountiful UT, *41301* **122** B3
Bowers Beach DE, *305* **50** D3
Bowie MD, *50269* **74** B5
Bowling Green KY, *49296* **68** D3
Bowling Green OH, *29636* **104** B2
Bowman ND, *1600* **102** D1
Box Elder SD, *2841* **116** C1
Bozeman MT, *27509* **86** C3
Bradenton FL, *49504* **52** D3
Bradford PA, *9175* **110** A2
Bradford RI, *1497* **112** E2
Brainerd MN, *13178* **80** D3
Brandon SD, *5693* **116** C5
Brandon VT, *1684* **124** D2
Branson MO, *6050* **84** E2
Brattleboro VT, *8289* **124** F3
Brawley CA, *22052* **44** F5
Brazil IN, *8188* **62** D2
Brazos R., *river* **7** E6
Bremerton WA, *37259* **128** B2
Bren Mar Park VA, **136** D2
Brentwood MD, *2844* **136** B4
Brevard NC, *6789* **100** B2
Brewton AL, *5498* **36** E3
Bridgeport CT, *139529* **48** D2
Bridgeport WV, *7306* **130** C3
Bridgeton NJ, *22771* **94** E2
Bridgeville DE, *1436* **50** E2
Bridgewater MA, *6664* **76** C5
Brigantine NJ, *12594* **94** E3
Brigham City UT, *17411* **122** B2
Bristol CT, *60062* **48** B3
Bristol NH, *1670* **92** D3
Bristol RI, *22469* **112** C4
Bristol TN, *24821* **119** A9
Bristol VT, *1800* **124** C2
Bristol VA, *17367* **126** D2
Britton SD, *1328* **116** A4
Brockton MA, *94304* **76** B5
Broken Arrow OK, *74859* **106** B5
Broken Bow NE, *3491* **88** C3
Brookhaven MS, *9861* **82** E3
Brookings OR, *5447* **108** D1
Brookings SD, *18504* **116** B5
Brooks Range, *mountains* **6** E1
Browning MT, *1065* **86** A2
Browns Mills NJ, *11257* **94** D3
Brownsville TN, *10748* **118** B2
Brownsville TX, *139722* **120** F5
Broyhill Park VA, *17000* **136** C1
Brunswick GA, *15600* **54** E5
Brunswick ME, *14816* **72** E2
Brunswick MD, *4894* **74** B3
Brush CO, *5117* **46** A4
Bryan TX, *65660* **120** D5
Buckhannon WV, *5725* **130** C3
Bucyrus OH, *13224* **104** C3
Buena Vista CO, *2195* **46** C3
Buena Vista VA, *6349* **126** C4
Buffalo MN, *10097* **80** E3
Buffalo NY, *292648* **98** C2
Buffalo SD, *380* **116** A1
Buffalo WY, *3900* **134** A4
Bullhead City AZ, *33769* **40** C1
Bunkie LA, *4662* **70** C2
Burley ID, *9316* **58** F3
Burlington CO, *3678* **46** B5
Burlington IA, *26839* **64** D5
Burlington NJ, *9736* **94** D3
Burlington NC, *44917* **100** A5
Burlington VT, *38889* **124** B2
Burns OR, *3064* **108** C4
Butler PA, *15121* **110** C1
Butte MT, *34606* **86** C2

C

Cabin John MD, *1734* **136** A2
Cabo Rojo PR, *10610* **136** F1
Cadillac MI, *10000* **78** D3
Caguas PR, *88680* **136** F3
Cairo GA, *9239* **54** E2
Cairo IL, *3632* **60** F3
Calais ME, *3447* **72** D5
Caldwell ID, *25967* **58** E1
Calhoun GA, *10667* **54** A1
Caliente NV, *1123* **90** D5
Cal Nev Ari NV, *278* **90** F4
Camarillo CA, *57077* **44** E3
Camas WA, *12534* **128** D2
Cambria CA, *6232* **44** E2
Cambridge MD, *10911* **75** C6
Cambridge MA, *101355* **76** B5
Cambridge OH, *11520* **104** D4
Camden AR, *13154* **42** E2
Camden DE, *2100* **50** D3
Camden NJ, *79904* **94** D2
Camden SC, *6682* **114** B3
Cameron MO, *8312* **84** B2
Camilla GA, *5669* **54** E2
Campbellsville KY, *10498* **68** C4
Camp Springs MD, *17968* **136** D4
Camp Verde AZ, *9451* **40** C3
Canaan CT, *1288* **48** A2
Canadian R., *river* **7** D6
Canandaigua NY, *11264* **98** C3
Canaveral, C., *cape* **7** E9
Cando ND, *1342* **102** B4
Canon City CO, *15431* **46** C3
Canton MS, *12911* **82** D3
Canton NY, *5882* **98** A5
Canton OH, *80806* **104** C4
Canton SD, *3110* **116** C5
Cape Coral FL, *102286* **52** E3
Cape Girardeau MO, *35349* **84** D5
Cape May NJ, *4034* **94** F2
Capital Hill MP, *1496* **137** C5
Capitol Heights MD, *4138* **136** C4
Captain Cook HI, *3206* **56** E4
Carbondale IL, *20681* **60** F3
Carbondale PA, *9804* **111** B6
Caribou ME, *8312* **72** A4
Carlin NV, *2161* **90** B4
Carlinville IL, *5685* **60** D3
Carlisle PA, *17970* **110** C4
Carlsbad CA, *78247* **44** F4
Carlsbad NM, *25625* **96** E4
Carmel IN, *37733* **62** C3
Carmi IL, *5422* **60** E4
Carolina PR, *168164* **136** E4
Carrington ND, *2268* **102** C4
Carroll IA, *10106* **64** B2
Carrollton GA, *19843* **54** B1

Carson City NV, *52457* **90** C1
Cartersville GA, *15925* **54** B2
Carthage MO, *12668* **84** D2
Caruthersville MO, *6760* **84** E5
Cary NC, *94536* **100** B5
Casa Grande AZ, *25224* **40** E3
Cascade Range, *mountains* **6** B2
Casper WY, *49644* **134** C4
Castle Dale UT, *1657* **122** D3
Castle Rock CO, *20224* **46** B3
Cataño PR, *30071* **136** E3
Cathedral City CA, *42647* **44** F4
Cavalier ND, *1537* **102** A5
Cayey PR, *19940* **136** F3
Cedar City UT, *20527* **122** F2
Cedar Falls IA, *36145* **64** B4
Cedar Rapids IA, *120758* **64** B4
Cedar R., *river* **7** B7
Ceiba PR, *3698* **136** F4
Celina OH, *10303* **104** C1
Centerville IA, *5924* **64** D3
Central City KY, *5893* **68** C3
Central City NE, *2998* **88** C4
Central Falls RI, *18928* **112** B3
Centralia IL, *14136* **60** E3
Centralia WA, *14742* **128** C2
Central Lowland, *plain* **7** C7
Central Val., *valley* **6** C2
Centreville MD, *1970* **75** B6
Chadron NE, *5634* **88** A1
Chalan Kanoa MP, *3108* **137** C4
Chama NM, *1199* **96** A3
Chamberlain SD, *2338* **116** C4
Chambersburg PA, *17862* **110** D3
Champaign IL, *67518* **60** C4
Champlain, L., *lake* **7** B9
Channel Is., *islands* **6** D2
Chanute KS, *9411* **66** C5
Chapel Hill NC, *48715* **100** B5
Charles City IA, *7812* **64** A4
Charleston IL, *21039* **60** D4
Charleston SC, *96650* **114** D4
Charleston WV, *53421* **130** D2
Charlestown IN, *5993* **62** F4
Charlestown RI, *950* **112** E2
Charles Town WV, *2907* **130** C5
Charlotte NC, *540828* **100** C4
Charlotte Amalie VI, *11004* **137** D1
Charlottesville VA, *45049* **126** B5
Chattahoochee R., *river* **7** E8
Chattanooga TN, *155554* **119** C6
Cheboygan MI, *5295* **78** B4
Chehalis WA, *7057* **128** C2
Chelan WA, *3522* **128** B3
Cheney WA, *8832* **128** B5
Cheraw SC, *5524* **114** B4
Cherokee IA, *5369* **64** B1
Cherrydale VA, **136** B2
Cherry Hill NJ, *69965* **94** D2
Chesapeake VA, *199184* **127** D6
Chesapeake Bay, *bay* **7** C10
Chesapeake Beach MD, *3180* **74** C5
Chester IL, *5185* **60** E3
Chester PA, *36854* **111** D6
Chester SC, *6476* **114** B3
Chester VT, *999* **124** E3
Chesterbrook VA, **136** B2
Chestertown MD, *4746* **75** B6
Cheverly MD, *6433* **136** B4
Chevy Chase MD, *2726* **136** A2
Cheyenne WY, *53011* **134** D5
Cheyenne R., *river* **6** B5
Chicago IL, *2896016* **60** A4
Chickasha OK, *15850* **106** C4
Chico CA, *59954* **44** B2
Chicopee MA, *54653* **76** B2
Childress TX, *6778* **120** B3
Chillicothe MO, *8968* **84** B2
Chillicothe OH, *21796* **104** E3
Chillum MD, *34252* **136** A4
Chimayo NM, *2924* **96** B3
Chinle AZ, *5366* **40** B5
Chinook MT, *1386* **86** A3
Chino Valley AZ, *7835* **40** C3
Chippewa Falls WI, *12925* **132** C2
Chisholm MN, *4960* **80** C3
Choteau MT, *1781* **86** B2
Chowchilla CA, *11127* **44** D3
Christiansburg VA, *16947* **126** C3
Christiansted VI, *2637* **137** F2
Chula Vista CA, *173556* **44** F4
Ciales PR, *3082* **136** E2
Cimarron R., *river* **7** D6
Cincinnati OH, *331285* **104** E1
Circleville OH, *13485* **104** E3
Clanton AL, *7800* **36** C3
Claremont NH, *13151* **92** E2
Claremore OK, *15873* **107** B6
Clarendon VA, **136** C2
Clarinda IA, *5690* **64** D2
Clarion PA, *6185* **110** B2
Clark SD, *1285* **116** B5
Clark Fork, *river* **6** A3
Clarksburg WV, *16743* **130** C3
Clarksdale MS, *20645* **82** B2
Clarkston WA, *7337* **128** C5
Clarksville AR, *7719* **42** C2
Clarksville TN, *103455* **118** A4
Clay Center KS, *4564* **66** B4
Claymont DE, *9220* **50** A3
Clayton DE, *1273* **50** C2
Clayton NM, *2524* **96** A5
Clearfield PA, *6631* **110** B3
Clearlake CA, *13142* **44** C1
Clear Lake IA, *8161* **64** A3
Clear Lake SD, *1335* **116** B5
Clearwater FL, *108787* **52** C3
Clemson SC, *11939* **114** B1
Cleveland MS, *13841* **82** B2
Cleveland OH, *478403* **104** B4
Cleveland TN, *37192* **119** C6
Cleveland Heights OH, *49958* **104** B4
Clifton NJ, *78672* **94** B4
Clinton CT, *3516* **48** C4
Clinton IA, *27772* **64** C5
Clinton MD, *26064* **74** C4
Clinton MA, *7884* **76** B4
Clinton MO, *9311* **84** C2
Clinton NC, *8600* **101** C6
Clinton OK, *8833* **106** B3
Clinton SC, *8091* **114** B2
Clinton TN, *9409* **119** B7
Cloquet MN, *11201* **80** C4
Clovis CA, *68468* **44** D3
Clovis NM, *32667* **96** C5
Coamo PR, *12356* **136** F3
Coast Ranges, *mountains* **6** C2
Cod, C., *cape* **7** B10
Cody WY, *8835* **134** A2
Coeur d'Alene ID, *34514* **58** B2
Coffeyville KS, *11021* **66** D5
Colby KS, *5450* **66** B1
Colchester CT, *3200* **48** B4
Colebrook NH, *1400* **92** B3
College AK, *11402* **38** B3
College Park MD, *24657* **136** A4
Collinsville IL, *24707* **60** E3
Colmar Manor MD, *1257* **136** B4
Colorado Plat., *plateau* **6** D4
Colorado R., *river* **6** D3
Colorado R., *river* **7** E6
Colorado Springs CO, *360890* **46** C4
Colstrip MT, *2346* **86** C4
Columbia MD, *88254* **74** B4
Columbia MS, *6603* **82** E3
Columbia MO, *84531* **84** B3
Columbia SC, *116278* **114** C3
Columbia TN, *33055* **118** B4
Columbia Plat., *plateau* **6** A3
Columbia R., *river* **6** A2
Columbus GA, *186291* **54** D1
Columbus IN, *39059* **62** D4
Columbus MS, *25944* **82** C5
Columbus NE, *20971* **88** C4
Columbus OH, *711470* **104** D3
Colville WA, *4988* **128** B5
Conception, Pt., *cape* **6** D2
Concord CA, *121780* **44** C2
Concord MA, *3500* **76** B4
Concord NH, *40687* **92** E3
Concord NC, *55977* **100** B4
Concordia KS, *5714* **66** B3
Conneaut OH, *12485* **104** A5
Connecticut R., *river* **7** B10
Connellsville PA, *9146* **110** D2
Connersville IN, *15411* **62** D4
Conrad MT, *2753* **86** B2
Conroe TX, *36811* **121** D6
Conway AR, *43167* **42** C3
Conway NH, *1692* **92** D4
Conway SC, *11788* **114** C5
Cookeville TN, *23923* **118** B5
Coon Rapids MN, *61607* **80** E3
Cooperstown ND, *1053* **102** C4
Coos Bay OR, *15374* **108** C1
Copper Harbor MI, *50* **78** A1
Coquille OR, *4184* **108** C1
Coral Gables FL, *42249* **52** E5
Coral Hills MD, *10720* **136** C4
Coral Springs FL, *117549* **52** E5
Corbin KY, *7742* **69** D6
Cordele GA, *11608* **54** D3
Corinth MS, *14054* **82** A4
Corning CA, *6741* **44** B2
Corning NY, *10842* **98** D3
Corpus Christi TX, *277454* **120** E5
Corry PA, *6834* **110** A2
Cortez CO, *7977* **46** D1
Cortland NY, *18740* **98** D4
Corvallis OR, *49322* **108** B1
Coshocton OH, *11682* **104** D4
Cottage City MD, *1136* **136** B4
Cottage Grove OR, *8445* **108** C1
Cottonwood AZ, *9179* **40** C3
Council Bluffs IA, *58268* **64** C1
Covington GA, *11547* **54** B2
Covington KY, *43370* **68** A5
Covington TN, *8463* **118** B1
Covington VA, *6303* **126** C4
Cozad NE, *4163* **88** C3
Craig CO, *9189* **46** A2
Cranston RI, *79269* **112** B3
Crawfordsville IN, *15243* **62** C3
Crescent City CA, *4006* **44** A1
Creston IA, *7597* **64** C2
Crestview FL, *14766* **52** E2
Crete NE, *6028* **88** C5
Crisfield MD, *2723* **75** D6
Crookston MN, *8192* **80** B1
Crosby ND, *1089* **102** A1
Crossett AR, *6097* **42** E3
Crossville TN, *8981* **119** B6
Crowley LA, *14225* **70** D2
Crown Point IN, *19806* **62** A2
Cruz Bay VI, *2743* **137** D2
Crystal City VA, **136** C3
Crystal Springs MS, *5873* **82** D3
Cuero TX, *6571* **120** E5
Culebra PR, *1418* **136** F5
Cullman AL, *13995* **36** B3
Culpeper VA, *9664* **126** B5
Cumberland MD, *21518* **74** A2
Cumberland Plat., *plateau* **7** D8
Cumberland R., *river* **7** D7
Cushing OK, *8371* **106** B5
Custer SD, *1860* **116** C1
Cut Bank MT, *3105* **86** A2
Cuyahoga Falls OH, *49374* **104** B4
Cynthiana KY, *6258* **68** B5

D

Dahlonega GA, *3638* **54** A2
Dale City VA, *55971* **127** B6
Dalhart TX, *7237* **120** A3
Dallas OR, *12459* **108** B1
Dallas TX, *1188580* **120** C5
Dalton GA, *27912* **54** A1
Dalton MA, *4100* **76** B1
Damascus MD, *11430* **74** B4
Danbury CT, *74848* **48** C1
Danielson CT, *4265* **48** B5
Danville IL, *33904* **60** C4
Danville KY, *15477* **68** C5
Danville VA, *48411* **126** D4
Darien CT, *19607* **48** D1
Darlington SC, *6720* **114** B4
Davenport IA, *98359* **64** C5
Davis CA, *60308* **44** C2
Dawson GA, *5058* **54** D2
Dayton OH, *166179* **104** D2
Dayton TN, *6180* **119** B6
Daytona Beach FL, *64112* **52** B4
Deadwood SD, *1380* **116** B1
Deale MD, *4796* **74** C5
Dearborn MI, *97775* **78** F5
Death Val., *valley* **6** D2
Decatur AL, *53929* **36** A3
Decatur GA, *18147* **54** B2
Decatur IL, *81860* **60** D3
Decorah IA, *8172* **64** A4
Dededo GU, *3181* **137** E4
Deep River CT, *2470* **48** C4
Deer Lodge MT, *3421* **86** C2
Defiance OH, *16465* **104** B1
De Kalb IL, *39018* **60** A4
Delano CA, *38824* **44** D3
Delaware OH, *25243* **104** D3
Delaware Bay, *bay* **7** C10
Delaware City DE, *1453* **50** B2
Delaware R., *river* **7** B9
Dell Rapids SD, *2980* **116** C5
Delmar DE, *1407* **50** F2
Delmar MD, *1859* **75** C6
Delray Beach FL, *60020* **52** E5
Del Rio TX, *33867* **120** E3
Delta CO, *6400* **46** C1
Delta UT, *3209* **122** D2
Deltona FL, *69543* **52** B4
Deming NM, *14116* **96** E2
Demopolis AL, *7540* **36** D2
Denison IA, *7339* **64** B2
Denmark SC, *3328* **114** C3
Denton MD, *2960* **75** B6
Denton TX, *80537* **120** C5
Denver CO, *554636* **46** B3
De Pere WI, *20559* **132** D4
De Queen AR, *5765* **42** D1
Derby KS, *17807* **66** C4
DeRidder LA, *9808* **70** C1
Derry NH, *22661* **92** F3
De Smet SD, *1164* **116** B5
Des Moines IA, *198682* **64** C3
Des Moines R., *river* **7** B6
De Soto MO, *6375* **84** C4
Detroit MI, *951270* **78** F5
Detroit Lakes MN, *7348* **80** C2
Devils Lake ND, *7222* **102** B4
Dewey Beach DE, *301* **50** E4
Dexter MO, *7356* **84** D5
Dickinson ND, *16010* **102** C1
Dickson TN, *12244* **118** B4
Dillon MT, *3752* **86** C2
Dillon SC, *6316* **114** B4
District Heights MD, *5958* **136** C5
Dodge City KS, *25176* **66** C2
Dodge Park MD, **136** B5
Dothan AL, *57737* **36** E4
Douglas AZ, *14312* **40** F5
Douglas GA, *10639* **54** E3
Douglas WY, *5288* **134** C4
Dover DE, *32135* **50** C3
Dover NH, *26884* **92** E4
Dover NJ, *18188* **94** B3
Dover-Foxcroft ME, *2592* **72** D3
Doylestown PA, *8227* **111** C6
Dublin GA, *15857* **54** D3
DuBois PA, *8123* **110** B2
Dubois WY, *962* **134** B2
Dubuque IA, *57686* **64** B5
Duluth MN, *86918* **80** C4
Dumas AR, *5238* **42** E4
Duncan OK, *22505* **106** C4
Dundalk MD, *62306* **74** B5
Dunkirk NY, *13131* **98** D1
Dunn NC, *9196* **100** B5
Dunn Loring VA, *7861* **136** B1
Durango CO, *13922* **46** D1
Durant OK, *13549* **106** D5
Durham NH, *9024* **92** E4
Durham NC, *187035* **100** B5
Dyersburg TN, *17452* **118** B2

E

Eagle WI, *1707* **132** E4
Eagle Pass TX, *22413* **120** E3
Easley SC, *17754* **114** B1
East Falls Church VA, **136** B2
East Grand Forks MN, *7501* **80** B1
East Greenwich RI, *4300* **112** C3
Easthampton MA, *15994* **76** B2
East Hartford CT, *49575* **48** B3
East Haven CT, *28189* **48** C3
East Lansing MI, *46525* **78** E4
East Liverpool OH, *13089* **104** C5
Eastman GA, *5440* **54** D3
Easton MD, *11708* **75** C6
Easton PA, *26263* **111** C6
Eastport ME, *1640* **72** D5
East Providence RI, *48688* **112** B3
East St. Louis IL, *31542* **60** E2
Eatonton GA, *6764* **54** C3
Eau Claire WI, *61704* **132** C2
Eden NC, *15908* **100** A4
Edenton NC, *5394* **101** B7
Edgartown MA, *1100* **77** D6
Edinboro PA, *6950* **110** A1
Edison NJ, *97687* **94** C3
Edmond OK, *68315* **106** B4
Edmonds WA, *39515* **128** B2
Edmonston MD, *959* **136** B4
Edwards Plat., *plateau* **6** E5
Effingham IL, *12384* **60** D4
Elbert, Mt., *peak* **6** C4
Elberton GA, *4743* **54** B3
El Cajon CA, *94869* **44** F4
El Centro CA, *37835* **44** F5
El Dorado AR, *21530* **42** E3
El Dorado KS, *12057* **66** C4
Elgin IL, *94487* **60** A4
Elizabeth NJ, *120568* **94** B4
Elizabeth City NC, *17188* **101** A7
Elizabethton TN, *13372* **119** A9
Elizabethtown KY, *22542* **68** C4
Elk City OK, *10510* **106** C3
Elkhart IN, *51874* **62** A4
Elkins WV, *7032* **130** C3
Elko NV, *16708* **90** B4
Elk Point SD, *1714* **116** D5
Elk River MN, *16447* **80** D3
Elkton MD, *11893* **75** A6
Ellendale DE, *327* **50** E3
Ellendale ND, *1559* **102** D4
Ellensburg WA, *15414* **128** C3
Ellsworth ME, *6456* **72** D4
Elmira NY, *30940* **98** D3
Eloy AZ, *10375* **40** E3
El Paso TX, *563662* **120** C1
El Reno OK, *16212* **106** B4
Elsmere DE, *5800* **50** A2
Ely MN, *3724* **80** B4
Ely NV, *4041* **90** C4
Elyria OH, *55953* **104** B4
Emmaus PA, *11313* **111** C6
Empire NV, *499* **90** B2
Emporia KS, *26760* **66** C4
Emporia VA, *5665* **126** D5
Encinitas CA, *58014* **44** F4
Enfield CT, *8125* **48** A3
Englewood CO, *31727* **46** B3
Enid OK, *47045* **106** B4
Enterprise AL, *21178* **36** E4
Enterprise OR, *1895* **108** A5
Enterprise UT, *1285* **122** F1
Ephraim UT, *4505* **122** D3
Ephrata PA, *13213* **110** C5
Ephrata WA, *6808* **128** C4
Erie PA, *103717* **110** A1
Erie, L., *lake* **7** B8
Erwin TN, *5610* **119** B9
Escalante UT, *818* **122** F3
Escanaba MI, *13140* **78** B2
Escondido CA, *133559* **44** F4
Espanola NM, *9688* **96** B3
Essex MD, *39078* **74** B5
Essex Junction VT, *8591* **124** B2
Estes Park CO, *5413* **46** A3
Estherville IA, *6656* **64** A2
Euclid OH, *52717* **104** B4
Eufaula AL, *13908* **36** D5
Eugene OR, *137893* **108** B1
Eunice LA, *11499* **70** C2
Eunice NM, *2562* **96** E5
Eureka CA, *26128* **44** B1
Eureka NV, *550* **90** C4
Evanston IL, *74239* **60** A4
Evanston WY, *11507* **134** D1
Evansville IN, *121582* **62** F2
Everett WA, *91488* **128** B2
'Ewa Beach HI, *14650* **56** D2
Exeter NH, *9759* **92** F4

Figures after entries indicate population, page number, and grid reference.

F

Fagasa AS, *900* **137** C1
Fagatogo AS, *2096* **137** C2
Fairbanks AK, *30224* **38** B3
Fairbury NE, *4262* **88** D4
Fairfax VA, *21498* **127** B6
Fairfield CT, *57340* **48** D2
Fairfield IA, *9509* **64** C4
Fairfield OH, *42097* **104** E1
Fair Haven VT, *2435* **124** D2
Fairmont MN, *10889* **80** F2
Fairmont WV, *19097* **130** B3
Fairmount Heights MD, *1508* **136** B4
Fajardo PR, *33286* **136** E4
Faleniu AS, *2056* **137** C1
Fallon NV, *7536* **90** C2
Fall River MA, *91938* **76** C5
Falls Church VA, *10377* **136** B1
Falls City NE, *4671* **88** D5
Falmouth MA, *4115* **77** D6
Fargo ND, *90599* **102** C5
Faribault MN, *20818* **80** E3
Farmington ME, *4098* **72** D2
Farmington MO, *13924* **84** D4
Farmington NH, *3468* **92** E4
Farmington NM, *37844* **96** A1
Farmington UT, *12081* **122** B3
Farmville VA, *6845* **126** C5
Fayetteville AR, *58047* **42** B1
Fayetteville GA, *11148* **54** C2
Fayetteville NC, *121015* **100** C5
Fayetteville TN, *6994* **118** C4
Fayetteville WV, *2754* **130** D2
Fear, C., *cape* **7** D9
Federalsburg MD, *2620* **75** C6
Federal Way WA, *83259* **128** C2
Felton DE, *784* **50** D2
Fergus Falls MN, *13471* **80** D1
Fernandina Beach FL, *10549* **52** A4
Ferndale WA, *8758* **128** A2
Fernley NV, *8543* **90** C2
Festus MO, *9660* **84** C4
Fillmore UT, *2253* **122** D2
Findlay OH, *38967* **104** C2
Fitchburg MA, *39102* **76** A4
Fitzgerald GA, *8758* **54** D3
Flagstaff AZ, *52894* **40** C3
Flandreau SD, *2376* **116** C5
Flattery, C., *cape* **6** A2
Flint MI, *124943* **78** E4
Flint Hills, *hills* **7** D6
Flint R., *river* **7** E8
Florence AL, *36264* **36** A2
Florence AZ, *17054* **40** E4
Florence KY, *23551* **68** A5
Florence OR, *7263* **108** C1
Florence SC, *30248* **114** B4
Florida Keys, *islands* **7** F9
Florida, Straits of, *strait* **7** F9
Florissant MO, *50497* **84** C4
Fond du Lac WI, *42203* **132** D4
Forest MS, *5987* **82** D3
Forest Heights MD, *2585* **136** D3
Forestville MD, *12707* **136** C5
Forks WA, *3120* **128** B1
Forrest City AR, *14774* **42** C4
Forsyth MT, *1944* **86** C4
Fort Benton MT, *1594* **86** B3
Fort Bragg CA, *7026* **44** B1
Fort Collins CO, *118652* **46** A3
Fort Dodge IA, *25136* **64** B2
Fort Kent ME, *1978* **72** A4
Fort Lauderdale FL, *152397* **52** E5
Fort Madison IA, *10715* **64** D5
Fort Morgan CO, *11034* **46** A4
Fort Myers FL, *48208* **52** D4
Fort Payne AL, *12938* **36** A4
Fort Peck L., *lake* **6** A4
Fort Pierce FL, *37516* **52** D5
Fort Pierre SD, *1991* **116** B3
Fort Scott KS, *8297* **66** C5
Fort Smith AR, *80268* **42** C1
Fort Stockton TX, *7846* **120** D2
Fortuna CA, *10497* **44** B1
Fort Valley GA, *8005* **54** D2
Fort Walton Beach FL, *19973* **52** E2
Fort Wayne IN, *205727* **62** B4
Fort Worth TX, *534694* **120** C5
Fountain CO, *15197* **46** C4
Foxboro MA, *5509* **76** C5
Framingham MA, *66910* **76** B4
Franconia VA, *31907* **136** D2
Frankford DE, *714* **50** F4
Frankfort IN, *16662* **62** C3
Frankfort KY, *27741* **68** B5
Franklin KY, *7996* **68** D3
Franklin LA, *8354* **70** D3
Franklin MA, *29560* **76** B4
Franklin NH, *8405* **92** E3
Franklin PA, *7212* **110** B1
Franklin TN, *41842* **118** B4
Franklin VA, *8346* **127** D6
Franklin WV, *797* **130** C4
Frederica DE, *648* **50** D3
Frederick MD, *52767* **74** A4
Frederick OK, *4637* **106** D3
Fredericksburg VA, *19279* **126** B5
Frederiksted VI, *732* **137** F1
Fredonia NY, *10706* **98** D1
Freehold NJ, *10976* **94** C4
Freeport IL, *26443* **60** A3
Freeport TX, *12708* **121** E6
Fremont NE, *25174* **88** C5
Fremont OH, *17375* **104** B3
Fresno CA, *427652* **44** D3
Front Range, *mountains* **6** C4
Front Royal VA, *13589* **126** B5
Frostburg MD, *7873* **74** A1
Fulton NY, *11855* **98** C4

G

Gabbs NV, *318* **90** C3
Gadsden AL, *38978* **36** B4
Gaffney SC, *12968* **114** A2
Gahanna OH, *32636* **104** D3
Gainesville FL, *95447* **52** B3
Gainesville GA, *25578* **54** B2
Gaithersburg MD, *52613* **74** B4
Galax VA, *6837* **126** D3
Galesburg IL, *33706* **60** B2
Galion OH, *11341* **104** C3
Gallatin TN, *23230* **118** A5
Gallup NM, *20209* **96** B1
Galveston TX, *57247* **121** D6
Galveston Bay, *bay* **7** E6
Garapan MP, *3588* **137** C4
Garden City KS, *28451* **66** C1
Gardiner ME, *6198* **72** E2
Gardner MA, *20770* **76** A3
Gardnerville NV, *3357* **90** C1
Garrison ND, *1318* **102** B2
Gary IN, *102746* **62** A2
Gastonia NC, *66277* **100** B3
Genesee R., *river* **7** B9
Geneseo NY, *7579* **98** C2
Geneva NE, *2226* **88** C4
Geneva NY, *13617* **98** C3
Georgetown DE, *4643* **50** E3
Georgetown SC, *8950* **114** C5
Gering NE, *7751* **88** B1
Germantown TN, *37348* **118** C1
Gettysburg PA, *7490* **110** D4
Gettysburg SD, *1352* **116** B3
Gila Bend AZ, *1980* **40** E3
Gila R., *river* **6** D3
Gillette WY, *19646* **134** A4
Gilroy CA, *41464* **44** D2
Glasgow KY, *13019* **68** D4
Glasgow MT, *3253* **86** B4
Glassboro NJ, *19068* **94** E2
Glassmanor MD, *35355* **136** D3
Glenarden MD, *6318* **136** B5
Glen Burnie MD, *38922* **74** B5
Glendale AZ, *218812* **40** D3
Glendive MT, *4729* **86** B5
Glen Echo MD, *242* **136** A2
Glen Echo Heights MD, **136** A2
Glenpool OK, *8123* **106** B5
Glenrock WY, *2231* **134** C4
Glens Falls NY, *14354* **99** C6
Glenwood Springs CO, *7736* **46** B2
Globe AZ, *7486* **40** D4
Gloucester MA, *30273* **77** A6
Gold Beach OR, *1897* **108** D1
Goldfield NV, *175* **90** D3
Goldsboro NC, *39043* **101** B6
Gonzales LA, *8156* **70** D3
Gooding ID, *3384* **58** F3
Goodland KS, *4948* **66** B1
Goose Creek SC, *29208* **114** D4
Gorham NH, *1773* **92** C4
Gothenburg NE, *3619* **88** C3
Grafton ND, *4516* **102** B5
Grafton WV, *5489* **130** B3
Grambling LA, *4693* **70** A2
Grand Canyon AZ, *1460* **40** B3
Grand Canyon, *canyon* **6** D3
Grand Forks ND, *49321* **102** B5
Grand Island NE, *42940* **88** C4
Grand Junction CO, *41986* **46** B1
Grand Portage MN, *100* **80** B5
Grand Rapids MI, *197800* **78** E3
Grand Rapids MN, *7764* **80** C3
Grand R., *river* **7** B8
Grandview WA, *8377* **128** C4
Grangeville ID, *3228* **58** C2
Granite Peak, *peak* **6** B4
Grants NM, *8806* **96** B2
Grants Pass OR, *23003* **108** D1
Grass Valley CA, *10922* **44** B2
Great Barrington MA, *2459* **76** B1
Great Basin, *basin* **6** C3
Great Bend KS, *15345* **66** C3
Great Falls MT, *56690* **86** B2
Great Plains, *plain* **6** B5
Great Salt L., *lake* **6** B3
Great Salt Lake Desert, *desert* **6** C3
Greeley CO, *76930* **46** A4
Green Bay WI, *102313* **132** D4
Greeneville TN, *15198* **119** A8
Greenfield CA, *12583* **44** D2
Greenfield MA, *13716* **76** A2
Green Mts., *mountains* **7** B10
Green R., *river* **6** B4
Green R., *river* **7** C8
Green River UT, *973* **122** D4
Green River WY, *11808* **134** D2
Greensboro NC, *223891* **100** B4
Greensburg IN, *10260* **62** D4
Greensburg PA, *15889* **110** C2
Green Valley AZ, *17283* **40** F4
Greenville AL, *7228* **36** D3
Greenville MS, *41633* **82** C2
Greenville NC, *60476* **101** B7
Greenville OH, *13294* **104** D1
Greenville RI, *8626* **112** B3
Greenville SC, *56002* **114** B2
Greenwich CT, *61101* **48** D1
Greenwood IN, *36037* **62** D3
Greenwood MS, *18425* **82** C3
Greenwood SC, *22071* **114** B2
Greer SC, *16843* **114** B2
Gregory SD, *1342* **116** C4
Grenada MS, *14879* **82** B3
Gresham OR, *90205* **108** A2
Gretna LA, *17423* **70** D4
Greybull WY, *1815* **134** A3
Griffin GA, *23451* **54** C2
Grinnell IA, *9105* **64** C4
Groton CT, *10010* **48** C5
Groveton NH, *1197* **92** B3
Guadalupe CA, *5659* **44** E2
Guadalupe Peak, *peak* **6** E5
Guánica PR, *9247* **136** F2
Guayama PR, *21624* **136** F3
Guaynabo PR, *78806* **136** E3
Guernsey WY, *1147* **134** C5
Gulf Coastal Plain, *plain* **7** E6
Gulfport MS, *71127* **82** F4
Gunnison CO, *5409* **46** C2
Guntersville AL, *7395* **36** B3
Guthrie OK, *9925* **106** B4
Guymon OK, *10472* **106** A2

H

Hackettstown NJ, *10403* **94** B3
Hagåtña (Agana) GU, *1122* **137** F4
Hagerstown MD, *36687* **74** A3
Hailey ID, *6200* **58** E3
Hamden CT, *56913* **48** C3
Hamilton AL, *6786* **36** B2
Hamilton MT, *3705* **86** C1
Hamilton OH, *60690* **104** E1
Hammond IN, *83048* **62** A2
Hammond LA, *17639* **70** D4
Hammonton NJ, *12604* **94** E3
Hampstead MD, *5060* **74** A4
Hampton NH, *9126* **92** F4
Hampton VA, *146437* **127** C6
Hanamaulu HI, *3272* **56** C5
Hancock MD, *1725* **74** A3
Hanford CA, *41686* **44** D3
Hanna WY, *873* **134** C4
Hannibal MO, *17757* **84** B4
Hanover NH, *8162* **92** D2
Hanover PA, *14535* **110** D4
Hardin MT, *3384* **86** C4
Harlan IA, *5282* **64** C2
Harlingen TX, *57564* **120** F5
Harpers Ferry WV, *307* **130** B5
Harrington DE, *3174* **50** D2
Harrisburg PA, *48950* **110** C4
Harrison AR, *12152* **42** B2
Harrisonburg VA, *40468* **126** B4
Harrisville RI, *1561* **112** A2
Harrisville WV, *1842* **130** C2
Hartford CT, *121578* **48** B3
Hartsville SC, *7556* **114** B4
Harvey ND, *1989* **102** B3
Hastings NE, *24064* **88** C4
Hatteras, C., *cape* **7** D10
Hattiesburg MS, *44779* **82** E4
Havelock NC, *22442* **101** C7
Haverhill MA, *58969* **76** A5
Havre MT, *9621* **86** A3
Havre de Grace MD, *11331* **75** A6
Hawai'i, *island* **6** F4
Hawthorne NV, *3311* **90** D2
Hays KS, *20013* **66** B2
Haysville KS, *8502* **66** C4
Hayward WI, *2129* **132** B2
Hazard KY, *4806* **69** C6
Hazen ND, *2457* **102** C2
Hazleton PA, *23329* **110** B5
Healdsburg CA, *10722* **44** C1
Heber City UT, *7291* **122** C3
Heber Springs AR, *6432* **42** C3
Helena AR, *6323* **42** D4
Helena MT, *25780* **86** C2
Helper UT, *2025* **122** C3
Hempstead NY, *56554* **98** B2
Henderson KY, *27373* **68** C2
Henderson NV, *175381* **90** F4
Henderson NC, *16095* **101** A6
Hendersonville NC, *10420* **100** B2
Hendersonville TN, *40620* **118** A4
Henryetta OK, *6096* **106** C5
Heppner OR, *1395* **108** A3
Hereford TX, *14597* **120** B3
Hermantown MN, *7448* **80** C4
Hermiston OR, *13154* **108** A4
Hershey PA, *12771* **110** C4
Hettinger ND, *1307* **102** D2
Hialeah FL, *226419* **52** E5
Hiawatha KS, *3417* **66** A5
Hibbing MN, *17071* **80** C3
Hickory NC, *37222* **100** B3
High Point NC, *85839* **100** B4
Hillcrest Heights MD, *16359* **136** C4
Hillsboro ND, *1563* **102** C5
Hillsboro OR, *70186* **108** A2
Hillsborough NH, *1842* **92** E2
Hilo HI, *40759* **56** E5
Hilton Head Island SC, *33862* **114** E3
Hinesville GA, *30392* **54** D5
Hinton WV, *2880* **130** E2
Hobbs NM, *28657* **96** E5
Hodgenville KY, *2874* **68** C4
Holbrook AZ, *4917* **40** C4
Holdrege NE, *5636* **88** C3
Holland MI, *35048* **78** E3
Hollister CA, *34413* **44** D2
Holly Springs MS, *7957* **82** A4
Hollywood FL, *139357* **52** E5
Holualoa HI, *6107* **56** E4
Holyoke MA, *39838* **76** B2
Homer AK, *3946* **38** C3
Homestead FL, *31909* **52** F5
Honesdale PA, *4874* **111** B6
Honolulu HI, *371657* **56** D2
Hood, Mt., *peak* **6** A2
Hood River OR, *5831* **108** A2
Hoover AL, *62742* **36** C3
Hopatcong NJ, *15888* **94** B3
Hope AR, *10616* **42** E2
Hope Valley RI, *1649* **112** D2
Hopewell VA, *22354* **127** C6
Hopkinsville KY, *30089* **68** D3
Hoquiam WA, *9097* **128** C1
Hornell NY, *9019* **98** D3
Hot Springs AR, *35750* **42** D2
Hot Springs SD, *4129* **116** C1
Houghton MI, *7010* **78** A1
Houlton ME, *5270* **72** B4
Houma LA, *32393* **70** D4
Houston TX, *1953631* **121** D6
Hudson NY, *7524* **99** D6
Hudson WI, *8775* **132** C1
Hudson R., *river* **7** B9
Hugo OK, *5536* **107** D6
Hugoton KS, *3708* **66** D1
Humacao PR, *20682* **136** F4
Humboldt TN, *9467* **118** B2
Humphreys Peak, *peak* **6** D3
Huntingdon PA, *6918* **110** C3
Huntington IN, *17450* **62** B4
Huntington VA, *8325* **136** D3
Huntington WV, *51475* **130** D1
Huntsville AL, *158216* **36** A3
Huntsville TX, *35078* **120** D5
Huron SD, *11893* **116** B4
Huron, L., *lake* **7** B8
Hutchinson KS, *40787* **66** C3
Hyannis MA, *14100* **77** C6
Hyattsville MD, *14733* **136** A4

I

Idabel OK, *6952* **107** D6
Idaho Falls ID, *50730* **58** E4
Idylwood VA, *16005* **136** B1
Illinois R., *river* **7** C7
Immokalee FL, *19763* **52** E4
Inarajan GU, *686* **137** F4
Independence KS, *9846* **66** D5
Independence MO, *113288* **84** B2
Indiana PA, *14895* **110** C2
Indianapolis IN, *791926* **62** D3
Indian Head MD, *3422* **74** C4
Indianola IA, *12998* **64** C3
Indianola MS, *12066* **82** C2
Indio CA, *49116* **44** F4
International Falls MN, *6703* **80** B3
Inverness FL, *6789* **52** C3
Iola KS, *6302* **66** C5
Ionia MI, *10569* **78** E3
Iowa City IA, *62220* **64** C4
Iowa Falls IA, *5193* **64** B3
Iowa R., *river* **7** B6
Irmo SC, *11039* **114** B3
Irondequoit NY, *52354* **98** C3
Iron Mountain MI, *8154* **78** B1
Ironton OH, *11211* **104** F3
Ironwood MI, *6293* **78** A4
Irvine CA, *143072* **44** F4
Isabela PR, *12818* **136** E1
Ishpeming MI, *6686* **78** B2
Island Pond VT, *849* **124** A4
Isle Royale, *island* **7** A7
Ithaca NY, *29287* **98** D4

J

Jackpot NV, *1100* **90** A4
Jackson AL, *5419* **36** E2
Jackson MI, *36316* **78** F4
Jackson MS, *184256* **82** D3
Jackson MO, *11947* **84** D5
Jackson TN, *59643* **118** B2
Jackson WY, *8647* **134** B1
Jacksonville AL, *8404* **36** B4
Jacksonville FL, *735617* **52** A4
Jacksonville IL, *18940* **60** D2
Jacksonville NC, *66715* **101** C6
Jaffrey NH, *2802* **92** F2

Jal NM, *1996* 96 E5
James R., *river* 7 B6
James R., *river* 7 C9
Jamestown NY, *31730* 98 D1
Jamestown ND, *15527* 102 C4
Jamestown RI, *5622* 112 D3
Jamestown VA, *90* 127 C6
Janesville WI, *59498* 132 F4
Jasper AL, *14052* 36 B2
Jasper IN, *12100* 62 F2
Jasper TX, *8247* 121 D6
Jefferson City MO, *39636* 84 C3
Jeffersontown KY, *26633* 68 B4
Jerome ID, *7780* 58 F3
Jersey City NJ, *240055* 94 B4
Jesup GA, *9279* 54 E4
Jewett City (Griswold) CT, *3053* 48 B5
John Day OR, *1821* 108 B4
Johnson City TN, *55469* 119 A9
Johnstown PA, *23906* 110 C2
Joliet IL, *106221* 60 B4
Jonesboro AR, *55515* 42 B4
Joplin MO, *45504* 84 D1
Jordan Valley OR, *239* 108 C5
Juan de Fuca, Str. of, *strait* 6 A2
Julesburg CO, *1467* 46 A5
Junction City KS, *18886* 66 B4
Juneau AK, *30711* 38 C5
Jupiter FL, *39328* 52 D5

K

Kaho'olawe, *island* 6 F3
Kahului HI, *20146* 56 E2
Kailua HI, *36513* 56 D3
Kailua-Kona HI, *9870* 56 E4
Kalaheo HI, *3913* 56 C5
Kalamazoo MI, *77145* 78 F3
Kalaoa HI, *6794* 56 E4
Kalispell MT, *14223* 86 B1
Kanab UT, *3564* 122 F2
Kāne'ohe HI, *34970* 56 D3
Kankakee IL, *27491* 60 B4
Kannapolis NC, *36910* 100 B4
Kansas City KS, *146866* 66 B5
Kansas City MO, *441545* 84 B1
Kansas R., *river* 7 C6
Kapaa HI, *9472* 56 C5
Kaskaskia R., *river* 7 C7
Kaua'i, *island* 6 F3
Kaunakakai HI, *2726* 56 E1
Kayenta AZ, *4922* 40 A4
Kearney NE, *27431* 88 C3
Keene NH, *22563* 92 F2
Kekaha HI, *3175* 56 C4
Kellogg ID, *2395* 58 B2
Kelso WA, *11895* 128 D2
Kemmerer WY, *2651* 134 D1
Kenai AK, *6942* 38 C3
Kenai Pen., *peninsula* 6 F2
Kendallville IN, *9616* 62 A4
Kenmare ND, *1081* 102 A2
Kennebunkport ME, *1376* 72 F2
Kenner LA, *70517* 70 D4
Kennett MO, *11260* 84 E5
Kennewick WA, *54693* 128 C4
Kenosha WI, *90352* 132 F5
Kent WA, *79524* 128 B2
Kentland MD, 136 B5
Kentucky R., *river* 7 C8
Keokuk IA, *11427* 64 D5
Kerrville TX, *20425* 120 D4
Ketchikan AK, *7922* 38 D5
Ketchum ID, *3003* 58 E3
Kettering OH, *57502* 104 D2
Kewanee IL, *12944* 60 B3
Key Largo FL, *11886* 52 F5
Keyser WV, *5303* 130 B4
Key West FL, *25478* 52 F4
Kihei HI, *16749* 56 F2
Killeen TX, *86911* 120 D5
Kimball NE, *2559* 88 C1
King City CA, *11094* 44 D2
Kingman AZ, *20069* 40 C2
Kingsburg CA, *9199* 44 D3
Kingsland GA, *10506* 54 E5
Kings Peak, *peak* 6 C4
Kingsport TN, *44905* 119 A8
Kingston NY, *23456* 99 D6
Kingston RI, *5446* 112 D3
Kingstree SC, *3496* 114 C4
Kingsville TX, *25575* 120 E5
Kinston NC, *23688* 101 B6
Kirkland WA, *45054* 128 B2
Kirksville MO, *16988* 84 A3
Kissimmee FL, *47814* 52 C4
Kittanning PA, *4787* 110 C2
Kittery ME, *4884* 72 F1
Klamath Falls OR, *19462* 108 D2
Knoxville IA, *7731* 64 C3
Knoxville TN, *173890* 119 B7
Kodiak AK, *6334* 38 C3
Kodiak I., *island* 6 F1
Kokomo IN, *46113* 62 C3
Kosciusko MS, *7372* 82 C3
Kotzebue AK, *3082* 38 B2

L

Lackawanna NY, *19064* 98 C2
Laconia NH, *16411* 92 E3
La Crosse WI, *51818* 132 D2
La Fayette GA, *6702* 54 A1
Lafayette IN, *56397* 62 C3
Lafayette LA, *110257* 70 D2
La Follette TN, *7926* 119 A7
La Grande OR, *12327* 108 A4
LaGrange GA, *25998* 54 C1
La Grange KY, *5676* 68 B4
Lahaina HI, *9118* 56 E2
La Junta CO, *7568* 46 C4
Lake Barcroft VA, *8906* 136 C1
Lake Charles LA, *71757* 70 D1
Lake City FL, *9980* 52 A3
Lake City SC, *6478* 114 C4
Lake Havasu City AZ, *41938* 40 C1
Lakeland FL, *78452* 52 C3
Lake Providence LA, *5104* 70 A3
Lakeview OR, *2474* 108 D3
Lakewood CO, *144126* 46 B3
Lakewood NJ, *36065* 94 D4
Lamar CO, *8869* 46 C5
Lāna'i, *island* 6 F3
Lancaster CA, *118718* 44 E4
Lancaster NH, *1695* 92 C3
Lancaster OH, *35335* 104 D3
Lancaster PA, *56348* 110 D5
Lancaster SC, *8177* 114 B3
Lander WY, *6867* 134 C2
Landover MD, *22900* 136 B5
Landover Hills MD, *1534* 136 B5
Langdon ND, *2101* 102 A4
Langley VA, *3500* 136 B1
Langley Park MD, *16214* 136 A4
Lansing MI, *119128* 78 E4
Lapeer MI, *9072* 78 E5
Laplace LA, *27684* 70 D4
La Plata MD, *6551* 74 C4
Laramie WY, *27204* 134 D4
Laredo TX, *176576* 120 E4
Lares PR, *7042* 136 F2
Largo MD, *8408* 74 B5
Larimore ND, *1433* 102 B5
Larned KS, *4236* 66 C3
Las Animas CO, *2758* 46 C5
Las Cruces NM, *74267* 96 E2
Las Vegas NV, *478434* 90 F4
Las Vegas NM, *14565* 96 B4
Laughlin NV, *7076* 90 F5
Laurel DE, *3668* 50 F2
Laurel MD, *19960* 74 B4
Laurel MS, *18393* 82 E4
Laurel MT, *6255* 86 C3
Laurens SC, *9916* 114 B2
Laurinburg NC, *15874* 100 C5
Lawrence IN, *38915* 62 D4
Lawrence KS, *80098* 66 B5
Lawrence MA, *72043* 76 A5
Lawrenceburg TN, *10796* 118 C4
Lawton OK, *92757* 106 C4
Layton UT, *58474* 122 B3
Lead SD, *3027* 116 B1
Leadville CO, *2821* 46 B3
Leavenworth IN, *353* 62 F3
Leavenworth KS, *35420* 66 B5
Lebanon IN, *14222* 62 C3
Lebanon KY, *5718* 68 C4
Lebanon MO, *12155* 84 D3
Lebanon NH, *12568* 92 D2
Lebanon OR, *12950* 108 B2
Lebanon PA, *24461* 110 C5
Lebanon TN, *20235* 118 B5
Leesburg VA, *28311* 126 A5
Lees Summit MO, *70700* 84 C2
Leesville LA, *6753* 70 C1
Lehi UT, *19028* 122 C3
Leitchfield KY, *6139* 68 C4
Leland MS, *5502* 82 C2
Le Mars IA, *9237* 64 B1
Lemmon SD, *1398* 116 A2
Lemoore CA, *19712* 44 D3
Lennox SD, *2037* 116 C5
Lenoir NC, *16793* 100 B3
Lenoir City TN, *6819* 119 B7
Leominster MA, *41303* 76 A4
Leonardtown MD, *1896* 74 D5
Leone AS, *3568* 137 C1
Lewes DE, *2932* 50 E4
Lewisburg PA, *5620* 110 B4
Lewisburg TN, *10413* 118 C4
Lewisburg WV, *3624* 130 D3
Lewisdale MD, 136 A4
Lewiston ID, *30904* 58 C1
Lewiston ME, *35690* 72 E2
Lewistown MT, *5813* 86 B3
Lewistown PA, *8998* 110 C4
Lexington KY, *260512* 68 B5
Lexington MA, *30355* 76 B5
Lexington NE, *10011* 88 C3
Lexington SC, *9793* 114 C3
Lexington TN, *7393* 118 B3
Lexington VA, *6867* 126 C4
Lexington Park MD, *11021* 74 D5
Libby MT, *2626* 86 A1
Liberal KS, *19666* 66 D1
Liberty MO, *26232* 84 B2
Lihue HI, *5674* 56 C5
Lima OH, *40081* 104 C2
Limon CO, *2071* 46 B4
Lincoln ME, *2933* 72 C4
Lincoln NE, *225581* 88 C5
Lincoln NH, *750* 92 C3
Lincoln City IN, *150* 62 F2
Lincoln City OR, *7437* 108 B1
Lincolnia VA, *15788* 136 C2
Lincolnton NC, *9965* 100 B3
Lindenwold NJ, *17414* 94 D2
Linton ND, *1321* 102 D3
Lisbon NH, *1070* 92 C3
Lisbon ND, *2292* 102 C5
Litchfield CT, *1328* 48 B2
Litchfield IL, *6815* 60 D3
Little Falls MN, *7719* 80 D2
Littlefield TX, *6507* 120 B3
Little Missouri R., *river* 6 B5
Little Rock AR, *183133* 42 D3
Littleton NH, *4431* 92 C3
Livingston MT, *6851* 86 C3
Livonia MI, *100545* 78 F5
Llano Estacado, *plain* 6 D5
Loa UT, *525* 122 E3
Lock Haven PA, *9149* 110 B4
Lockport NY, *22279* 98 C2
Lodi CA, *56999* 44 C2
Logan UT, *42670* 122 A3
Logan WV, *1630* 130 D1
Logansport IN, *19684* 62 B3
Lolo MT, *3388* 86 B1
Lompoc CA, *41103* 44 E2
London KY, *5692* 69 D6
Long Beach CA, *461522* 44 F3
Long Branch NJ, *31340* 94 C4
Long I., *island* 7 B10
Long Island Sound, *bay* 7 B10
Longmont CO, *71093* 46 B3
Longview TX, *73344* 121 C6
Longview WA, *34660* 128 D2
Lorain OH, *68652* 104 B4
Lordsburg NM, *3379* 96 E1
Los Alamos NM, *11909* 96 B3
Los Angeles CA, *3694820* 44 E3
Los Banos CA, *25869* 44 D2
Los Lunas NM, *10034* 96 C3
Louisville KY, *529548* 68 B4
Louisville MS, *7006* 82 C4
Loup R., *river* 7 C6
Loveland CO, *50608* 46 A3
Lovell WY, *2281* 134 A2
Lovelock NV, *2003* 90 B2
Lovington NM, *9471* 96 D5
Lowell MA, *105167* 76 A5
Lower Pen., *peninsula* 7 B8
Lubbock TX, *199564* 120 B3
Ludington MI, *8357* 78 D2
Lufkin TX, *32709* 121 C6
Lumberton NC, *20795* 100 C5
Luquillo PR, *7947* 136 E4
Luray VA, *4871* 126 B5
Lusk WY, *1447* 134 C5
Lyman WY, *1938* 134 D1
Lynchburg VA, *65269* 126 C4
Lynden WA, *9020* 128 A2
Lyndonville VT, *1227* 124 B4
Lynn MA, *89050* 76 B5
Lyons KS, *3732* 66 C3

M

Machias ME, *1376* 72 D5
Mackinaw City MI, *859* 78 B4
Macomb IL, *18558* 60 C2
Macon GA, *97255* 54 C3
Macon MO, *5538* 84 B3
Madawaska ME, *3326* 72 A4
Madera CA, *43207* 44 D3
Madison IN, *12004* 62 E4
Madison SD, *6540* 116 C5
Madison WV, *2677* 130 D1
Madison WI, *208054* 132 E3
Madisonville KY, *19307* 68 C3
Madras OR, *5078* 108 B3
Magnolia AR, *10858* 42 E2
Maine, G. of, *gulf* 7 B10
Makawao HI, *6327* 56 E2
Malone NY, *6075* 98 A5
Malta MT, *2120* 86 A4
Malvern AR, *9021* 42 D2
Manassas VA, *35135* 126 B5
Manatí PR, *16173* 136 E2
Manchester CT, *30595* 48 B4
Manchester IA, *5257* 64 B4
Manchester NH, *107006* 92 F3
Manchester VT, *602* 124 E2
Mandan ND, *16718* 102 C3
Mangilao GU, *7794* 137 F4
Manhattan KS, *44831* 66 B4
Manistee MI, *6586* 78 D2
Manistique MI, *3583* 78 B3
Manitowoc WI, *34053* 132 D5
Mankato MN, *32427* 80 E3
Manning SC, *4025* 114 C4
Mansfield LA, *5582* 70 B1
Mansfield OH, *49346* 104 C3
Manteca CA, *49258* 44 C2
Manti UT, *3040* 122 D3
Manville RI, *3800* 112 A3
Maquoketa IA, *6112* 64 B5
Marathon FL, *10255* 52 F4
Marco Island FL, *14879* 52 E4
Marianna AR, *5181* 42 D4
Marianna FL, *6230* 52 A1
Maricao PR, *1123* 136 F1
Marietta GA, *58748* 54 B2
Marietta OH, *14515* 104 E4
Marina CA, *25101* 44 D2
Marinette WI, *11749* 132 C5
Marion AL, *3511* 36 D2
Marion IL, *16035* 60 F3
Marion IN, *31320* 62 C4
Marion IA, *26294* 64 B4
Marion OH, *35318* 104 C3
Marion SC, *7042* 114 B4
Marion VA, *6349* 126 D2
Marksville LA, *5537* 70 C2
Marlborough MA, *36255* 76 B4
Marlow Heights MD, *6059* 136 C4
Marquette IA, *421* 64 A5
Marquette MI, *19661* 78 B2
Marshall MN, *12735* 80 E2
Marshall MO, *12433* 84 B2
Marshalltown IA, *26009* 64 B3
Marshfield WI, *18800* 132 D3
Martin SD, *1106* 116 C2
Martin TN, *10515* 118 A2
Martins Additions MD, *875* 136 A3
Martinsburg WV, *14972* 130 B5
Martinsville VA, *15416* 126 D4
Marysville CA, *12268* 44 C2
Marysville KS, *3271* 66 A4
Maryville MO, *10581* 84 A1
Maryville TN, *23120* 119 B7
Mason City IA, *29172* 64 A3
Massena NY, *11209* 98 A5
Massillon OH, *31325* 104 C4
Matamoras PA, *2312* 111 B6
Mattoon IL, *18291* 60 D4
Maui, *island* 6 F3
Maumee OH, *15237* 104 B2
Maunabo PR, *2075* 136 F4
Mauna Kea, *peak* 6 F4
Mayagüez PR, *78647* 136 F1
Mayfield KY, *10349* 68 D2
Maysville KY, *8993* 69 B6
Mayville ND, *1953* 102 B5
McAlester OK, *17783* 106 C5
McAllen TX, *106414* 120 F4
McCall ID, *2084* 58 D2
McComb MS, *13337* 82 E3
McCook NE, *7994* 88 D2
McDermitt NV, *269* 90 A3
McGill NV, *1054* 90 C4
McKenzie TN, *5295* 118 B2
McKinley, Mt., *peak* 6 E2
McLean VA, *38929* 136 B1
McMinnville OR, *26499* 108 B1
McMinnville TN, *12749* 118 B5
McPherson KS, *13770* 66 C3
Mead, L., *lake* 6 D3
Meadville PA, *13685* 110 B1
Medford MA, *55765* 76 B5
Medford OR, *63154* 108 D2
Medina OH, *25139* 104 B4
Melbourne FL, *71382* 52 C5
Memphis TN, *650100* 118 C1
Mena AR, *5637* 42 D1
Mendocino, C., *cape* 6 B1
Mendota CA, *7890* 44 D2
Menominee MI, *9131* 78 C2
Menomonee Falls WI, *32647* 132 E4
Menomonie WI, *14937* 132 C1
Mentor OH, *50278* 104 B4
Merced CA, *63893* 44 D2
Meriden CT, *58244* 48 C3
Meridian ID, *34919* 58 E2
Meridian MS, *39968* 82 D4
Merizo GU, *1587* 137 F4
Merrifield VA, *11170* 136 C1
Merrill WI, *10146* 132 C3
Merrillville IN, *30560* 62 A2
Merrimack R., *river* 7 B10
Merritt Island FL, *36090* 52 C4
Mesa AZ, *396375* 40 D3
Mesabi Range, *mountains* 7 A6
Mesquite NV, *9389* 90 E5
Metairie LA, *146136* 70 D4
Methuen MA, *43789* 76 A5
Metropolis IL, *6482* 60 F4
Mexico MO, *11320* 84 B3
Mexico, G. of, *gulf* 7 F8
Miami FL, *362470* 52 E5
Miami OK, *13704* 107 A6
Miami Beach FL, *87933* 52 E5
Michigan City IN, *32900* 62 A3
Michigan, L., *lake* 7 B7
Middleboro MA, *6913* 76 C5
Middlebury VT, *6252* 124 C2
Middlesboro KY, *10384* 69 D6
Middletown CT, *43167* 48 C3
Middletown DE, *6161* 50 B2
Middletown NY, *25388* 98 A1
Middletown OH, *51605* 104 E1
Middletown PA, *9242* 110 C4
Middletown RI, *17334* 112 D4
Midland MI, *41685* 78 D4
Midland TX, *94996* 120 C3
Midwest City OK, *54088* 106 C4
Milan TN, *7664* 118 B2
Milbank SD, *3640* 116 B5
Miles City MT, *8487* 86 C5
Milford CT, *52305* 48 D2
Milford DE, *6732* 50 D3
Milford MA, *24230* 76 B4

142 Index

Figures after entries indicate population, page number, and grid reference.

Milford NH, *8293* **92** F3
Milford UT, *1451* **122** E2
Mililani Town HI, *28608* **56** C2
Milk R., *river* **6** A4
Milledgeville GA, *18757* **54** C3
Miller SD, *1530* **116** B4
Millington TN, *10433* **118** C1
Millinocket ME, *5190* **72** C3
Mills WY, *2591* **134** C4
Millsboro DE, *2360* **50** F3
Millville NJ, *26847* **94** E2
Milpitas CA, *62698* **44** C2
Milton DE, *1657* **50** E3
Milton VT, *1537* **124** B2
Milton-Freewater OR, *6470* **108** A4
Milwaukee WI, *596974* **132** E5
Minden LA, *13027* **70** A1
Minden NE, *2964* **88** C3
Minneapolis MN, *382618* **80** E3
Minnesota R., *river* **7** B6
Minot ND, *36567* **102** B2
Mississippi Delta, *delta* **7** E7
Mississippi R., *river* **7** E7
Missoula MT, *57053* **86** B1
Missouri R., *river* **7** C6
Mitchell SD, *14558* **116** C4
Mitchell, Mt., *peak* **7** D8
Moab UT, *4779* **122** E5
Moberly MO, *11945* **84** B3
Mobile AL, *198915* **36** F2
Mobile Bay, *bay* **7** E8
Mobridge SD, *3574* **116** A3
Modesto CA, *188856* **44** C2
Mojave Desert, *desert* **6** D2
Moline IL, *43768* **60** B2
Moloka'i, *island* **6** F3
Moncks Corner SC, *5952* **114** C4
Monessen PA, *8669* **110** D1
Monett MO, *7396* **84** D2
Monmouth OR, *7741* **108** B1
Monroe GA, *11407* **54** B3
Monroe LA, *53107* **70** A2
Monroe MI, *22076* **78** F5
Monroe NC, *26228* **100** C4
Monroe WI, *10843* **132** F3
Monroeville AL, *6862* **36** E2
Monroeville PA, *29349* **110** C1
Monterey CA, *29674* **44** D2
Monterey Bay, *bay* **6** C2
Montevideo MN, *5346* **80** E2
Monte Vista CO, *4529* **46** D3
Montgomery AL, *201568* **36** D3
Monticello AR, *9146* **42** E3
Monticello KY, *5981* **68** D5
Monticello NY, *6512* **98** A1
Monticello UT, *1958* **122** E5
Montpelier ID, *2785* **58** F5
Montpelier VT, *8035* **124** C3
Montrose CO, *12344* **46** C1
Moore OK, *41138* **106** C4
Moorefield WV, *2375* **130** C4
Moorhead MN, *32177* **80** C1
Moosup CT, *3237* **48** B5
Morehead KY, *5914* **69** B6
Morehead City NC, *7691* **101** C7
Moreno Valley CA, *142381* **44** E4
Morgan City LA, *12703* **70** D3
Morgan Hill CA, *33556* **44** D2
Morgantown WV, *26809* **130** B3
Morningside MD, *1295* **136** C5
Morrilton AR, *6550* **42** C2
Morris IL, *11928* **60** B4
Morris MN, *5068* **80** D2
Morristown NJ, *18544* **94** B3
Morristown TN, *24965* **119** A8
Morrisville VT, *2009* **124** B3
Morro Bay CA, *10350* **44** E2
Moscow ID, *21291* **58** C1
Moses Lake WA, *14953* **128** C4
Moultrie GA, *14387* **54** E3
Moundsville WV, *9998* **130** B2
Mountain Home AR, *11012* **42** B3
Mountain Home ID, *11143* **58** E2
Mountain View HI, *2799* **56** E5
Mountain View WY, *1153* **134** D1
Mount Airy NC, *8484* **100** A4
Mount Holly NJ, *10600* **94** D3
Mount Pleasant IA, *8751* **64** C4
Mount Pleasant MI, *25946* **78** D4
Mount Pleasant SC, *47609* **114** D4
Mount Rainier MD, *8498* **136** B4
Mount Vernon IL, *16269* **60** E3
Mount Vernon OH, *14375* **104** C3
Mount Vernon VA, *28582* **127** B6
Mount Vernon WA, *26232* **128** B2
Mullins SC, *5029* **114** B5
Muncie IN, *67430* **62** C4
Munising MI, *2539* **78** B2
Murfreesboro TN, *68816* **118** B5
Murray KY, *14950* **68** D2
Muscatine IA, *22697* **64** C5
Muscle Shoals AL, *11924* **36** A2
Muskegon MI, *40105* **78** E2
Muskogee OK, *38310* **107** B6
Myrtle Beach SC, *22759* **114** C5
Mystic CT, *4001* **48** C5

N

Nacogdoches TX, *29914* **121** C6
Nags Head NC, *2700* **101** B8
Naguabo PR, *4432* **136** F4
Nampa ID, *51867* **58** E2
Nanticoke PA, *10955* **110** B5
Nantucket MA, *3830* **77** D7
Napa CA, *72585* **44** C2
Naperville IL, *128358* **60** B4
Naples FL, *20976* **52** E4
Narragansett Pier RI, *3671* **112** E3
Nashua NH, *86605* **92** F3
Nashville TN, *569891* **118** B4
Natchez MS, *18464* **82** E2
Natchitoches LA, *17865* **70** B2
Naugatuck CT, *30989* **48** C2
Nebraska City NE, *7228* **88** C5
Neenah WI, *24507* **132** D4
Neosho MO, *10505* **84** D2
Nephi UT, *4733* **122** C3
Nevada MO, *8607* **84** D2
New Albany IN, *37603* **62** F4
New Albany MS, *7607* **82** A4
Newark DE, *28547* **50** A2
Newark NJ, *273546* **94** B4
Newark OH, *46279* **104** D3
New Bedford MA, *93768* **76** C5
New Bern NC, *23128* **101** C7
Newberry SC, *10580* **114** B2
New Britain CT, *71538* **48** B3
New Brunswick NJ, *48573* **94** C3
Newburgh NY, *28259* **98** A2
Newburyport MA, *17189* **76** A5
New Canaan CT, *6600* **48** D1
New Castle DE, *4862* **50** A2
New Castle IN, *17780* **62** C4
New Castle PA, *26309* **110** B1
Newcastle WY, *3065* **134** B5
New City NY, *34038* **98** A2
New Haven CT, *123626* **48** C3
New Iberia LA, *32623* **70** D3
New London CT, *25671* **48** C5
New Martinsville WV, *5984* **130** B2
New Milford CT, *6633* **48** B1
Newnan GA, *16242* **54** C2
New Orleans LA, *484674* **70** D4
New Philadelphia OH, *17056* **104** C4
Newport AR, *7811* **42** C4
Newport KY, *17048* **68** A5
Newport NH, *4008* **92** E2
Newport OR, *9532* **108** B1
Newport RI, *26475* **112** D4
Newport VT, *5005* **124** A4
Newport News VA, *180150* **127** D6
New Port Richey FL, *16117* **52** C3
New Roads LA, *4966* **70** C3
New Rochelle NY, *72182* **98** B2
New Rockford ND, *1463* **102** B4
Newton IA, *15579* **64** C3
Newton KS, *17190* **66** C4
Newton MA, *83829* **76** B5
Newton NJ, *8244* **94** A3
New Town ND, *1367* **102** B2
New Ulm MN, *13594* **80** E2
New York NY, *8008278* **98** B2
Niagara Falls NY, *55593* **98** C1
Niantic CT, *3085* **48** C4
Niceville FL, *11684* **52** E2
Nicholasville KY, *19680* **68** C5
Ni'ihau, *island* **6** F3
Nikiski AK, *4327* **38** C3
Niles MI, *12204* **78** F2
Niobrara R., *river* **6** C5
Noblesville IN, *28590* **62** C3
Nogales AZ, *20878* **40** F4
Nome AK, *3505* **38** B2
Norfolk NE, *23516* **88** B4
Norfolk VA, *234403* **127** D6
Normal IL, *45386* **60** C3
Norman OK, *95694* **106** C4
Norristown PA, *31282* **111** D6
North Adams MA, *14681* **76** A1
Northampton MA, *28978* **76** B2
North Augusta SC, *17574* **114** C2
North Bend OR, *9544* **108** C1
North Bennington VT, *1428* **124** F2
North Brentwood MD, *469* **136** B4
North Charleston SC, *79641* **114** D4
North Chevy Chase MD, *465* **136** A3
North Conway NH, *2069* **92** C4
Northfield MN, *17147* **80** E3
Northfield VT, *3208* **124** C3
North Haven CT, *23035* **48** C3
North Las Vegas NV, *115488* **90** E4
North Little Rock AR, *60433* **42** D3
North Myrtle Beach SC, *10974* **114** C5
North Platte NE, *23878* **88** C2
North Platte R., *river* **6** B4
North Providence RI, *32411* **112** B3
North Sioux City SD, *2288* **116** D5
North Springfield VA, *9173* **136** D1
Norton KS, *3012* **66** A2
Norton VA, *3904* **126** D1
Norwalk CT, *82951* **48** D1
Norwalk OH, *16238* **104** B3
Norwich CT, *36117* **48** C5
Norwich NY, *7355* **98** D4
Norwood MA, *28587* **76** B5
Novato CA, *47630* **44** C1
Nueces R., *river* **7** F6
Nuuuli AS, *5154* **137** C2

O

Oahe, L., *lake* **6** B5
O'ahu, *island* **6** F3
Oakdale LA, *8137* **70** C2
Oakes ND, *1979* **102** D4
Oak Harbor WA, *19795* **128** B2
Oak Hill WV, *7589* **130** D2
Oakland CA, *399484* **44** C2
Oakland MD, *1930* **74** A1
Oakley KS, *2173* **66** B1
Oak Ridge TN, *27387* **119** B7
Oakview MD, **136** A4
Oakville CT, *8618* **48** B2
Ocala FL, *45943* **52** B3
Ocean City MD, *7173* **75** D7
Ocean City NJ, *15378* **94** F3
Oceanside CA, *161029* **44** F4
Ocmulgee R., *river* **7** D8
Oconee R., *river* **7** D8
Odessa DE, *286* **50** B2
Odessa TX, *90943* **120** C3
Oelwein IA, *6692* **64** B4
Ogallala NE, *4930* **88** C2
Ogden UT, *77226* **122** B3
Ogdensburg NY, *12364* **98** A4
Ohio R., *river* **7** C8
Oil City PA, *11504* **110** B1
Oildale CA, *27885* **44** E3
Okanogan WA, *2484* **128** B4
Okeechobee, L. of the, *lake* **7** F9
Oklahoma City OK, *506132* **106** C4
Okmulgee OK, *13022* **106** B5
Olathe KS, *92962* **66** B5
Old Saybrook CT, *1962* **48** C4
Olean NY, *15347* **98** D2
Olney IL, *8631* **60** E4
Olympia WA, *42514* **128** C2
Omaha NE, *390007* **88** C5
Omak WA, *4721* **128** B4
O'Neill NE, *3733* **88** B4
Oneonta NY, *13292* **98** D5
Ontario OR, *10985* **108** B5
Ontario, L., *lake* **7** B9
Ontonagon MI, *1769* **78** A5
Opelika AL, *23498* **36** D4
Opelousas LA, *22860* **70** C2
Opp AL, *6607* **36** E3
Orangeburg SC, *12765* **114** C3
Ord NE, *2269* **88** B3
Oregon OH, *19355* **104** B2
Oregon City OR, *25754* **108** A2
Orem UT, *84324* **122** C3
Orland CA, *6281* **44** B2
Orlando FL, *185951* **52** C4
Orleans MA, *1716* **77** C7
Orocovis PR, *909* **136** F3
Orofino ID, *3247* **58** C2
Orono ME, *8253* **72** D3
Oroville CA, *13004* **44** B2
Osceola AR, *8875* **42** C5
Oshkosh WI, *62916* **132** D4
Oskaloosa IA, *10938* **64** C4
Oswego NY, *17954* **98** C4
Othello WA, *5847* **128** C4
Ottawa IL, *18307* **60** B3
Ottawa KS, *11921* **66** B5
Ottumwa IA, *24998* **64** C4
Ouachita Mts., *mountains* **7** D6
Ouachita R., *river* **7** D7
Overland Park KS, *149080* **66** B5
Owatonna MN, *22434* **80** E3
Owensboro KY, *54067* **68** C3
Owosso MI, *15713* **78** E4
Owyhee NV, *1017* **90** A4
Owyhee R., *river* **6** B3
Oxford MS, *11756* **82** B3
Oxford OH, *21943* **104** E1
Oxnard CA, *170358* **44** E3
Oxon Hill MD, *35355* **136** D4
Ozark AL, *15119* **36** E4
Ozark MO, *9665* **84** D2
Ozark Plat., *plateau* **7** D7
Ozarks, L. of the, *lake* **7** D6

P

Paden City WV, *2860* **130** B2
Padre I., *island* **7** F6
Paducah KY, *26307* **68** D2
Page AZ, *6809* **40** A4
Pago Pago AS, *4278* **137** C2
Pahrump NV, *24631* **90** E4
Painesville OH, *17503* **104** B5
Paintsville KY, *4132* **69** C7
Palestine TX, *17598* **120** C5
Palm Bay FL, *79413* **52** C5
Palm Coast FL, *32732* **52** B4
Palmdale CA, *116670* **44** E4
Palmer AK, *4533* **38** C3
Palmer Park MD, *7000* **136** B5
Palm Springs CA, *42807* **44** F4
Pampa TX, *17887* **120** A3
Panaca NV, *550* **90** D5
Panama City FL, *36417* **52** F2
Panguitch UT, *1623* **122** E2
Paola KS, *5011* **66** B5
Papillion NE, *16363* **88** C5
Paragould AR, *22017* **42** B5
Paramus NJ, *25737* **94** B4
Paris IL, *9077* **60** D4
Paris TN, *9763* **118** A3
Paris TX, *25898* **120** B5
Park City UT, *7371* **122** B3
Parkersburg WV, *33099* **130** C2
Park Hills MO, *7861* **84** C4
Park River ND, *1535* **102** B5
Parkston SD, *1674* **116** C4
Parma OH, *85655* **104** B4
Parowan UT, *2565* **122** E2
Parsons KS, *11514* **66** C5
Pascagoula MS, *26200* **82** F4
Pasco WA, *32066* **128** C4
Pascoag RI, *4742* **112** A2
Passaic NJ, *67861* **94** B4
Paterson NJ, *149222* **94** B4
Patillas PR, *4091* **136** F3
Pauls Valley OK, *6256* **106** C4
Pavaiai AS, *2200* **137** C1
Pawcatuck CT, *5474* **48** C5
Pawtucket RI, *72958* **112** B3
Payette ID, *7054* **58** E1
Payson AZ, *13620* **40** D4
Payson UT, *12716* **122** C3
Peabody MA, *48129* **76** A5
Pearl City HI, *30976* **56** D2
Pearl R., *river* **7** E7
Pecos TX, *9501* **120** C2
Pecos R., *river* **6** D5
Pee Dee R., *river* **7** D9
Pekin IL, *33857* **60** C3
Pella IA, *9832* **64** C3
Pendleton OR, *16354* **108** A4
Penns Grove NJ, *4886* **94** E1
Penn Yan NY, *5219* **98** D3
Penobscot R., *river* **7** A10
Pensacola FL, *56255* **52** E1
Peoria IL, *112936* **60** C3
Perry FL, *6847* **52** A2
Perry GA, *9602* **54** D3
Perry IA, *7633* **64** C2
Perryton TX, *7774* **120** A3
Perryville MO, *7667* **84** D5
Perth Amboy NJ, *47303* **94** C4
Peru IN, *12994* **62** B3
Petaluma CA, *54548* **44** C1
Peterborough NH, *2944* **92** F2
Petersburg AK, *3224* **38** C5
Petersburg VA, *33740* **127** C6
Petersburg WV, *2423* **130** C4
Petoskey MI, *6080* **78** C3
Phenix City AL, *28265* **36** D5
Philadelphia MS, *7303* **82** C4
Philadelphia PA, *1517550* **111** D6
Philippi WV, *2870* **130** C3
Phillipsburg KS, *2668* **66** A2
Phillipsburg NJ, *15166* **94** B2
Phoenix AZ, *1321045* **40** D3
Picayune MS, *10535* **82** F3
Piedmont, *highlands* **7** D9
Pierre SD, *13876* **116** B3
Pikes Peak, *peak* **6** C5
Pikeville KY, *6295* **69** C7
Pimmit Hills VA, *6152* **136** B1
Pine Bluff AR, *55085* **42** D3
Pine Bluffs WY, *1153* **134** D5
Pinedale WY, *1412* **134** C2
Pinehurst NC, *9706* **100** C5
Pine Ridge SD, *3171* **116** D2
Pineville LA, *13829* **70** C2
Pioche NV, *475* **90** D5
Piqua OH, *20738* **104** D1
Pismo Beach CA, *8551* **44** E2
Piti GU, *706* **137** F4
Pittsburg KS, *19243* **66** C5
Pittsburgh PA, *334563* **110** C1
Pittsfield MA, *45793* **76** B1
Pittston PA, *8104* **110** B5
Placerville CA, *9610* **44** C2
Plainfield NJ, *47829* **94** C3
Plainfield VT, *850* **124** C3
Plainview TX, *22336* **120** B3
Plano TX, *222030* **120** C5
Plaquemine LA, *7064* **70** D3
Platte SD, *1367* **116** C4
Platte R., *river* **7** C6
Platteville WI, *9989* **132** F3
Plattsburgh NY, *18816* **99** A6
Plattsmouth NE, *6887* **88** C5
Pleasantville NJ, *19012* **94** E3
Plentywood MT, *2061* **86** A5
Plymouth IN, *9840* **62** A3
Plymouth MA, *7658* **77** C6
Plymouth NH, *3528* **92** D3
Pocahontas AR, *6518* **42** B4
Pocatello ID, *51466* **58** F4
Pocomoke City MD, *4098* **75** D6
Point Pleasant NJ, *19306* **94** D4
Point Pleasant WV, *4637* **130** C1
Polson MT, *4041* **86** B1
Pompano Beach FL, *78191* **52** E5
Ponca City OK, *25919* **106** A5
Ponce PR, *155038* **136** F2
Pontchartrain, L., *lake* **7** E7
Pontiac IL, *11864* **60** B4
Pontiac MI, *66337* **78** E5
Poplar Bluff MO, *16651* **84** D4
Poplarville MS, *2601* **82** F3
Portage MI, *44897* **78** F3
Portage WI, *9728* **132** E3

Portales NM, *11131* **96** C5
Port Angeles WA, *18397* **128** B1
Port Arthur TX, *57755* **121** D6
Port Charlotte FL, *46451* **52** D3
Porterville CA, *39615* **44** D3
Port Huron MI, *32338* **78** E5
Port Jervis NY, *8860* **98** A1
Portland ME, *64249* **72** F2
Portland OR, *529121* **108** A2
Port Orange FL, *45823* **52** B4
Port St. Lucie FL, *88769* **52** D5
Portsmouth NH, *20784* **92** F4
Portsmouth OH, *20909* **104** F3
Portsmouth RI, *2700* **112** C4
Portsmouth VA, *100565* **127** D6
Port Sulphur LA, *3115* **70** E5
Port Townsend WA, *8334* **128** B2
Post Falls ID, *17247* **58** B1
Poteau OK, *7939* **107** C6
Potomac R., *river* **7** C9
Pottstown PA, *21859* **110** C5
Pottsville PA, *15549* **110** C5
Poughkeepsie NY, *29871* **98** A2
Powder R., *river* **6** B4
Powell WY, *5373* **134** A2
Powell, L., *lake* **6** C4
Pownal VT, *700* **124** F2
Prairie du Chien WI, *6018* **132** E2
Pratt KS, *6570* **66** C3
Prescott AZ, *33938* **40** C3
Prescott Valley AZ, *23535* **40** C3
Presque Isle ME, *9511* **72** B4
Price UT, *8402* **122** D3
Prichard AL, *28633* **36** F2
Prince Frederick MD, *1432* **74** C5
Princess Anne MD, *2313* **75** D6
Princeton IN, *8175* **62** F2
Princeton KY, *6536* **68** D2
Princeton NJ, *14203* **94** C3
Princeton WV, *6347* **130** E2
Prineville OR, *7356* **108** B3
Proctor VT, *1700* **124** D2
Prosser WA, *4838* **128** C4
Providence RI, *173618* **112** B3
Provincetown MA, *3192* **77** B7
Provo UT, *105166* **122** C3
Pryor OK, *8659* **107** B6
Pueblo CO, *102121* **46** C4
Puget Sound, *bay* **6** A2
Pukalani HI, *7380* **56** E2
Pulaski TN, *7871* **118** C4
Pulaski VA, *9473* **126** D3
Pullman WA, *24675* **128** C5
Punxsutawney PA, *6271* **110** B2
Putnam CT, *6746* **48** A5
Putney VT, *800* **124** F3
Puyallup WA, *33011* **128** C2

Q

Quakertown PA, *8931* **111** C6
Questa NM, *1864* **96** A3
Quincy IL, *40366* **60** C1
Quincy MA, *88025* **76** B5
Quincy WA, *5044* **128** C4
Quitman GA, *4638* **54** F3
Quoddy Head, *cape* **7** A10

R

Racine WI, *81855* **132** F5
Radcliff KY, *21961* **68** C4
Radford VA, *15859* **126** C3
Rainier, Mt., *peak* **6** A2
Raleigh NC, *276093* **100** B5
Ramsey NJ, *14351* **94** A4
Randallstown MD, *30870* **74** B5
Randolph MA, *30963* **76** B5
Randolph VT, *1900* **124** C3
Rapid City SD, *59607* **116** C1
Raton NM, *7282* **96** A4
Ravenswood WV, *4031* **130** C1
Ravensworth VA, **136** D1
Rawlins WY, *8538* **134** D3
Raymond WA, *2975* **128** C1
Reading PA, *81207* **110** C5
Red Bank NJ, *11844* **94** C4
Red Bluff CA, *13147* **44** B2
Red Cloud NE, *1131* **88** D4
Redding CA, *80865* **44** B2
Redfield SD, *2897* **116** B4
Red Lodge MT, *2177* **86** C3
Redmond OR, *13481* **108** B3
Red Oak IA, *6197* **64** C2
Red R., *river* **7** D6
Red R. of the North, *river* **7** A6
Red Wing MN, *16116* **80** E4
Reedsport OR, *4378* **108** C1
Rehoboth Beach DE, *1495* **50** E4
Reidsville NC, *14485* **100** A5
Reisterstown MD, *22438* **74** A5
Reno NV, *180480* **90** C1
Renton WA, *50052* **128** B2
Rexburg ID, *17257* **58** E4
Rhinelander WI, *7735* **132** C3
Rice Lake WI, *8320* **132** C2
Richfield UT, *6847* **122** D2
Richford VT, *1400* **124** A3
Richland WA, *38708* **128** C4
Richmond IN, *39124* **62** D5
Richmond KY, *27152* **68** C5
Richmond VA, *197790* **127** C6
Ridgecrest CA, *24927* **44** E4
Ridgway PA, *4591* **110** B2
Rifle CO, *6784* **46** B2
Rincón PR, *1436* **136** E1
Ringwood NJ, *12396* **94** A4
Rio Grande, *river* **7** F6
Rio Rancho NM, *51765* **96** B3
Ripley TN, *7844* **118** B1
Ripley WV, *3263* **130** C2
Ripon WI, *6828* **132** D4
Ritchie MD, **136** C5
Riverdale Heights MD, **136** A4
Riverdale Park MD, *6690* **136** A4
River Falls WI, *12560* **132** C1
Riverhead NY, *10513* **98** B3
Riverside CA, *255166* **44** E4
Riverton WY, *9310* **134** C2
Roanoke AL, *6563* **36** C4
Roanoke VA, *94911* **126** C4
Roanoke Rapids NC, *16957* **101** A6
Roanoke R., *river* **7** C9
Rochester IN, *6414* **62** B3
Rochester MN, *85806* **80** E4
Rochester NH, *28461* **92** E4
Rochester NY, *219773* **98** C3
Rockford IL, *150115* **60** A3
Rock Hill SC, *49765* **114** B3
Rockingham NC, *9672* **100** C4
Rock Island IL, *39684* **60** B2
Rockland ME, *7609* **72** E3
Rockport MA, *5606* **77** A6
Rock R., *river* **7** C7
Rock Springs WY, *18708* **134** D2
Rockville MD, *47388* **74** B4
Rocky Ford CO, *4286* **46** C4
Rocky Mount NC, *55893* **101** B6
Rocky Mts., *mountains* **6** A4
Rogers AR, *38829* **42** B1
Rolla MO, *16367* **84** C3
Rolla ND, *1417* **102** A3
Rome GA, *34980* **54** B1
Rome NY, *34950* **98** C4
Roosevelt UT, *4299* **122** C4
Roseau MN, *2756* **80** A2
Rosebud SD, *1557* **116** C3
Roseburg OR, *20017* **108** C1
Rosedale Estates MD, **136** D4
Rose Hill VA, *15058* **136** D2
Roseville CA, *79921* **44** C2
Rosslyn VA, **136** B3
Roswell GA, *79334* **54** B2
Roswell NM, *45293* **96** D4
Roundup MT, *1931* **86** C4
Roxboro NC, *8696* **100** A5
Roy UT, *32885* **122** B2
Rugby ND, *2939* **102** B3
Ruidoso NM, *7698* **96** D3
Rumford ME, *4795* **72** D2
Rupert ID, *5645* **58** F3
Russell KS, *4696* **66** B3
Russellville AL, *8971* **36** A2
Russellville AR, *23682* **42** C2
Russellville KY, *7149* **68** D3
Ruston LA, *20546* **70** A2
Ruth NV, *500* **90** C4
Rutland VT, *17292* **124** D2

S

Sabine R., *river* **7** E6
Saco ME, *16822* **72** F2
Sacramento CA, *407018* **44** C2
Sacramento R., *river* **6** C2
Safford AZ, *9232* **40** E5
Saginaw MI, *61799* **78** E4
St. Albans VT, *7650* **124** A2
St. Albans WV, *11567* **130** D1
St. Anthony ID, *3342* **58** E4
St. Augustine FL, *11592* **52** B4
St. Charles MD, *33379* **74** C4
St. Charles MO, *60321* **84** C4
St. Clair, L., *lake* **7** B8
St. Cloud MN, *59107* **80** D3
St. Croix R., *river* **7** B6
St. George UT, *49663* **122** F1
St. Helens OR, *10019* **108** A2
St. Helens, Mt., *peak* **6** A2
St. Ignace MI, *2678* **78** B4
St. John R., *river* **7** A10
St. Johns AZ, *3269* **40** C5
St. Johnsbury VT, *6319* **124** B4
St. Johns R., *river* **7** E9
St. Joseph MI, *8789* **78** F2
St. Joseph MO, *73990* **84** B1
St. Lawrence I., *island* **6** E1
St. Lawrence R., *river* **7** A9
St. Louis MO, *348189* **84** C5
St. Maries ID, *2652* **58** B2
St. Marys GA, *13761* **54** F5
St. Marys PA, *14502* **110** B3
St. Marys WV, *2017* **130** B2
St. Mary's City MD, *900* **74** D5
St. Paul MN, *287151* **80** E3
St. Petersburg FL, *248232* **52** C3
Sakakawea, L., *lake* **6** A5
Salamanca NY, *6097* **98** D2
Salem IN, *6172* **62** E3
Salem MA, *40407* **76** A5
Salem NH, *28112* **92** F4
Salem NJ, *5857* **94** E1
Salem OR, *136924* **108** B2
Salem SD, *1371* **116** C5
Salem VA, *24747* **126** C3
Salida CO, *5504* **46** C3
Salina KS, *45679* **66** B3
Salina UT, *2393* **122** D3
Salinas CA, *151060* **44** D2
Salisbury MD, *23743* **75** C6
Salisbury NC, *26462* **100** B4
Sallisaw OK, *7989* **107** B6
Salmon ID, *3122* **58** D3
Salmon R., *river* **6** B3
Salt Lake City UT, *181743* **122** B3
Salton Sea, *lake* **6** D3
Salt R., *river* **6** D3
San Angelo TX, *88439* **120** C3
San Antonio MP, *4741* **137** C4
San Antonio TX, *1144646* **120** D4
San Bernardino CA, *185401* **44** E4
San Clemente CA, *49936* **44** F4
Sandersville GA, *6144* **54** C3
Sand Hills, *hills* **6** C5
San Diego CA, *1223400* **44** F4
Sandpoint ID, *6835* **58** A2
Sand Springs OK, *17451* **106** B5
Sandusky MI, *2745* **78** E5
Sandusky OH, *27844* **104** B3
Sandwich MA, *3058* **77** C6
Sandy UT, *88418* **122** B3
Sanford FL, *38291* **52** C4
Sanford ME, *10133* **72** F1
Sanford NC, *23220* **100** B5
San Francisco CA, *776733* **44** C2
San Francisco Bay, *bay* **6** C2
Sanger CA, *18931* **44** D3
San Germán PR, *12033* **136** F1
Sangre de Cristo, *mountains* **6** C5
San Joaquin R., *river* **6** C2
San Jose CA, *894943* **44** D2
San Jose MP, *787* **137** C4
San Jose MP, *1361* **137** D4
San Juan PR, *421958* **136** E3
San Juan R., *river* **6** D4
San Lorenzo PR, *8947* **136** F4
San Luis AZ, *15322* **40** E1
San Luis Obispo CA, *44174* **44** E2
San Marcos CA, *54977* **44** F4
San Marcos TX, *34733* **120** D4
San Mateo CA, *92482* **44** C2
San Roque MP, *983* **137** C5
San Sebastián PR, *11598* **136** E1
Santa Barbara CA, *92325* **44** E3
Santa Cruz CA, *54593* **44** D2
Santa Fe NM, *62203* **96** B3
Santa Isabel PR, *6993* **136** F3
Santa Maria CA, *77423* **44** E2
Santa Monica CA, *84084* **44** E3
Santa Paula CA, *28598* **44** E3
Santa Rita GU, *1205* **137** F4
Santa Rosa CA, *147595* **44** C1
Santa Rosa NM, *2744* **96** C4
San Vicente MP, *3494* **137** C5
Saranac Lake NY, *5041* **99** B6
Sarasota FL, *52715* **52** D3
Saratoga WY, *1726* **134** D4
Saratoga Springs NY, *26186* **99** C6
Sartell MN, *9641* **80** D3
Sauk Rapids MN, *10213* **80** D3
Sault Ste. Marie MI, *16542* **78** B4
Savannah GA, *131510* **54** D5
Savannah TN, *6917* **118** C3
Savannah R., *river* **7** D8
Sayre PA, *5813* **110** A5
Sayreville NJ, *40377* **94** C3
Schenectady NY, *61821* **99** C6
Schuyler NE, *5371* **88** C4
Scioto R., *river* **7** C8
Scituate MA, *5069* **77** B6
Scott City KS, *3855* **66** B1
Scottsbluff NE, *14732* **88** B1
Scottsboro AL, *14762* **36** A4
Scottsdale AZ, *202705* **40** D3
Scranton PA, *76415* **110** B5
Seaford DE, *6699* **50** F2
Sea Isle City NJ, *2835* **94** F3
Searcy AR, *18928* **42** C3
Seaside OR, *5900* **108** A1
Seat Pleasant MD, *4885* **136** B5
Seattle WA, *563374* **128** B2
Sebastopol CA, *7774* **44** C1
Sebring FL, *9667* **52** D4
Sedalia MO, *20339* **84** C2
Sedona AZ, *10192* **40** C3
Sedro-Woolley WA, *8658* **128** B2
Selah WA, *6310* **128** C3
Selbyville DE, *1645* **50** F4
Selma AL, *20512* **36** D3
Seminole OK, *6899* **106** C5
Seneca SC, *7652* **114** B1
Sequim WA, *4334* **128** B2
Seven Corners VA, *8701* **136** C1
Severna Park MD, *28507* **74** B5
Sevierville TN, *11757* **119** B7
Seward AK, *2830* **38** C3
Seward NE, *6319* **88** C4
Seward Pen., *peninsula* **6** E1
Seymour IN, *18101* **62** E4
Shakopee MN, *20568* **80** E3
Shamokin PA, *8009* **110** C5
Sharon PA, *16328* **110** B1
Shasta, Mt., *peak* **6** B2
Shawano WI, *8298* **132** C4
Shawnee OK, *28692* **106** C5
Sheboygan WI, *50792* **132** D5
Shelburne VT, *1700* **124** B2
Shelby MT, *3216* **86** A2
Shelby NC, *19477* **100** B3
Shelbyville IN, *17951* **62** D4
Shelbyville TN, *16105* **118** B5
Shelton CT, *38101* **48** C2
Shelton WA, *8442* **128** C2
Shenandoah IA, *5546* **64** D2
Sheridan WY, *15804* **134** A3
Sherman TX, *35082* **120** B5
Shiprock NM, *8156* **96** A1
Shirlington VA, **136** C2
Show Low AZ, *7695* **40** D5
Shreveport LA, *200145* **70** A1
Sidney MT, *4774* **86** B5
Sidney NE, *6282* **88** C1
Sidney OH, *20211* **104** D2
Sierra Nevada, *mountains* **6** C2
Sierra Vista AZ, *37775* **40** F4
Sikeston MO, *16992* **84** D5
Silver City NM, *10545* **96** E1
Silver Hill MD, *33515* **136** C4
Silver Spring MD, *76540* **74** B4
Silverton OR, *7414* **108** B2
Simpsonville SC, *14352* **114** B2
Simsbury CT, *5603* **48** B3
Sinajana GU, *2101* **137** F4
Sioux Center IA, *6002* **64** A1
Sioux City IA, *85013* **64** B1
Sioux Falls SD, *123975* **116** C5
Sisseton SD, *2572* **116** A5
Sitka AK, *8835* **38** C5
Skowhegan ME, *6696* **72** D2
Slidell LA, *25695* **70** D4
Smithfield NC, *11510* **101** B6
Smithfield UT, *7261* **122** A3
Smoky Hill R., *river* **7** C6
Smyrna DE, *5679* **50** C2
Smyrna GA, *40999* **54** B2
Smyrna TN, *25569* **118** B4
Snake R., *river* **6** B3
Snake R. Plain, *plain* **6** B3
Snohomish WA, *8494* **128** B2
Snow Hill MD, *2409* **75** D7
Socorro NM, *8877* **96** C2
Soda Springs ID, *3381* **58** F4
Soddy-Daisy TN, *11530* **119** C6
Soldotna AK, *3759* **38** C3
Soledad CA, *11263* **44** D2
Somerset KY, *11352* **68** D5
Somerset MD, *1124* **136** A2
Somerset MA, *18234* **76** C5
Somerset PA, *6762* **110** D2
Somersworth NH, *11477* **92** E4
Somerville NJ, *12423* **94** C3
Songsong MP, *1411* **137** D4
Sonoran Desert, *desert* **6** D3
South Bend IN, *107789* **62** A3
South Boston VA, *8491* **126** D4
Southbridge MA, *12878* **76** B3
South Burlington VT, *15814* **124** B2
South Haven MI, *5021* **78** F2
Southington CT, *39728* **48** B3
South Lake Tahoe CA, *23609* **44** C3
South Platte R., *river* **6** C5
South Portland ME, *23324* **72** F2
South Sioux City NE, *11925* **88** B5
Spanish Fork UT, *20246* **122** C3
Sparks NV, *66346* **90** C1
Sparta NJ, *9755* **94** A3
Sparta WI, *8648* **132** D2
Spartanburg SC, *39673* **114** B2
Spearfish SD, *8606* **116** B1
Spencer IA, *11317* **64** A2
Spencer MA, *6032* **76** B3
Spencer WV, *2352* **130** C2
Spokane WA, *195629* **128** B5
Spokane Valley WA, *80700* **128** B5
Springdale AR, *45798* **42** B1
Springfield CO, *1562* **46** D5
Springfield IL, *111454* **60** D3
Springfield MA, *152082* **76** B2
Springfield MO, *151580* **84** D2
Springfield OH, *65358* **104** D2
Springfield OR, *52864* **108** B2
Springfield TN, *14329* **118** A4
Springfield VT, *3938* **124** E3
Spring Hill FL, *69078* **52** C3
Springhill LA, *5439* **70** A1
Spring Hill VA, **136** A1
Stafford Springs CT, *4100* **48** A4
Stamford CT, *117083* **48** D1
Stanley ND, *1279* **102** B2
Starkville MS, *21869* **82** C4
State College PA, *38420* **110** C3
Statesboro GA, *22698* **54** D4
Statesville NC, *23320* **100** B4
Staunton VA, *23853* **126** B4
Stayton OR, *6816* **108** B2
Steamboat Springs CO, *9815* **46** A2
Stephenville TX, *14921* **120** C4
Sterling CO, *11360* **46** A5
Sterling IL, *15451* **60** B3
Sterling Heights MI, *124471* **78** E5
Steubenville OH, *19015* **104** C5
Stevens Point WI, *24551* **132** D3
Stillwater OK, *39065* **106** B5
Stockbridge MA, *900* **76** B1

Figures after entries indicate population, page number, and grid reference.

Stockton CA, 243771.........44 C2
Storm Lake IA, 10076.........64 B2
Storrs CT, 10996.........48 B4
Stoughton MA, 11200.........76 B5
Stowe VT, 500.........124 B3
Stratford CT, 49976.........48 D2
Streator IL, 14190.........60 B3
Stroudsburg PA, 5756.........111 B6
Sturbridge MA, 2047.........76 B3
Sturgeon Bay WI, 9437.........132 C5
Sturgis MI, 11285.........78 F3
Sturgis SD, 6442.........116 B1
Stuttgart AR, 9745.........42 D4
Suffolk VA, 63677.........127 D6
Suitland MD, 33515.........136 C4
Sulphur LA, 20512.........70 D1
Summersville WV, 3294.........130 D2
Summerville SC, 27752.........114 C4
Sumter SC, 39643.........114 C4
Sunbury PA, 10610.........110 C4
Sundance WY, 1161.........134 A5
Sunland Park NM, 13309.........96 E3
Sunnyside WA, 13905.........128 C4
Sun Valley ID, 1427.........58 E3
Superior WI, 27368.........132 A1
Superior, L., lake.........7 A7
Susanville CA, 13541.........44 B2
Susquehanna R., river.........7 C9
Sutherlin OR, 6669.........108 C1
Sutton WV, 1011.........130 C2
Swainsboro GA, 6943.........54 C4
Swanton VT, 2548.........124 A2
Sweet Home OR, 8016.........108 C2
Sylacauga AL, 12616.........36 C3
Sylvester GA, 5990.........54 E2
Syracuse NY, 147306.........98 C4

T

Tacoma WA, 193556.........128 C2
Tafuna AS, 8409.........137 C1
Tahlequah OK, 14458.........107 B6
Tahoe, L., lake.........6 C2
Takoma Park MD, 17299.........136 A3
Talladega AL, 15143.........36 C4
Tallahassee FL, 150624.........52 A2
Tallulah LA, 9189.........70 B3
Talofofo GU, 2340.........137 F4
Tamaqua PA, 7174.........110 C5
Tampa FL, 303447.........52 C4
Tampa Bay, bay.........7 F9
Tamuning GU, 10833.........137 F4
Tanapag MP, 3318.........137 C5
Taneytown MD, 5128.........74 A4
Taos NM, 4700.........96 A3
Tarpon Springs FL, 21003.........52 C3
Taunton MA, 55976.........76 C5
Tawas City MI, 2005.........78 D4
Taylorville IL, 11427.........60 D3
Tehachapi CA, 10957.........44 E3
Tell City IN, 7845.........62 F3
Telluride CO, 2221.........46 C1
Temecula CA, 57716.........44 F4
Tempe AZ, 158625.........40 D3
Temple TX, 54514.........120 D5
Temple Hills MD, 7792.........136 D4
Tennessee R., river.........7 D8
Terre Haute IN, 59614.........62 D2
Texarkana AR, 26448.........42 E1
Texarkana TX, 34782.........121 B6
The Dalles OR, 12156.........108 A3
Thermopolis WY, 3172.........134 B3
Thibodaux LA, 14431.........70 D4
Thief River Falls MN, 8410.........80 B1
Thomaston CT, 3200.........48 B2
Thomaston GA, 9411.........54 C2
Thomasville GA, 18162.........54 E2
Thompson Falls MT, 1321.........86 B1
Thomson GA, 6828.........54 C4
Thousand Oaks CA, 117005.........44 E3
Tiffin OH, 18135.........104 B3
Tifton GA, 15060.........54 E3
Tillamook OR, 4352.........108 A1
Tioga ND, 1125.........102 B1
Titusville FL, 40670.........52 C4
Titusville PA, 6146.........110 B2
Tiverton RI, 7282.........112 C4
Toccoa GA, 9323.........54 A3

Toledo OH, 313619.........104 B2
Tolland CT, 800.........48 B4
Tombigbee R., river.........7 D7
Tombstone AZ, 1504.........40 F5
Toms River NJ, 86327.........94 D4
Tonopah NV, 2627.........90 D3
Tooele UT, 22502.........122 C2
Topeka KS, 122377.........66 B5
Toppenish WA, 8946.........128 C3
Torrance CA, 137946.........44 F3
Torrington CT, 35202.........48 B2
Torrington WY, 5776.........134 C5
Townsend MT, 1867.........86 C2
Towson MD, 51793.........74 A5
Tracy CA, 56929.........44 C2
Traverse City MI, 14532.........78 C3
Tremonton UT, 5592.........122 A2
Trenton MO, 6216.........84 A2
Trenton NJ, 85403.........94 C3
Trinidad CO, 9078.........46 D4
Trinity R., river.........7 E6
Troy AL, 13935.........36 E4
Troy NY, 49170.........99 C6
Troy OH, 21999.........104 D2
Trujillo Alto PR, 50841.........136 E3
Trumann AR, 6889.........42 C5
Trumbull CT, 34243.........48 D2
Truth or Consequences NM, 7289.........96 D2
Tuba City AZ, 8225.........40 B4
Tucson AZ, 486699.........40 E4
Tucumcari NM, 5989.........96 B5
Tulare CA, 43994.........44 D3
Tularosa NM, 2864.........96 D3
Tullahoma TN, 17994.........118 C5
Tulsa OK, 393049.........106 B5
Tumwater WA, 12698.........128 C2
Tupelo MS, 34211.........82 B4
Tupper Lake NY, 3935.........98 B5
Turlock CA, 55810.........44 C2
Tuscaloosa AL, 77906.........36 C2
Tuskegee AL, 11846.........36 D4
Twin Falls ID, 34469.........58 F3
Two Harbors MN, 3613.........80 C4
Two Rivers WI, 12639.........132 D5
Tyler TX, 83650.........121 C6
Tyndall SD, 1239.........116 D4
Tysons Corner VA, 18540.........136 B1

U

Ukiah CA, 15497.........44 B1
Ulysses KS, 5960.........66 C1
Umatac GU, 564.........137 F4
Unalaska AK, 4283.........38 D1
Union SC, 8793.........114 B2
Union City TN, 10876.........118 A2
Uniontown PA, 12422.........110 D1
University Park MD, 2318.........136 A4
Upper Pen., peninsula.........7 B7
Upton WY, 872.........134 B5
Urbana IL, 36395.........60 C4
Utica NY, 60651.........98 C5
Utuado PR, 9887.........136 F2
Uvalde TX, 14929.........120 E4

V

Vacaville CA, 88625.........44 C2
Vail CO, 4531.........46 B2
Valdez AK, 4036.........38 C3
Valdosta GA, 43724.........54 E3
Vale OR, 1976.........108 C5
Valentine NE, 2820.........88 A2
Vallejo CA, 116760.........44 C2
Valley City ND, 6826.........102 C4
Van Buren AR, 18986.........42 C1
Van Buren ME, 2369.........72 A4
Vancouver WA, 143560.........128 C2
Vandalia IL, 6975.........60 D3
Van Horn TX, 2435.........120 D1
Van Wert OH, 10690.........104 C1
Vega Baja PR, 28811.........136 E3
Venice FL, 17764.........52 D3
Ventura CA, 100916.........44 E3
Verde R., river.........6 D3

Vergennes VT, 2741.........124 C2
Vermillion SD, 9765.........116 D5
Vernal UT, 7714.........122 C5
Vernon CT, 28063.........48 B4
Vero Beach FL, 17705.........52 D5
Versailles KY, 7511.........68 B5
Vicksburg MS, 26407.........82 D2
Victoria TX, 60603.........120 E5
Victorville CA, 64029.........44 E4
Vidalia GA, 10491.........54 D4
Vidalia LA, 4543.........70 B3
Vienna WV, 10861.........130 B2
Vieques PR, 4325.........136 F5
Villalba PR, 4388.........136 F2
Ville Platte LA, 8145.........70 C2
Vincennes IN, 18701.........62 E2
Vineland NJ, 56271.........94 E2
Vinita OK, 6472.........107 A6
Vinton IA, 5102.........64 B4
Virginia MN, 9157.........80 C4
Virginia Beach VA, 425257.........127 D7
Virginia City NV, 800.........90 C1
Virginia Hills VA.........136 D2
Visalia CA, 91565.........44 D3
Vista CA, 89857.........44 F4
Volga SD, 1435.........116 B5

W

Wabash IN, 11743.........62 B4
Wabash R., river.........7 C7
Waco TX, 113726.........120 C5
Wagner SD, 1675.........116 D4
Wagoner OK, 7669.........107 B6
Wahiawā HI, 16151.........56 C2
Wahoo NE, 3942.........88 C5
Wahpeton ND, 8586.........102 D5
Wailuku HI, 12296.........56 C3
Waimea (Kamuela) HI, 7028.........56 D4
Waipahu HI, 33108.........56 D2
Wakefield RI, 8468.........112 E3
Waldorf MD, 22312.........74 C4
Walker Mill MD, 11104.........136 C5
Walkersville MD, 5192.........74 A4
Wall SD, 818.........116 C2
Walla Walla WA, 29686.........128 D5
Wallingford CT, 17509.........48 C3
Wallingford VT, 948.........124 C3
Walsenburg CO, 4182.........46 D4
Walterboro SC, 5153.........114 D3
Wareham MA, 2874.........77 C6
Warner Robins GA, 48804.........54 C3
Warren AR, 6442.........42 E3
Warren MI, 138247.........78 E5
Warren OH, 46832.........104 B5
Warren PA, 10259.........110 A2
Warren RI, 11360.........112 C4
Warrensburg MO, 16340.........84 C2
Warrenton VA, 6670.........126 B5
Warsaw IN, 12415.........62 B4
Warwick RI, 85808.........112 C3
Wasatch Range, mountains.........6 C3
Wasco CA, 21263.........44 E3
Washburn ND, 1389.........102 C2
Washington DC, 572059.........136 B3
Washington IN, 11380.........62 E2
Washington IA, 7047.........64 C4
Washington MO, 13243.........84 C4
Washington NJ, 6712.........94 B2
Washington NC, 9583.........101 B7
Washington PA, 15268.........110 D1
Washington UT, 8186.........122 F1
Washington Court House OH, 13524.........104 E2
Washington, Mt., peak.........7 A10
Wasilla AK, 5469.........38 C3
Waterbury CT, 107271.........48 C2
Waterbury VT, 1706.........124 B3
Waterloo IA, 68747.........64 B4
Watertown NY, 26705.........98 B4
Watertown SD, 20237.........116 B5
Watertown WI, 21598.........132 E4
Waterville ME, 15605.........72 D2
Watford City ND, 1435.........102 B1
Watseka IL, 5670.........60 C4
Watsonville CA, 44265.........44 D2
Waukegan IL, 87901.........60 A4
Waukesha WI, 64825.........132 E4

Wausau WI, 38426.........132 C3
Waverly IA, 8968.........64 B4
Waycross GA, 15333.........54 E4
Wayne NE, 5583.........88 B4
Waynesboro GA, 5813.........54 C4
Waynesboro MS, 5197.........82 E4
Waynesboro PA, 9614.........110 D4
Waynesboro VA, 19520.........126 B4
Waynesburg PA, 4184.........110 D1
Weatherford OK, 9859.........106 B4
Webb City MO, 9812.........84 D1
Webster SD, 1952.........116 B5
Webster City IA, 8176.........64 B3
Weirton WV, 20411.........130 A3
Weiser ID, 5343.........58 D1
Welch WV, 2683.........130 E2
Wellfleet MA, 1000.........77 C7
Wellington KS, 8647.........66 D4
Wells NV, 1346.........90 B4
Wellsboro PA, 3328.........110 A4
Wenatchee WA, 27856.........128 B3
Wendover UT, 1537.........122 C1
West Allis WI, 61254.........132 E4
West Bend WI, 28152.........132 E4
Westbrook ME, 16142.........72 F2
West Des Moines IA, 46403.........64 C3
Westerly RI, 17682.........112 E1
Westernport MD, 2104.........74 A1
Westerville OH, 35318.........104 C4
West Fargo ND, 14940.........102 C5
Westfield MA, 40072.........76 B2
West Hartford CT, 63589.........48 B3
West Haven CT, 52360.........48 C3
West Helena AR, 8689.........42 D4
West Lafayette IN, 28778.........62 C2
West Memphis AR, 27666.........42 C5
West Palm Beach FL, 82103.........52 D5
West Plains MO, 10866.........84 E3
West Point MS, 12145.........82 C4
West Point NE, 3660.........88 B5
West Valley City UT, 108896.........122 B3
West Warwick CT, 29581.........112 C3
West Wendover NV, 4721.........90 B5
Wethersfield CT, 26271.........48 B3
Wheatland WY, 3548.........134 C5
Wheaton MD, 57694.........74 A4
Wheeler Peak, peak.........6 D4
Wheeling WV, 31419.........130 B2
Whitefish NH, 1089.........92 C3
White Mts., mountains.........7 A10
White Plains NY, 53077.........98 B3
White R., river.........6 B5
White R., river.........7 C8
White R., river.........7 D7
White River Junction VT, 2569.........124 D3
White Sulphur Springs WV, 2315.........130 D3
Whiteville NC, 5148.........100 D5
Whitewater WI, 13437.........132 E4
Whitney, Mt., peak.........6 C2
Wichita KS, 344284.........66 C4
Wichita Falls TX, 104197.........120 B4
Wickenburg AZ, 5082.........40 D3
Wickford RI, 1900.........112 C3
Wiggins MS, 3849.........82 F4
Wildwood NJ, 5436.........94 F3
Wilkes-Barre PA, 43123.........110 B5
Williamsburg KY, 5143.........68 D5
Williamsburg VA, 11998.........127 C6
Williamson WV, 3414.........130 D1
Williamsport PA, 30706.........110 B4
Williamston NC, 5843.........101 B7
Williamstown MA, 4754.........76 A1
Williamstown WV, 2907.........130 B2
Williston ND, 12512.........102 B1
Willits CA, 5073.........44 B1
Willmar MN, 18351.........80 E2
Wilmington DE, 72664.........50 A3
Wilmington NC, 90486.........101 C6
Wilmington OH, 11921.........104 E2
Wilson NC, 44405.........101 B6
Winchester KY, 16724.........68 C5
Winchester TN, 7329.........118 C5
Winchester VA, 23585.........126 A5

Windsor CT, 3600.........48 B3
Windsor VT, 2200.........124 D3
Windsor Locks CT, 12043.........48 A3
Winfield KS, 12206.........66 D4
Winnemucca NV, 7174.........90 B3
Winner SD, 3137.........116 C3
Winnfield LA, 5749.........70 B2
Winnsboro LA, 5344.........70 B3
Winnsboro SC, 3599.........114 B3
Winona MN, 27069.........80 E4
Winona MS, 5482.........82 C3
Winooski VT, 6561.........124 B2
Winslow AZ, 9520.........40 C4
Winsted CT, 7321.........48 B2
Winston-Salem NC, 185776.........100 B4
Wisconsin Dells WI, 2418.........132 E3
Wisconsin Rapids WI, 18435.........132 D3
Wisconsin R., river.........7 B7
Woburn MA, 37258.........76 B5
Wolfeboro NH, 2979.........92 D4
Wolf Point MT, 2663.........86 B5
Woodburn OR, 20100.........108 B2
Woodbury NJ, 10307.........94 D2
Woodland CA, 49151.........44 C2
Woods, L. of the, lake.........7 A6
Woodsville NH, 1081.........92 C2
Woodward OK, 11853.........106 A3
Woonsocket RI, 43224.........112 A3
Wooster OH, 24811.........104 C4
Worcester MA, 172648.........76 B4
Worland WY, 5250.........134 B3
Worthington MN, 11283.........80 F2
Wright WY, 1347.........134 B4
Wynne AR, 8615.........42 C4
Wyoming DE, 1141.........50 D3
Wyoming MI, 69368.........78 E3
Wytheville VA, 7804.........126 D3

X

Xenia OH, 24164.........104 D2

Y

Yabucoa PR, 6636.........136 F4
Yakima WA, 71845.........128 C3
Yankton SD, 13528.........116 D5
Yauco PR, 19609.........136 F2
Yazoo City MS, 14550.........82 C3
Yazoo R., river.........7 E7
Yellowstone L., lake.........6 B4
Yellowstone R., river.........6 B4
Yerington NV, 2883.........90 C2
Yigo GU, 6391.........137 E4
Yona GU, 2332.........137 F4
Yonkers NY, 196086.........98 B2
York NE, 8081.........88 C4
York PA, 40862.........110 D4
York SC, 6985.........114 A3
Youngstown OH, 82026.........104 C5
Yreka CA, 7290.........44 A2
Yuba City CA, 36758.........44 C2
Yukon R., river.........6 E1
Yuma AZ, 77515.........40 E1
Yuma CO, 3285.........46 B5

Z

Zanesville OH, 25586.........104 D4
Zuni Pueblo NM, 6367.........96 C1

Abbreviations

AS............American Samoa
GU............Guam
MP............Northern Mariana Islands
PR............Puerto Rico
VI............Virgin Islands